Critical Muslim 33

Relics

Critical Muslim is published quarterly by C. Hurst & Co. (Publishers) Ltd. on behalf of and in conjunction with Critical Muslim Ltd. and the Muslim Institute, London.

All editorial correspondence to Muslim Institute, CAN Mezzanine, 49–51 East Road, London N1 6AH, United Kingdom.
E-mail: editorial@criticalmuslim.com

C. Hurst & Co (Publishers) Ltd., 41 Great Russell Street, London WC1B 3PL

ISBN: 978-1-787-38332-6 ISSN: 2048-8475

To subscribe or place an order by credit/debit card or cheque (pounds sterling only) please contact Kathleen May at the Hurst address above or e-mail kathleen@hurstpub.co.uk

Tel: 020 7255 2201

A one-year subscription, inclusive of postage (four issues), costs £50 (UK), £65 (Europe) and £75 (rest of the world), this includes full access to the *Critical Muslim* series and archive online. Digital only subscription is £3.30 per month.

Critical Muslim

Subscribe to Critical Muslim

Now in its ninth year in print, *Critical Muslim* is also available online. Users can access the site for just £3.30 per month – or for those with a print subscription it is included as part of the package. In return, you'll get access to everything in the series (including our entire archive), and a clean, accessible reading experience for desktop computers and handheld devices — entirely free of advertising.

Full subscription

The print edition of *Critical Muslim* is published quarterly in January, April, July and October. As a subscriber to the print edition, you'll receive new issues directly to your door, as well as full access to our digital archive.

United Kingdom £50/year
Europe £65/year
Rest of the World £75/year

Digital Only

Immediate online access to *Critical Muslim*

Browse the full *Critical Muslim* archive

Cancel any time

£3.30 per month

www.criticalmuslim.io

CM33

WINTER 2020

CONTENTS

RELICS

REVIEWS

ET CETERA

RELICS

INTRODUCTION: THINGS TO REMEMBER

Samia Rahman

A few years ago, while visiting Sudan, I travelled the short distance from my hotel in Khartoum, overlooking the Nile, to Omdurman. The heat was hard to bear, I am far more suited to cold climates and love nothing better than venturing out under cloudy skies, all wrapped up and grappling with a gloriously brisk wind. It was the middle of the day on a Friday and I was struggling to maintain composure. The men and women of Khartoum were always impeccably turned out in traditional dress of long flowing robes that contained not a single crease or smudge despite the dust and detritus that never failed to besmirch me mere moments after stepping out. In particular I was fascinated by the unspecked and immaculate whiteness of the men's *thobes* (head-to-toe robes) as they went about their business. As someone who has the good fortune to lead a relatively ironing-free existence after wholeheartedly embracing the crumpled look, I spent much of my time in Sudan gazing in wonderment at the creaseless appearance of the citizens of Khartoum and despairing at the absolute mess of me.

Clambering out of the taxi as elegantly as I could, despite feeling the onset of sunstroke, I saw that I had arrived at the tomb of the nineteenth century Qadiriyyah leader Sheikh Hamad al-Nil. Located in a large mausoleum on the edge of a vast cemetery of simple headstones it was overlooked by a gleaming mosque with three green domes. The only other time I had visited a Sufi shrine was the Ajmer Sharif Dargah in India, resting place of the thirteenth century Sufi mystic and philosopher Moinuddin Chishti. Pilgrims of all faiths gathered to pay their respects, to pray that the soul of the saint would intercede on their behalf and provide balm for all that ailed their existence and that of those they loved. I had not experienced this before, the worship of a Muslim shrine by people of varying religions drawn to a sacred relic simply to revel in its sanctity. Just as Yovanka Paquete Perdigao describes in her essay on the festival of Touba in Senegal, a journey of pilgrimage can transcend faith and become a celebration of the diversity of what it is that offers meaning to people's lives. She notes that despite the fact that the Grand Magal's date is based on the Hijri calendar, it is ostensibly a Muslim festival, the two day celebration is embraced by all of Senegal's people from myriad backgrounds. 'It can best be described as an intricate ceremony featuring religious rituals and a festival with a dizzying array of entertainment. It is greatly anticipated by all religious as well as non-religious communities in Senegal and is a tremendous fixture in any Senegalese person's calendar.'

Hundreds of thousands of pilgrims of all faiths and none descend on the holy city of Touba, founded in the twentieth century by the anti-colonial icon Cheikh Ahmadou Bambou. Dakar becomes markedly deserted as the majority of the population relocates. The arduous journey to attend the Grand Magal is a crucial aspect of the experience, emulating the laborious journey Muslims would undertake, traversing the globe and withstanding all manner of obstacles and setbacks, focused on their desire to perform the Hajj in Mecca. That the Hajj was such a major physical, spiritual and emotional commitment rendered it a once-in-a-lifetime endeavour, the pinnacle of a person's life, the ultimate goal to tick off on their bucket list. Of course, this was before fast travel and luxury package trips commodified a journey of piety, stripping it of much of its spiritual dimension.

Back in Omdurman, followers of the al-Qadiriya al-Arkiya order began to gather as a growing crowd of locals and curious tourists, myself included, looked on as the ceremony unfolded to a cacophony of sound and colour. Men in glistening white as well as green thobes swayed in unison. Dhakirs adorning beaded jewellery and elegant figures with dreadlocked hair joined the throng. Purposeful and yet utterly absorbed by their internal connection with their creator, they marched to the saint's tomb, chanting rhythmically *la illaha illallah* 'there is no God but Allah'. The voices became hypnotic and increasingly frenetic, bodies in rapture as the disciples honoured their spiritual guide. I found the scene desperately moving and also exalting. I forgot the unease I felt about the cemetery setting and instead allowed myself to embrace the mystical, introspective atmosphere.

That evocative scene dancing about in my mind, I wonder what it is about our attachments to relics, whether they be buildings, fragments of our past, or symbols of our religious identity, that provoke such strength of feeling. Relics become a medium through which we venerate the sacred and honour spiritual saviours; they become the focus of our attempts to seek salvation and relief. In the *Narratives* issue of *Critical Muslim*, Nicholas Masterton of Turner Prize-nominated and Emmy award-winning investigative agency Forensic Architecture, explores the way in which narratives are held within structures. Masterton asks us to look upon structures with a new perspective, 'the idea that a building is a witness of an event.' The job of the architecture or art appreciator also changes, for as a building lacks language, 'it becomes necessary to interrogate the architecture to let it tell the story of what it has seen.'

The stories locked within relics are there for us to excavate, often bringing unknown implications for our contemporary existences. In the gripping Turkish fantasy drama Gift, we meet Atiye, an acclaimed painter living a seemingly perfect and indulgent life as part of Istanbul's elite. Her art has centred on a symbol that she believed she had invented, plucking it from the recesses of her imagination. To her great shock, the exact symbol is found at Göbeklitepe, an archaeological site located in the Southeastern Anatolia Region of Turkey, bordering Syria. The ancient temple dates back 11,500 years and is thought to be the oldest religious monument in the world. A vast complex comprising T-shaped pillars displaying animal carvings, a maze of rectangular rooms as well as huge stone rings, it is believed to have been the stage for rituals and sacrifice. When the symbol is uncovered by the conveniently handsome archaeologist Erhan, links to Atiye's ancestry and her family's past cause her life to be thrown into disarray in a sequence of gripping events. The past seeps into the present and there is a sense that relics are more than inanimate objects from long ago. Rather, they have a timeless quality that engenders a unique significance to the context into which they find themselves in. In his fascinating essay on archaeology and jihad, Aaron Tugendhaft explores the way in which contemporary powers continue to use relics and archaeology for their own geopolitical ends. ISIS and the Taliban are the sensationalistic tabloid fodder of the jihad against relics, attempting to eradicate what they perceive to be incitements to idolatry. However, Tugendhaft considers the discovery in 1899 of the Tell Halaf archaeological site in Syria, on the other side of the border from Göbeklitepe, by the controversial German diplomat and member of the Oppenheim banking dynasty Max van Oppenheim. The neolithic artefacts excavated from the site, which dates back to 6000 BC, revealed an insight into prehistoric Halaf Culture for the very first time. Oppenheim believed they were better protected in Berlin, only for them to be destroyed by allied bombs in the Second World War. It wasn't until ten years after the fall of the Berlin Wall that work began at the Pergamon Museum to restore the artefacts. A team of four archaeologists began painstakingly sifting through the 27,000 pieces of debris, using photographs and their own knowledge, to put together a mind-bogglingly complex series of jigsaw puzzles. Contemporary artist Rayyane Tabet was inspired by the momentous project to create an exhibition exploring issues arising from the looting of artefacts during colonial times, and the eventual fate of the Halaf antiquities. 'When the conservators in Berlin began reassembling the Tell Halaf fragments, they laid out each piece on wooden pallets that filled a vast workspace. Tabet's work *Basalt Shards* (2017) transforms that step in the reconstruction process into its own object of reflection.' In the process of reconstructing the shattered pieces, they were almost lifted beyond their original station, granted a new fulfilment in the unfulfillable as a new relic in itself. A relic that derived its own meaning for the puzzle solvers and a new meaning for those who will be able to look upon the shards after their near fatal run in with British munitions. 'Each fragment is granted an individual dignity that disrupts our desire to possess things whole. As works on paper, they make no claim to permanence. Rather, the rubbings reveal the ephemerality even of stone.'

The individual dignity of each fragment, rendering it impossible to entirely possess, is a breathtaking description that illuminates the manner in which relics absorb meaning according to the changing course of history. Just like buildings that speak, relics are witness to the passage of time, and harbour secrets that are continuously unlocking and revealing themselves. Perdigao celebrates the opening of the Museum of Black Civilizations in Dakar and reflects on Senegal's call for the return of its cultural heritage looted during the colonial era and languishing in European Museums. It is not dissimilar to Oppenheim's view that a

Museum in Berlin would be a more natural home for the treasures he excavated, albeit from an entirely different country and culture: 'Tabet's work acknowledges the fraught history that surrounds the ancient objects that we admire in our museums. They neither seek to obscure that history in veneration nor escape it through iconoclasm. Rather, his drawings inhabit the uncomfortable space between destruction and preservation. They help us engage the past without an encumbering injunction to preserve it.'

Yet I had always bought into the narrative of relics as entities that must be conserved and fastidiously kept intact so as to not impinge upon their authenticity. How many times have we watched one of those daytime television programmes where excited members of the public bring along an heirloom, passed down over generations, perhaps locked away in the attic and long-forgotten, to find out how much it is worth. The joy and surprise on their faces as they are told the rather ugly ornament inherited from grandma is priceless. And then the chastisement of realising that the slightly ragged doll beloved of their now adult children could have been worth so much more if it had been kept in pristine condition and never played with. But at what cost? Is it more important for relics to be sanitised and untouched as an indicator of their value or for them to be cherished and put to use? As a child I remember visiting the home of family friends who proudly showed off their newly acquired dining table and chairs, complete with the plastic wrapping still on the seats so they are not adversely impacted by everyday use. In some similar way, how can relics take on meaning in our lives if they are closeted away and rendered remote.

I am reminded of months meandering through the narrow streets in the Old City in Cairo, when I felt as if I was wandering through a living, breathing, working museum. Isn't this how relics can form a part of the evolving landscape? Hafeez Burhan Khan vividly illustrates, in his account of an emotional visit to Jerusalem, how relics can become part of the fabric of our lives. Not static, but in harmony with a changing society. When a vicious fire tore through medieval French Cathedral Notre Dame, there was widespread sorrow at the loss of an iconic structure and a proud history disintegrated to ashes. But let us stop to think for a moment. Notre Dame is no less likely to fall than the Ottoman Empire before it, or any other Empire you care to mention. What we experience at moments of loss such as the fall of this emblem of power is the next shedding of a city's skin. After loss let there be growth. Notre Dame represented a moment in a culture and religion's past and from the charred remains a new skin will develop. If we don't allow this organic process to take place, all we are left with is stagnation. Notre Dame is a symbol of power that lies at the centre of France's complicity in a savage colonial campaign that oversaw the devastation of entire African civilisations and theft of its ancient relics. Its destruction and planned restoration reflects the violence of this history and now that we have the potential for renewal, perhaps this is a metaphor for the opportunity France now has to make reparations by returning the artefacts it plundered to their places of origin.

By mourning and then letting go of our attachment to relics as being fixed exactly as we remember them, such as Notre Dame, we empower them to exist beyond us. This beckons Tugendhaft's observation of the 'individual dignity' of each Tell Halaf fragment 'that disrupts our desire to possess things whole'. Because that desire may encourage us to harbour unrealistic hopes for attachments to remain the same, prompting an unhealthy synergy that benefits no-one. Sahil Warsi recounts visiting his grandparents house one day to find that a shield and two curved swords that had been in his family for generations and had mesmerised him since he was a child, had been sent to Dewa near Lucknow, to be displayed at the entrance of the shrine of saint Waris Ali Shah. The impact of the loss surprised even him. His grandfather counselled that the swords had been given a new lease of life in their new home, appreciated by far more people than when they were rusting away in a seldom entered room in their home. Later when reflecting on the fate of a cherished box of *tabarrukat* (blessed items) including a *mohr* (tablet used in prayer) made from the soil of Karbala, Sahil realised his grandfather hoped that he would take custody of the sacred relics after his death. The unending complexity of family politics meant that Sahil knew he would never be able to fulfil this wish and that the heirloom would be passed on to his uncle. It weighed heavily on him that he was unable to make the promise to his grandfather, but found solace in his earlier words. 'I thought about what Papa had said to me about the swords, how in letting go of an object, we may allow it to live on. What made the *tabarrukat* valuable to Papa is perhaps not exactly what makes them valuable to my uncle or relatives who visit him. Yet through their gaze and reverence, the objects live on.'

The idea that we may live on through material objects that mean something to us, is one way in which we grapple with the existential crisis of finding purpose in our existence. Creating a legacy to pass on, something to pass down so that it may become an esteemed relic for future generations, is a compulsive ideal. How many people are seeking to create a legacy so that they may not be forgotten in the annals of time. When it became apparent I was not destined to contribute to the creation of the next generation, I remember feeling overwhelming sadness that there would be no one who would be excited to read my old letters or delight in my childhood photographs in the same way my siblings and I marvel at my parents' life's paper trail. Who will care about my achievements, never mind the minutiae of my life, once I am no longer here to remind the universe of my presence? But I cannot wonder if this is simply a tainted image of where I and others of my generation find ourselves. Yet again in another of those transitional periods. The physical does not bear the same value it did to my parents and we would be naïve to believe it will not bear less and less value to subsequent generations. What will children of the future marvel over? Our social media feeds? Digitised images of structures and objects lain waste to the sands of callous time? In an applaudable act of irony, the selfies of today desecrate the sacred and dehumanise the self as we all rush to show the rest of the world that we had accomplished something and that our lives mattered. I take solace though in that as our lives become more digitised, we will see that 'oh so familiar' of value bequeathed inanimate things which we will come to know as digital relics. Let us just hope we don't note these wonders in parody. There is a beauty in what digital humanities promise. The ability to see what would otherwise be lost through war or natural disaster (both unfortunately of our own doing). It offers a chance to connect to something beyond ourselves and our increasingly busy lives, beyond our income levels, and beyond the number of followers we have accumulated. Despite what our situation and circumstance bring the human race to next, we will continue to latch onto that which allows us to transcend.

Relics, whether they are intimate or monumental, signify the transience and also the regenerative quality of life. Warsi captures this view: 'As containers of meaning and sentiments, relics reflect our relationships to ourselves, to others, and to the world around us. In this way they ask us to make a decision about what we hold on to through them and what we let fall away. In the case of objects, perhaps sometimes letting go is part of letting things live on in different ways or allow others to hold on to something they need.' What is it that we need from relics? Is it the feeling of rootedness, being part of a moment in time? In *The Gift*, Atiye's life was simultaneously turned upside down and given new meaning by the archaeological discovery at Göbeklitepe. Evidently, relics can enrich as well as provoke, but only if we give them the space to breathe and similarly create the space in our lives into which they can be curated.

THE LOST MOSAIC

Boyd Tonkin

Then

At first it felt like a wild goose chase – a wasted journey uphill through spitting late-summer rain across the scrappy northern suburbs of Palermo. Once we had left the old markets of the city centre, where the drizzle had turned stallholders short-tempered behind their dampened tables of spices, fruit and fish, the most striking landmark along the way was the hulking Palace of Justice. Built and fenced to withstand a siege, this concrete fortress housed a coven of Mafia godfathers during the historic trials of the 1980s and 1990s that had, in part but not entirely, broken the crime families' stranglehold on everyday life in Sicily.

I urged my partner to press on. Further up, beyond the shabby apartment blocks and corner groceries in neighbourhoods where African and Middle Eastern faces became more and more common, I promised that there stood a fairy-tale palace. And within it lay a relic that spoke across nine centuries of a glorious epoch of inter-cultural peace and concord. At that time, the Kingdom of Sicily led the Mediterranean – arguably, all Europe – in the splendour of its arts and sciences.

At last, we reached La Zisa. The squat, imposing Norman palace sits at the top of a modern geometrical park laid out in vaguely Islamic style. It gestures, in its austere municipal regularity, to the lush gardens filled with streams, orchards and game that would once have surrounded it on every side. La Zisa carries a name that derives from the Arabic *al-Aziz*, the Magnificent – a title supposedly given to it by the skilled Berber farmworkers who cultivated the lands around.

Construction began around 1165 in the reign of King William I – one of the Hauteville family of warlords from Normandy to rule as kings of the island, of Apulia on the Italian mainland, of Malta, and even of a broad coastal stretch of north Africa in today's Tunisia and Libya. In the late eleventh century, the Hauteville warriors with their all-conquering cavalry had displaced the so-called 'Arab' rulers of Sicily: many, in fact, were Berbers. These 'Saracens' had captured Palermo in 831 and extended their dominion over the island during the next decades. Muslim governance had supplanted the Greek Christianity of the Byzantine Empire. Then an invasion in 1061, led by the Norman leader Robert Guiscard, had exploited the quarrels of the island's two senior emirs, Ibn al-Hawas and Ibn al-Timnah. Latin Catholicism had, by the 1070s, eventually trumped Islam. It was a familiar enough cycle in the medieval Mediterranean, undergone with varying degrees of conflict or conciliation from Portugal to Palestine.

In the Kingdom of Sicily, however, something extraordinary happened. The Norman victors did not set out to suppress Islam and forcibly convert the people whose emirs they had defeated, instead they allowed Muslims to thrive, and to occupy high positions, so long as they stay loyal to the new regime. That, very occasionally, happened in Spain during the centuries of the 'Reconquista', notably with the eclectic culture fostered at the thirteenth-century court of Alfonso the Wise in Castile. But in Sicily, exchange and hybridisation went much further. While retaining their Catholic faith, the Norman elite effectively became Arab-Muslim in their manners, their customs, their dress – even their language. Nowhere else in Europe did such a thorough process of osmosis steep a Christian court in the social and intellectual world of their Muslim subjects. Ibn Jubayr, a Valencian scholar who worked as a court secretary in Granada, left a colourful and opinionated account of his travels through Sicily in 1185, soon after the completion of La Zisa. 'Their King, William, is admirable for his just conduct, and the use he makes of the industry of the Muslims', Ibn Jubayr writes. 'He has much confidence in Muslims, relying on them for his affairs, and the most important matters; even the supervisor of his kitchen being a Muslim...'

Unconverted Muslims served the Norman kings as governors, lawyers, courtiers, civil servants, farmers, merchants, as well as artisans and artists of every sort. Palermo continued to hosts scores of mosques (perhaps exaggerating, a chronicler during the period of Arab rule had counted 300 of them). Ibn Jubayr frets about the dangers of apostasy for Muslims in Sicily – a temptation aggravated by the easygoing lifestyle that saw citizens of different faiths share so much. 'The Christian women of the city,' he remarks in Palermo, 'follow the fashion of Muslim women, are fluent of speech, wrap their cloaks about them, and are veiled... Thus they parade to their churches... bearing all the adornments of Muslim women, including jewellery, henna on the fingers, and perfumes.' Outside Palermo, he visited a grand mosque that he ranked 'one of the finest... in the world... of a workmanship that I have never seen better'. John Julius Norwich's history *The Normans in Sicily*, a landmark in modern appreciation of the dynasty, concludes that the 'easy eclecticism' of the Hautevilles would make their island 'stand to the world as an example of culture and enlightenment, giving them an understanding and breadth of outlook which was to be the envy of civilised Europe'.

La Zisa, designed as a summer pleasure-palace open to cooling breezes from the mountains behind and the sea below, voices this age of symbiosis in stone. Facing the garden stands the open *diwan* hall, with its pointed archways and water-channel running across the floor from a fountain (*sadirwan*). Above the Byzantine mosaics of hunters and peacocks is the hall's most breathtaking feature: a vaulted honeycomb ceiling, or *muqarnas*, tumbling down in carved stalactites in the style of Persian and North African palaces and mosques. In Islamic architecture, the *muqarnas* decorated vault conveys a theological as well as an aesthetic meaning – as a portal of wonder that guides the viewer towards a sense of the beautiful intricacy of the divine creation. Around the entrance arch, stucco Arabic calligraphy – now removed – proclaimed that 'This is the earthly paradise that opens to the view; this King is the *Musta'iz* (Glorious One), this Palace the *Aziz*.'

La Zisa, though, was not only a luxury retreat for a Christian ruler but a secular entertainment complex. It served as a fun-house for feasting, music, poetry and dalliance with royal mistresses – all skills largely supplied to the Norman court, along with their architecture, their irrigation and much else, by Muslim professionals. Not surprisingly, when Enlightenment-era travellers from northern Europe discovered the dilapidated palace, they automatically described it as a refuge of the 'Muslim Emirs' of Sicily. Its arabesque ornaments inspired the flamboyant 'Arab Hall' designed in the 1860s by architect George Aitchison for Leighton House, the artist Lord Leighton's home in Kensington. In fact, this alleged epitome of Islamic exoticism was commissioned by descendants of the Vikings from northern France, whose kinsfolk at that time ruled England as well. Visitors sometimes remark that the pugnacious geometry of La Zisa's exterior resembles the White Tower, at the heart of the Tower of London. Branches of the same Norman clans built both. Indeed, English Norman clerics, soldiers and officials took key positions in the Kingdom of Sicily. John Julius Norwich comments that Walter of the Mill, the ambitious prelate-politician of Palermo who proved a near-fatal thorn in the side of the monarchy, became 'almost certainly the only Englishman in history regularly to sign himself "Emir and Archbishop".'

Today, set amid brownish, patchy lawns under showers that heralded autumn, La Zisa felt forlorn. Our trek through tatty suburbs to find a somewhat run-down historic site now engulfed by the mess of modernity reminded me of similar weary trudges in Indian cities. The region of Sicily, and Italy's national government, does now care for its Arab-Norman heritage. In 2015 a network of monuments – this palace among them – joined the UNESCO list of World Heritage sites. I had first come here in 2016 with the curators of a British Museum exhibition that showcased the wonders of Sicily and spotlit, among them, its medieval golden age of tolerance. Yet the Norman kingdom and its multi-faith flowering cannot yet match the fame of the fabled Muslim-led *convivencia* in medieval Spain.

Arab-Norman Palermo, though praised by Al-Jubayr as the equal of Cordoba in its treasures and amenities, attracts fewer of the seekers in search of a lost and longed-for multicultural ideal who flock to Andalusia. Europeans familiar with the legends of Granada seldom know much about the earlier glories of Palermo – although two fairly recent British novels, Barry Unsworth's *The Ruby in her Navel* and Tariq Ali's *A Sultan in Palermo*, have celebrated its age of marvels. Palermo fails to feature in Justin Marozzi's newly published *Islamic Empires*, his portrait of 'fifteen cities that define a civilisation', even though – first under Muslim, then Christian rule – its period as a hub of Arabic culture lasted almost four centuries, from the 830s to around 1200. Surely, though, this story of Western Christian overlords who not only protected, but eagerly adopted, the manners and graces of their Muslim neighbours and compatriots has as much to say to us today as the romance of medieval Andalusia.

But where was the relic that, I hoped, would compress this lost tradition of harmony into a single slab? The upper floors of La Zisa now house a small museum of Islamic art. Foremost among its exhibits, so I recalled, was a funerary tablet that commemorates the departed mother of a Catholic priest named Grisando. He served at the court of King Roger II, the Norman monarch whose enlightened curiosity made Palermo a citadel of learning. This royal patronage yielded results such as the unique *Book of Roger*, or *Nuzhat al-mushtāq fi'khtirāq al-āfāq*. This atlas and gazetteer was completed by the geographer Muhammad al-Idrisi in 1154 after the king, his friend, had authorised him to question seafarers in the port of Palermo about their homelands and journeys. Al-Idrisi's research revised the cartography handed down by the map-makers of antiquity (he depicted a spherical Earth, and calculated its circumference to within 10 per cent accuracy). The *Book of Roger* remained in use until the sixteenth century.

When Father Grisando's mother Anna died, he paid tribute to her in a way that befitted the eclectic culture of his time and place. Anna's memorial appears not only in the Latin, Greek and Arabic habitually found in Norman Sicily. One quadrant of the slab is inscribed in the Judaeo-Arabic spoken by the island's Jews – a dialect of Arabic, written in Hebrew script. The date of Anna's passing even appears according to four separate calendars: 1149 for Latin Christians, with the equivalent year for Greek Orthodox believers, Jews and Muslims. In Roger II's Sicily even the formal measurement of time, that marker of humankind's relationship with eternity, was allowed to have several parallel scales.

I found the room where I expected to see the Grisando slab. The vitrine, though, stood empty. Memories of disappointment after footsore slogs to other provincial museums in Italy came dripping back to me. Here, at least, a nearby placard offered hope. The tablet had apparently been moved into a long-term exhibition devoted to Arab-Norman Sicily in the Royal Palace, back in the city centre. And there, eventually, we found it.

It hangs in a chamber not far from the syncretic sumptuousness of Roger II's Cappella Palatina – a chapel with Norman spaces and proportions, radiant gilded mosaics of Biblical scenes in finest Byzantine style, and riotously Islamic *muqarnas* carved above. In its current home, the Grisando relic feels a little overshadowed by more glamorous artefacts from its era – jewels, textiles, weaponry, sculpture. But it sits in a spot where hosts of tourists in Palermo will have a fair chance of encountering it. Few ever go out to La Zisa.

Anna's memorial matters because it shows that the Arab-Norman elite not only accepted diversity of faith and culture as a matter of course. They advertised it on public and formal occasions. Inscriptions in Arabic still adorn churches and palaces of the time. In the nearby, smaller castle of La Cuba (Arabic *qubbat*, or 'vault'), an Arabic exhortation instructs us to stop and see 'the great room of the greatest of all kings, William II'.

In fact, the Arab-Norman heyday would prove brief. William II oversaw a period of decline and internecine disputes. It ended with the extinction of the Hauteville line and the crowning of the Holy Roman Emperor Henry VI of Hohenstaufen as King of Sicily in Palermo cathedral on Christmas Day 1194. As the Crusades carved deeper trenches between Muslim and Christian communities across the Mediterranean, what Norwich calls 'the happiest and most glorious chapter of the island's history' came to a swift close. A mixture of force, threat, inducement and deportation thinned out the numbers of the overtly Muslim population.

However, the specific Arab-Norman fusion survived in agriculture, in customs, in language – Sicilian remains peppered everywhere with Arabic – and, above all, in food. Citrus fruits, sugar-based desserts, ices, almonds, raisins, aubergines and spices (from chilli to saffron) serve as edible memorials to an Islamic past on the Sicilian table. So, supremely, does pasta. Dry pasta, *pasta asciutta*, was an Arab innovation. Before it spread to mainland Italy, it had a reputation as a solely Sicilian staple. Pasta's longevity and convenience suited a mobile society in need of portable nutrition for long voyages by sea or land. It might be argued that, in every mouthful of spaghetti or macaroni, we can taste a relic from the glory days of Muslim and multi-faith Sicily.

Now

Not far from the Royal Palace and Cathedral in downtown Palermo lies the district of Ballarò. Its picturesquely crumbling maze of narrow streets, punctuated here and there by grandiose Baroque churches and monasteries, has always been seen as a heartland of Palermitan popular culture – one of three rowdy, seething hubs of inner-city street life along with La Kalsa (Arabic *al-Khalesa*, 'the chosen') to the north and Vucciria to the west. These days, however, the markets and shops of Ballarò throb with a fresh pulse of imported energy. African hairdressers, Middle Eastern food stalls, Bangladeshi grocers and Indian sweet shops crowd the twisting lanes. Sicilian dialect joins Arabic and many languages of South Asia and Sub-Saharan Africa among the hubbub of vendors and shoppers.

Ballarò, close to the port, has always been a place for incomers to congregate. But the surge in informal migration to Sicily across the perilous seas from Tunisia and Libya has left central Palermo with a population probably more cosmopolitan today than at any time in its millennia-long history of transit and settlement. Although many migrants move on from Sicily to mainland Italy and elsewhere in Europe, tens of thousands do not. Since new arrivals may stay under the radar of officialdom for years, an estimate of 175,000 for the island's population of recent migrants most likely understates their numbers by a significant margin. Their visible presence, amid a network of storefront mosques, welfare centres, migrant-run restaurants and other social enterprises, has turned ramshackle Ballarò into the front line of the effort both to welcome the latest wave of Palermitans – a large proportion of them Muslims by background – and to resist the hostility of nativist Italian politicians and their local followers.

Old and new struggles for justice in Palermo have lately come together in a novel, and heartening, way. Ballarò is one of the city neighbourhoods where lower-league mafiosi – less almighty and well-connected than the great clans of former decades, but still a harmful brake on social progress – routinely try to bully locals. Always opportunistic, they have even sought to profit from the new migrations by combining with drug-dealers from a Nigerian gang. As elsewhere in Palermo, however, the mainstay of

Mafia income remains the regular protection money – the notorious *pizzo* – extracted from shopkeepers and other businesses.

In 2016, a Gambian migrant, Yusupha Susso, was shot and left in a coma after he refused to pay off the local mobsters. Soon after, a citizens' alliance led by Bangladeshi shopkeepers – along with Nigerians, Tunisians, Gambians and others – filed a lawsuit against known associates of the assailant. It was a turning-point. A group of marginal, often insecure new residents had dared to take on the semi-underground forces that have plagued all of Palermo's poor since the nineteenth century. The litigants, moreover, enjoyed the backing of the city government. Meanwhile, a Bangladeshi-born resident of Ballarò, Sumi Dali Aktar, became the first Bengali elected as a member of Sicily's assembly.

What role, though, does the memory of King Roger's enlightened hybrid kingdom have in these latest twists of community politics in a fluid, globalised society? A relic need not take the form of a physical object or place. It may survive as an idea. And the reclaimed legacy of Arab-Norman tolerance has become a weapon in the hands of Roger's pluralist successors in Sicily.

With intervals out of office, sometimes affiliated to a national party and sometimes as an independent, Leoluca Orlando has served as mayor of Palermo for most of the thirty-two years since 1987. He remains one of the most remarkable – and, for all his foibles, admirable – figures in contemporary European public life. For decades, Orlando risked his life as an anti-Mafia campaigner. He won, and retains, huge popularity in Sicily through his resistance to the mob. And he shamed politicians in Rome into tardy moves against it. As far back as the late 1980s, he figured among the top three Mafia targets for assassination. The other two, Palermo-born prosecutors and magistrates Paolo Borsellino and Giovanni Falcone, were notoriously slaughtered in 1992. Those murders finally accelerated state action against the major gangs. Orlando, however, lived.

And he has made Palermo – for all its enduring patches of sometimes charming, sometimes scary, disrepair – a place that tourists like to visit in fast-growing numbers. Whether they know it or not, the visitors who stroll safely from bar to café in the night-time streets of La Kalsa and Vucciria are beneficiaries of a bitter legal and political struggle for civility that has cost the lives of many activists. At least an anti-Mafia documentation centre stands on the pedestrianised main drag of the Corso Vittorio Emanuele to remind them of their debt.

Crucially, since his (fifth) re-election in 2017, Orlando has joined his career-long mission to curb organised crime and the social degradation it causes with support for Palermo's newest citizens and their needs. The anti-Mafia mayor has become the pro-migrant mayor. When Italy's former interior minister, the right-wing populist Matteo Salvini, forbade rescue boats from docking in Italian ports, Orlando ostentatiously announced that they would be welcome in Palermo. In his office hangs a portrait of St Benedict the Moor – a sixteenth-century Franciscan born to African slaves in Sicily.

Orlando himself links his twin campaigns. In a recent article, he argued that 'welcoming migrants benefits our city as a whole. Just as some years ago when convincing people to fight against the Mafia I had to explain why legality is economically beneficial, now I assure people that opening our city is beneficial too.' His Charter of Palermo, devised in 2015, defends mobility as an 'inalienable human right' and calls for the European Union to remove its restrictions on the ability of migrants to settle, move, work and reunite with families. He has established a 'council of cultures' whose members represent what he calls 'Palermo's mosaic', in which 'Each small piece of the mosaic has its own role… but only by looking at the full picture can you understand the beauty and balance of the image.'

Orlando's multicultural strategy can sound well-intentioned but naive, based on a (to British ears) old-fashioned definition of unified 'communities' with uncontested 'leaders'. Even here, however, he draws on the traditions of medieval Sicily: John Julius Norwich notes that, under the Normans, Latin, Greek or Muslim local magistrates were 'selected according to the race and language predominant in their district'. In practice, though, Orlando's inclusive vision does mean that incomers in Palermo have easy access to a range of services denied them elsewhere in Italy. And it's striking that he frequently invokes the island's storied medieval past as a foundation for his ideals. 'Palermo was a migrant city,' he recently told the New York Times. 'Arabs and the Normans lived together. I normally say, "In Palermo, the dog and the cat and the mouse work together."' Again in the vein of his Arab-Norman predecessors, he roots identity and belonging in commitment to a place and polity rather than an inheritance of blood and soil: 'It does not matter if my mother or

father are Sicilian. I am a Sicilian because I have decided to be here.' King
Roger II himself, the descendant of foreign usurpers maintained in power
by a mongrel coalition, could hardly have put it better.

Relics and icons, as any historian of religion will explain, change their
meaning over time. Like a liquid turning to a gas, they can move from
one medium to another. Previously neglected like the palace of La Zisa
itself, the physical traces of Christian, Muslim and Jewish co-existence
and cross-fertilisation in medieval Sicily now command a high prestige.
They help tell a story of diversity that the authorities in Palermo – if not
in every corner of the island – want to spread abroad. Hence the recent
transfer of the Grisando funerary slab from its little-frequented outpost
to the Royal Palace.

But the material evidence of medieval harmony now counts in Sicily
because an immaterial relic – the memory of a thriving multi-faith
community in which Muslims played an honoured part – has come to be
cherished as well. In traditional religious practice, the possession of relics
conferred legitimacy on their guardians. Relics established continuity with
a lineage of faith and worship. They symbolised the values that their
powerful keepers wished their communities to share. And, not least, they
attracted pilgrims from far and wide. The pilgrims' sojourns both boosted
the hosts' prosperity, and glorified their reputation across frontiers. In this
light, the 'Arab-Norman Itinerary' of UNESCO-registered sites in
Palermo and elsewhere, established in 2015, overtly echoes the pilgrimage
routes of the Middle Ages. This time, tourists come not just to revere the
sacred objects of one creed or another, they are invited to endorse the idea
of a fruitful historic partnership between faiths and cultures.

This appreciation came late to the rest of Europe. For travellers of the
Enlightenment, only the relics of Greek and Roman antiquity made Sicily
worth a visit. They saw monuments of the Middle Ages as barbarous
rubbish. In the Romantic era, a new respect began to dawn, but on an
aesthetic rather than a cultural plane. *The Normans in Sicily*, a pioneering
survey of 1838 by the writer-traveller Henry Gally Knight, argued that 'In
Sicily, and only in Sicily, the Greeks, the Saracens, and the Normans, were
united'. Thus 'the northern, the classic, and the oriental styles were
blended together... Nothing of the sort is to be seen anywhere else'.

At first, the fusion of architectural styles mostly struck outsiders. Only later did the fusion of peoples that must have underpinned it win respect. John Julius Norwich published the two volumes of *The Normans in Sicily* in 1967 and 1970. At that time, few other Western historians – especially medievalists – would have championed the plural civilisation of Arab-Norman Sicily as 'a sunburst of beauty and brilliance', and as 'an example of tolerance and enlightenment' that stood out against 'the whole bigoted medieval world'. Now such attitudes may sound commonplace. But Leoluca Orlando's deployment of historical memory as a defence against populist politics in Sicily, and Italy, shows that such 'relics' still have a talismanic power.

Relics always become focuses of myth – not in the sense of an untrue story, but an ideal one; a narrative that helps fix the values and beliefs of its audience. The relics, and myths, of Arab-Norman Sicily have a special salience right now. They tell of Christian courts and rulers who not merely granted tolerance to their Muslim populations but, in culture if not creed, became deeply Islamicised themselves. In Palermo's Royal Palace, the gold, green and turquoise mosaics of 'Roger's Room' portray, through exquisite Byzantine craft, the plants, trees and beasts of a purely Persian-Islamic 'paradise garden'. This tessellated paradise stands within the vaults and arches of a Norman architectural space. These relics speak of Islamic art and custom as an embedded part of European tradition, not an exotic addendum. Hence their value to Mayor Orlando and his allies. As for what Anna, the priest's mother with her quadrilingual memorial tablet, would have made of her modern renown – that's a story none of us can tell.

IGNORANT ANTIQUITIES

Aaron Tugendhaft

I.

A bearded man dressed in the black *taqiyah* and white *thawb* of a devout Muslim addresses the camera. He stands before the fragment of a large Assyrian sculpture known as a *lamassu* – a protective deity that combines a bull's body, an eagle's wings, and a human head. 'Oh Muslims, the remains that you see behind me are the idols of peoples of previous centuries, which were worshipped instead of God,' the man explains in Arabic, with the poise of a museum docent. 'The Prophet Muhammad commanded us to shatter and destroy statues. This is what his companions did when they conquered lands. Since God commanded us to shatter and destroy these statues, idols, and remains, it is easy for us to obey. We do not care what people think or if this costs us billions of dollars.'

When he finishes, the video transitions to a museum gallery. Three men topple a life-sized sculpture from its pedestal. Others look on. In the ensuing montage men overturn sculptures, smash them with sledgehammers, and mutilate them with pneumatic drills. For two and a half minutes, these images of destruction are interspersed with shots of decimated sculptures strewn across the floor – often rendered in slow motion, lending the sequence a lyrical quality. The audio is no less carefully crafted: A lone voice chants a Qur'anic verse and then the sound of a *nashid* weaves through the duration of the video. In haunting tones, the song declares: 'Demolish! Demolish! the state of idols / Hell is filled with idols and wood / Demolish the statues of America and its clan.' Even for those who cannot understand the Arabic lyrics, the music – punctuated by the sounds of shattering stone and machine-gun fire – is mesmerising.

Released onto the Internet on February 25, 2015, the Islamic State video of iconoclasm in Iraq's Mosul Museum provoked immediate outrage. The blogosphere began to teem with calls to action to protect antiquities from the locals – rehashing old imperial tropes about barbarism and civilisation. Some argued that teams should be sent into Iraq, 'Monuments Men' style, to rescue the cultural property that remained. 'Now that Islamist madmen are on the loose across great swathes of the Middle East,' Hudson Institute fellow Ann Marlowe reasoned in *The Daily Beast*, 'we have reason to value the cultural imperialism of years past. It was rationalized, then, as saving treasures from barbarians. Whatever the truth of the matter in those days, there is no doubt now that the barbarians are back with a vengeance.' In a lighter vein, cartoonist Patrick Chappatte depicted two jihadists leaving the Mosul Museum with sledgehammers in hand – one saying to the other, 'My first time in a museum. This was awesome!'

The day the video appeared, the director-general of UNESCO Irina Bokova condemned the event as 'a deliberate attack against Iraq's millennial history and culture'. She called the destruction 'a war crime' and insisted that 'there is absolutely no political or religious justification for the destruction of humanity's cultural heritage'. Cultural institutions followed with statements in short order: 'Speaking with great sadness on behalf of the Metropolitan, a museum whose collection proudly protects and displays the arts of ancient and Islamic Mesopotamia,' Metropolitan Museum of Art director Thomas P Campbell wrote in a press release, 'we strongly condemn this act of catastrophic destruction to one of the most important museums in the Middle East'. The 'mindless attack on great art, on history, and on human understanding', Campbell added, was 'a tragic assault not only on the Mosul Museum, but on our universal commitment to use art to unite people and promote human understanding'. The European Association of Archaeologists condemned the 'cultural arrogance facing the world's cultural heritage'. Cairo's al-Azhar issued a similar statement: 'The destruction of cultural heritage is forbidden in Islam and rejected in total,' declared Grand Imam Ahmed el-Tayeb. 'By claiming they are idols, Daesh is committing a major crime against the whole world.' Whereas ISIS spoke of the need to cleanse the world of idols, their critics referred to a moral and legal imperative to protect cultural heritage.

In the wake of the Islamic State's rampage through Syria and Iraq, the Louvre Museum in Paris spearheaded ALIPH (French acronym for the International Alliance for the Protection of Heritage in Conflict Areas) with support from the French government and the United Arab Emirates. Styled 'a response to barbarism' in its online manifesto, the global fund has committed itself to the rehabilitation of the Mosul Museum along with other projects to restore damaged cultural sites throughout the Middle East.

Royaumes oubliés (Forgotten Kingdoms), an exhibition of Iron Age Syrian sculpture at the Louvre this past summer, sought to reinforce ALIPH's efforts by enlisting visitors in the fight to protect a 'terribly fragile heritage common to all humanity'. The show highlighted basalt sculptures from Tell Halaf (ancient Guzana) that had shattered during an Allied bombing raid of Berlin during World War II. The fragments were stored in the basement of Berlin's Pergamon Museum for over fifty years until a conservation team began the painstaking effort of reconstituting the sculptures in 2001. Ten years later, a special exhibition unveiled thirty works that the team had been able to reconstruct. The Pergamon Museum is currently building a new gallery to house the resurrected sculptures. While they await their new home, some have gone on tour. In Paris, the Tell Halaf sculptures served to focus attention on the fragility of cultural heritage and the imperative to protect it.

But the Paris exhibit avoided addressing questions that its display provoked. The fact that the Tell Halaf sculptures were destroyed in Berlin disrupts the common assumption that Near Eastern antiquities are safer in Western museums than they are in their countries of origin. At the same time, the show's cultural heritage perspective set both the Islamic State's clickbait iconoclasm and the Allied effort to defeat Nazi Germany on the same side of barbarism.

2.

When Samuel Beckett visited the Tell Halaf Museum in Berlin's Charlottenburg district on 21 December 1936, he had the place to himself. The quirky institution was hardly a popular tourist destination. After Beckett rang for the key, he was left alone among colossal lions, scorpion-bird-men, griffons, and sphinxes. 'Superbly daemonic, sinister + implacable,' the yet unknown Irish writer wrote in his diary.

The museum's contents belonged to Baron Max von Oppenheim (1860–1946), and were acquired through self-funded excavations at Tell Halaf. Heir to one of Germany's wealthiest banking families, Oppenheim found the Orient more alluring than his father's banking business in Cologne. In 1892, he leased a house in an old Arab neighborhood of Cairo that served as a base for exploring the region and learning its ways. Oppenheim was a staunch patriot determined to serve his country as an expert on the Middle East. Though denied an official post in the German Foreign Office because of his Jewish background, in his role as attaché to the German Consulate-General he produced regular reports for the kaiser on contemporary Arab politics.

In 1899, Oppenheim was gathering information in northern Syria when Bedouin friends told him about extraordinary stone sculptures that had been found on a nearby hill. He resolved to see for himself. After three days of clandestine digging, Oppenheim recognised that he had made an important find. 'It was a turning point in my life,' he later recalled. But with neither proper tools nor permission to excavate, there was nothing more he could do. Only twelve years later – after being dismissed as attaché in Cairo for intrigues considered 'a perpetual danger [and] grave menace to peace' – did Oppenheim return to Tell Halaf with a permit from the Ottoman authorities. He excavated the site until the outbreak of World War I turned his attention back to politics.

Oppenheim believed Islam was the Achilles' heel of Germany's enemies. From Egypt to India, the British Empire ruled over a hundred million Muslim subjects. Tsarist Russia ruled nineteen million more, and there were nearly as many under French control. If these Muslims could be incited to rebel against their overlords, Oppenheim surmised, Germany would reap the benefits. In the hundred-page 'Memorandum Concerning the Revolutionizing of the Islamic Territories of Our Enemies', Oppenheim outlined a plan to foment a global jihad. It called for the Ottoman Sultan-Caliph to issue a German-prepared fatwa declaring a Holy War against the Entente powers and to flood Muslim lands with leaflets aimed at exploiting resentment against colonial rule.

With the backing of a Foreign Office now willing to overlook his Jewish origins, Oppenheim set up a jihad bureau in Berlin that mobilised German orientalists to produce thousands of pamphlets in the various languages of Muslim lands. 'O beloved Muslims, consider even for a brief moment the present condition of the Islamic world,' one typical pamphlet began. 'Wherever you look, you see that the enemies of the true religion, particularly the English, the Russians, and the French, have oppressed Islam. ... But the time has now come for the Holy War, and by this the land of Islam shall be forever freed from the power of the infidel who oppresses it. ... Know that the blood of infidels in the Islamic lands may be shed with impunity – except those to whom the Muslim power has promised security and who are allied with it.' (The final caveat was necessary to protect Germans and Austrians from the wrath that Oppenheim sought to unleash.)

Oppenheim also sought to enlist Muslim prisoners of war for his jihad. Both the French and the British used Muslim colonial troops – mainly from North Africa and India, respectively – in the trenches of the western front. Oppenheim thought he could radicalise captured colonial troops and send them back behind enemy lines. Germany's oldest mosque was built for this purpose at the so-called 'Half Moon Camp' in the town of Wünsdorf, forty kilometres south of Berlin. Additionally, beginning in March 1915, Oppenheim edited the multilingual *El Dschihad*, a propaganda newspaper aimed at motivating POWs to turn against the colonial powers. Despite these efforts, only a handful of prisoners got onboard the project.

Oppenheim's global jihad never ignited. The baron grossly misread the situation on the ground and despite a personal relationship with King Faisal, the son of Sharif Hussein of Mecca, he was ultimately outmanoeuvred by his British counterpart T E Lawrence in the race to win Arab support. (Oppenheim and Lawrence knew each other from before the war, when the Englishman was excavating at Carchemish, not far from Tell Halaf.) When Sharif sided with the British and declared an uprising against the Turks, the legitimacy of Oppenheim's jihad was fatally compromised. By 1915, Oppenheim's disillusioned protégé Curt Prüfer pronounced the Holy War 'a tragicomedy'.

After Germany's defeat, Oppenheim re-dedicated himself to archaeology. When Germany joined the League of Nations in 1926, Oppenheim was able to petition the French Mandate authorities for permission to return to Tell Halaf. He made a visit to assess the situation in 1927 and excavated again two years later. Oppenheim then arranged for part of his Tell Halaf finds to be shipped to Berlin, while the rest went to the nascent National Museum of Aleppo. The Aleppo museum, originally housed in an old Ottoman palace, moved into a purpose-built structure in 1966. The modern building, designed by Yugoslav architects Zdravko Bregovac and Vjenceslav Richter, reproduces the famed portico from Tell Halaf as its main entrance. The museum was hit by mortar fire in July 2016.

Oppenheim sought to display the sculptures he kept in the Pergamon Museum on Berlin's prestigious Museum Island. When negotiations fell through, he settled for a disused machine factory on the other side of town. The Tell Halaf Museum opened to the public on 15 July 1930 – the baron's seventieth birthday. Beckett was not the only notable visitor. According to the museum registry, the Expressionist painter Emile Nolde visited with his wife in January 1931. The mystery novelist Agatha Christie, who stopped by with her archaeologist husband Max Mallowan, records how the baron affectionately stroked one of the (in her opinion) 'extremely ugly' sculptures. Even Faisal bin Hussein, now king of Iraq, paid a visit. Presumably there were no hard feelings that he had opted to side with Lawrence and the British during the war.

The rise of National Socialism didn't disturb the old baron. Oppenheim quickly received honorary Aryan status and was put on the Nazi government payroll. When war broke out, he again composed a lengthy memorandum recommending ways to stir up trouble for the British in India and the Middle East. The Foreign Office ignored it. Hitler himself wasn't enthusiastic about encouraging darker peoples to rebel against their white masters (he had ridiculed the German Orientalists' Holy War in *Mein Kampf*) but did take a liking to Oppenheim's friend Amin al-Husseini, the Grand Mufti of Jerusalem. Repackaging Oppenheim's earlier efforts with Nazi support, the Berlin-based Mufti produced a series of wartime radio addresses exhorting the Arab world to join a global jihad against the Bolsheviks, British and Jews.

In 1943, an Allied incendiary bomb set Oppenheim's museum aflame. When firemen arrived, the cold water they used to extinguish the fire caused the museum's basalt sculptures to shatter into some 27,000 pieces. Oppenheim convinced Walter Andrae, director of the Pergamon Museum's Near Eastern collections, to salvage the remains. Nine truckloads of Oppenheim's treasures finally reached Museum Island, but in fragments. They lingered in a cellar there for the next half-century.

Oppenheim died of natural causes a year after the end of the war. He had devoted his life to recovering ancient monuments and instigating modern jihad. For Oppenheim, there was no tension between the two. And yet, his jihad pamphlets paved the way for today's Islamic State videos that provoke the colonial powers by destroying those antiquities that Oppenheim held so dear.

3.

'Demolish! Demolish! the state of idols,' repeats the *nasheed* that accompanies images of destruction in the Islamic State's February 2015 video from Iraq's Mosul Museum. The video presents the destruction as a re-enactment of Ibrahim's iconoclasm.

As the Qur'an relates, in 21: 52-56, the young Ibrahim lashed out against his neighbours' folly:

> Ibrahim said to his father and his people, 'What are these images to which you are so devoted?' They replied, 'We found our fathers serving them.' He said, 'You and your fathers have clearly gone astray.' They asked, 'Have you brought us the truth or are you just playing about?' He said, 'Listen! Your true lord is the lord of the heavens and the earth, He who created them, and I am a witness to this. By God I shall certainly outwit your idols as soon as you have turned your backs!'

Ibrahim goes on to smash all but the largest of the idols. When his neighbours return, they ask Ibrahim if he was responsible for the destruction. He says, no, it was done by the biggest of them, and they should just ask *him*. The townspeople reply that he knows these gods can't speak. Ibrahim's retort: 'How can you serve what can neither benefit nor harm you, instead of God? Shame on you and the things you serve instead of God. Have you no sense?' (21:66-67)

The ISIS video alludes to this story through the momentary on-screen appearance of 21:58: 'He reduced them to fragments.' An article published in *Dabiq* (the Islamic State's official magazine) soon after the video was released made the insidious connection more explicit. 'Erasing the Legacy of a Ruined Nation' celebrates how 'the soldiers of the Khalifah, with sledgehammers in hand, revived the Sunnah of their father Ibrahim (*'alayhis-salam*) when they laid waste to the *shirki* [idolatrous] legacy of a nation that had long passed from the face of the Earth'. The article favourably compares the destruction not only to Ibrahim's act but also to his attitude. Dismissing outrage about the destruction of ancient cultural heritage, the article explains that the Islamic State's fighters 'were not the least bit concerned about the feelings and sentiments of the *kuffar* [unbelievers], just as Ibrahim was not concerned about the feelings and sentiments of his people when he destroyed their idols'. Like Ibrahim, determined to cleanse the world of idols – violently, if necessary – ISIS would pay no heed to contemporary censures.

The story in the Qur'an begins with Ibrahim asking the people about the images to which they appear so devoted. The people tell him they serve them just as their fathers did. They attest a conservative practical wisdom. Though the verb *'ibada* is often translated as 'worship' when used with reference to gods, its basic meaning is 'to serve' – as a slave serves a master or a subject serves a king. If we resist our modern tendency to consign religion and politics to separate autonomous spheres, we can be better attuned to the term's political connotations. The images that the people serve are intimately connected to the political regime under which they live: to 'serve images' (which is the literal meaning of the Greek *idol-latria*) is to serve the sovereign who rules through them. By advocating submission to 'your true lord, the lord of the heavens and the earth', Ibrahim does not simply criticise the people's theology; he subverts their politics. He is calling for regime change.

In his *History of Prophets and Kings*, the polymath Muhammad ibn Jarir al-Tabari (839–923) embroidered a political context only hinted at in the Qur'an. He collected numerous traditions that placed Ibrahim's childhood during the reign of Nimrud, ancient Babylon's legendary king. Ibrahim's iconoclasm leads to a face-off between mighty ruler and upstart reformer. The images that Ibrahim smashed constituted a fundamental feature of Nimrud's regime. Traditions about the two men do not miss the political significance of Ibrahim's iconoclasm. As al-Tabari reports, astrologers told Nimrud that 'a boy will be born in this city of yours who will be called Ibrahim. He will abandon your religion and break your idols'. Nimrud commanded that in the foretold month every newborn boy be killed. Yet, Ibrahim manages to survive the king's murderous scheme. When Ibrahim is later found guilty of destroying the idols, Nimrud tries once more to execute him – this time by burning him alive. When that attempt, too, fails, an astounded Nimrud declares his willingness to offer a sacrifice to Ibrahim's god. 'God will not accept anything from you as long as you keep any vestige of this old religion of yours,' Ibrahim tells the king. 'You must leave it for my religion.'

Nimrud's reply is revealing: 'O Ibrahim! I cannot abandon my kingship, but I will slaughter the cattle for Him.' Nimrud understands that to abandon his religion with its idols is equivalent to forsaking his position as king – an equivalency implied earlier when the astrologers refer to 'your idols' and 'your religion' rather than 'our idols' and 'our religion'. Though impressed by Ibrahim's God, Nimrud is not prepared to dismantle his regime.

Nimrud has long served as an emblem of the monumental Mesopotamian civilisations that preceded Islam in Islamic poetic imagination. When the ISIS video's spokesman (somewhat inaccurately) identifies the images under attack as having belonged to 'the Assyrians, Akkadians, and others', he links them to Nimrud's reign. And yet, it is clearly not simply Nimrud's ancient kingdom that is under attack in the *nashid*'s refrain to demolish the state of idols. The ancient civilisations that Nimrud symbolises have been defunct for millennia. Their monuments weren't even visible in Muhammad's day. This point is emphasised in the video with a nineteenth-century photograph showing British excavators unearthing the *lamassu* sculpture that is later seen being destroyed. Nimrud's wasn't the only 'state of idols'; modern imperial powers have introduced a new idolatrous regime, not least in their fetishistic desire for ancient sculpture. Both idolatrous states are encapsulated in the term *jahiliyya*.

The *jahiliyya* or 'Age of Ignorance' refers, most narrowly, to the century or so of Arabian history that predates the arrival of Muhammad. With time, however, the term's meaning expanded to include the epoch before the establishment of Islam. In this sense, as peoples of the pre-Islamic past 'the Assyrians, Akkadians, and others' belong to the period of *jahiliyya*. In modern times, the reformers Muhammad 'Abduh (1849-1905) and Rashid Rida (1865-1935) also compared aspects of contemporary Muslim life with aspects of *jahili* society. A. Yusuf 'Ali (d. 1953), in a gloss on the word *jahiliyya* in his English translation of the Qur'an, comments: 'The Days of Ignorance were the days of tribalism, feuds, and selfish accentuation of differences in man. Those days are not really yet over. It is the mission of Islam to take us away from that false mental attitude.'

In the 1960s, Muslim Brotherhood theorist Sayyid Qutb (1906-66) popularised the term *jahiliyya* in his attempt to articulate what is wrong with modern life. Born in a village in Upper Egypt, Qutb actively participated in Cairo's literary scene from the mid-1920s through the early-1950s. As the story goes, repulsed by the loose mores he witnessed while on a government-sponsored study trip in the United States, Qutb began to develop the hardline brand of Islam for which he is best known. On his return to Egypt, Qutb joined the Muslim Brotherhood and became a fierce critic of the Egyptian government and the lingering influence of the imperial powers despite the country's nominal independence. After a failed attempt on Nasser's life in 1954, the Muslim Brotherhood was banned and Qutb imprisoned. He spent most of the rest of his life in jail, where he wrote a massive Qur'anic commentary called *In the Shade of the Qur'an*; his best-known book, *Milestones,* a call for Islamic revolution; and numerous other works. In August 1966, he was executed for plotting against the Egyptian government.

Qutb gives *jahiliyya* a central place in his more radical later writings. A society that fails to follow God's guidance in all areas of life, he argues, is *jahili* and engaged in the usurpation of God's sovereignty. *Jahili* societies are man-made imposter sovereignties — whether they take the form of tribes, clans, kingdoms, empires, or, as today, nation-states. 'The true character of Islam,' by contrast, he writes in *Milestones,* 'is a universal proclamation of the freedom of man from servitude to other men, the establishment of the sovereignty of God and His Lordship throughout the world, the end of man's arrogance and selfishness, and the implementation of the divine law in human affairs'.

In his commentary on the Qur'an, Qutb elaborates: '*Jahiliyya* – as God describes it and His Qur'an defines it – is the rule of humans by humans because it involves making some humans servants of others, rebelling against service to God, rejecting God's divinity and, in view of this rejection, ascribing divinity to some humans and serving them apart from God.' *Jahiliyya* is not a time period. It is 'a condition which existed yesterday, exists today, and will exist tomorrow'.

By filming the destruction of ancient Mesopotamian artefacts, ISIS produced an image that perfectly encapsulates the multivalent meaning of *jahiliyya*. Reenacting Ibrahim's iconoclasm against Nimrud's idols becomes a cipher for animosity towards today's political regimes. The shattered sculptures strewn on the museum's floor attest to an ignorance both ancient and modern.

4.

Since 2016, Lebanese artist Rayyane Tabet has been engaged in a series of works relating to Tell Halaf. His interest in the archaeological site began when he learned that his great-grandfather had once known Max von Oppenheim. In 1929, Faek Borkhoche had been appointed Oppenheim's personal secretary when the baron returned to excavate in Syria. Since the French Mandatory authorities suspected Oppenheim of being a secret agent with plans to radicalise local Bedouin tribes, they enlisted Borkhoche to keep a watchful eye. When Tabet found Oppenheim's calling card among his grandparents' papers, it introduced him to a world of archaeology and intrigue.

The thirty resurrected Tell Halaf sculptures had been unveiled in Berlin a few years earlier. Of the 27,000 sculptural fragments that were salvaged from the destroyed Tell Halaf Museum, the restorers were only able to recombine 25,000 of them. 2,000 fragments remained unidentified and unmatched. Intrigued by these sculptural leftovers, Tabet contacted the conservators in Berlin to ask if he could draw them. The restorers found the request perplexing, since to them these remainders marked a failure in their project. Still, they granted permission. In 2017, Tabet travelled to Berlin to produce charcoal rubbings of all the leftover basalt fragments.

When the conservators in Berlin began reassembling the Tell Halaf fragments, they laid out each piece on wooden pallets that filled a vast workspace. Tabet's work *Basalt Shards* (2017) transforms that step in the reconstruction process into its own object of reflection. His rubbings of the stone fragments, each on its own sheet of white paper, have been tacked onto similar wooden pallets, but now propped vertically from floor to ceiling along an entire wall. Each fragment is granted an individual dignity that disrupts our desire to possess things whole. As works on paper, they make no claim to permanence. Rather, the rubbings reveal the ephemerality even of stone.

Tabet's work acknowledges the fraught history that surrounds the ancient objects that we admire in our museums. They neither seek to obscure that history in veneration nor escape it through iconoclasm. Rather, his drawings inhabit the uncomfortable space between destruction and preservation. They help us engage the past without an encumbering injunction to preserve it.

The 2,000 shards that Tabet worked with come from inside the original Tell Halaf sculptures. As such, they lack ancient carving marks. This raises what Tabet has called 'a temporal mind-fuck' when trying to date the objects housed once more in the Pergamon's storage rooms. Should these stones be dated to the ninth-tenth century BC, along with the sculptures' surface fragments, even though they show no marks of workmanship from that time? Are they now just pieces of basalt, datable geologically as 350 million years old? Or should we rather consider them more modern works, made in 1943 by the combined artistry of an Allied bombing team and German firefighters?

The third option is intriguing. No longer merely the residue of destruction, the fragments take on the status of new creations. With Tabet's help, these 'fragment-sculptures' begin to appear as works in their own right. Like all good art, they stir us to reorient our experience – of war, of art, and of our relationship to the past. In a sense, they are not unlike the ISIS video that similarly transformed smashed sculptures into a new digital image. That image, too, has the force to reorient our experience. Nobody who has seen it can experience ancient Mesopotamian sculpture in quite the same way again.

Both the 'fragment-sculptures' and the Mosul Museum video attest to how iconoclasm does not eliminate images so much as it produces new ones. That, after all, is what Ibrahim the iconoclast did as well. He left the biggest idol standing among the rubble so that, when his neighbours returned, they could see and think.

LINGERING SCENTS OF HYDERABAD

Rita Sonal Panjatan

They say that scent elicits the strongest memories, can transport you back into times long relegated to a distant past, bring forth fragments of emotions thought buried under the merciless march of time. Stepping out of the airport in Hyderabad I would take a breath, a shallow breath on account of the pollution that is dimming the hues of what would otherwise be a blue sky, but enough of a breath to give me an ancient taste of home. I was not born in Hyderabad, and yet it lives inside me, in the mitochondria of my cells. I know little about the city and yet I know that I am woven into the fabric of its past and its culture. As we ride towards the family home I become a child again, gazing out of the window, my heart beginning to feel at ease, a sense of belonging giving refuge to my being.

The history of Hyderabad has always been one of defiance, against the Mughal Emperors far away in Delhi, against submission to the British, against the new republic. But its defiance was not merely one of belligerence, but rather one of culture, of 'culturedness', of knowing its place between the North and the South, not torn between them, but at ease with itself, relishing its achievements without the need to show them off. Rather than one-upmanship, its people show their pride through hospitality, for how much better to spend an evening with good food, poetry and laughter, rather than trying to prove a point. It is the stuff of legends, and on the wings of stories told and retold, Hyderabad's buoyant splendour is sinking into an ever more distant past. Today it seems to me a Camelot, one we can still reach through the relics of a generation born before India's independence, but which is slipping away fast.

I made the journey into the heart of my family many times, and yet not nearly often enough. The childhood memories are the fondest. My sitting next to my mother, my small face pressed against the window of the bouncy white ambassador car, we approach the house nestled among the rocks of Banjara Hills. A cousin would sprint to the gate and swing it wide open, then followed a steep descent on the dry earthen ground, and finally the car came to a halt. With big hellos we'd get out, having reached the place where home truly meant love, and approach the house. We would stop before entering to pay our respects to an old, small, bent man who was sitting on a little bench installed just for him, his back disfigured by spondylitis, leaning against the white wall of the house. 'Adaab, adaab!' he would exclaim enthusiastically, raising his frail right hand towards his forehead in the traditional manner of greeting. 'Adaab, Sheikh Ahmed Sahib!' we would reply and bow down so his old eyes could see us better, and we could bask in the light of his welcome. Sheikh Ahmed was my uncle's old cook, now retired, living out his days sitting on this bench, where he could see everyone, greet everyone, and chat with whoever wanted to hear his views on the world. He seemed timelessly ancient, and yet I remember him still cooking in the small kitchen when I was three years old, on a low wooden stool preparing the most delicious meals. The food, oh the food! Hyderabad is famous for a number of reasons, but foremost must stand its indelible love for its signature treats. The biryanis, *haleems* and *neharis* one eats at weddings, for Eid, at any reason for a festivity, are etched forever into my culinary memory.

Behind the house, there is a lake. At the time when it was built, it was a glistening pool of water with water lilies in which my cousins would swim. The house itself is modest. Designed as a bungalow for one family with two children, it soon housed three families, my aunts and uncles bringing up the next generation together. A separate apartment had been built on top, to accommodate the occupants, and what ensued was a lively hubbub of siblings and cousins. It was here that I first met my family, being only one year old. Many decades later, a new Spanish daughter-in-law was introduced here. After sometime she remarked how happy it made her to be in this house. My aunt apologised for its now somewhat dilapidated state. 'Oh no,' said the Spanish girl, 'in this house every brick is made of love.'

My uncle himself, in the words of my friend who knew him well, could make a morose donkey laugh. His marriage was an arranged one, and after they were betrothed he unleashed a festival of romance on his young bride, taking her for rides in an open car, and showering her with the attention, love and generosity that would become the bedrock of a lifetime together and the bedrock of our families' relationship to each other. His wife prays five times daily, while he happily offered a choice of scotch whiskies to whoever stepped through the door. Their son and his daughter have become scientists, having been fed a diet of books and learning, next to the delicious foods that ran aplenty.

One of the earliest memories I have is being taken as a little girl by my cousins, all grown up already and some having children of their own, and then put in the middle of a big bedspread. They would stand around it, grab the fabric and toss me high into the air, and there I was, bouncing up and down, surrounded by the laughter and love of cousin brothers and sisters. Me, the single child from Germany, a warm country here, a cold country there, a large family here, a small family there. Two worlds – of which the Hyderabad one seemed more humane, more alive.

From such fragments I piece together an image, trying to capture what it means to belong to one of the old families of Banjara Hills, whose fate was closely intertwined with the Nizams. Originally from Secunderabad, the sister city, tales have been handed down to me, while I filled my cheeks with biryani, by uncles, and old distant relations for whom my grandfather had provided a point of focus, of dazzle and of never faltering generosity. I recount them over and over, not knowing on which side of the cusp between myth and reality they are located. May I be forgiven if I stray too far into idealisation.

My great grandfather, Syed Siraj-ul Hassan, was a learned man, sent to undertake his studies in jurisprudence at Merton College Oxford in 1880. From descriptions of his last surviving son, he was quick witted already then, and not afraid of humorous confrontations. And so he gleefully recounted stories from his days as a student, which his son, himself an avid scholar, noted down:

> One of these which he recounted with particular relish related to the morning when he had over-slept somewhat and, in a rush to go over and register himself for breakfast in accordance with Merton College regulations, he hastily pulled a dressing-gown over his pyjamas and dashed out into the corridor. There he was promptly spotted by one of the 'Dons'. 'Hassan!' called out the crusty academician, 'you are not properly dressed'. To carry the situation off, Siraj-ul Hassan summoned all the jauntiness of which he was capable and answered:

'This is my national dress, Sir!', 'Well then, Mr Hassan' came the mildly sar-
donic reply, 'don't you think you'd better save it for State occasions?'

Siraj ul-Hassan drew out his studies to the limit, adding a PhD to his
titles, and returned with the Anglicised-Indian brand of rational humanism,
which shaped the coming elites of Indian administrators, and culminated
in the figure of Nehru. But this fusion of influences was part of a wider
theme that can still be found in Hyderabad today, the *tehzeeb* (etiquette),
the intertwinement and respect between Hindus and Muslims. I observed
it early when walking with my beloved aunt down a road in Bajara Hills,
by then dotted with a growing number of single family homes – white,
lovely buildings, the walls surrounding the individual compounds dripping
in pink bougainvilleas. For us, being Muslims, the greeting is *'Adaab arz
hey'* (our respects) accompanied with a slight bow, the right hand cusped
and slowly directed towards the forehead. For my aunt's acquaintances,
being Hindus, it is 'Namaskaar', accompanied by the palms of both hands
pressed against each other and held against the chest, this, too with a slight
bow of the head. 'Namaskaar' said my aunt and raised her hand towards
her forehead. *'Adaa barz hey'* replied her neighbours, their hands forming
the gesture of the 'Namaskaar' against their chests. And while we continued
on our way, my young mind marvelled at the mutual and natural respect
that this encounter illustrated.

Hyderabad's' location at the navel of India made it a great heaven of
pluralism, an example of what India could be at its finest. There seemed to
be a general embodied understanding of the mutual enrichment that the
various cultural and religious traditions had to offer. My father recounted
instances of his childhood in the 1930s and 40s where he was given access
to the kitchens of Hindu friends, spaces tightly guarded for their ritual
purity. At the protests of the children of the house who were denied such
access, their mother, having been witness to her own offspring's
mischievousness replied: 'You are not an honest boy, but he is. That is why
he can enter and you cannot.' Ironically, the same happened in the reverse,
when my father was denied a ritual feast, while the Hindu children of the
gardeners could partake. 'Their hearts are innocent, but you are a liar', my
grandmother simply stated, thus proving the universal truth that it is easier
to impress the parents of others, rather than one's own.

During the great flood of the Musi River in 1908 that brought the loss of tens of thousands of lives, the Nizam himself donned a *dhoti* and stepped into the river to perform a Hindu *puja* to appease the river goddess. He did that before embarking on a large scale infrastructure project which included dams and tanks, to prevent such a disaster from happening again. In recent commemorations of the event, interviews record the respect the Nizam is afforded for this action to this day. One could observe that a Muslim ruler performing a Hindu ritual for his Hindu subjects was simply the shrewd calculation of a politician wanting to keep his multi-ethnic and multi-faith populace appeased in the wake of a terrible disaster. But even if so, the symbolism of such an act is the kind of medicine that would be healing the world over. One does not have to look far to appreciate the need for such deeds.

Religiosity then, as I gather from such stories and by my own observations today, was lived as a state of honesty and respect, rather than an adherence to strict rules. It is little wonder that it was the particular brand of South Asian Sufism that took hold in such conditions, rather than more fervently dogmatic expressions of Islam. Today I relish in the Qawwalis performed at weddings or other occasions, their melodies transporting me into a realm of great peace while their lyrics of love to God are deeply moving.

My grandfather was not a religious man. He had been brought up by his mother; his father Siraj had left his mother early. So not wanting her only son to carry the unfaithful husband's name, she gave her son the surname 'Panjatan', referring to the five holy people of Islam: Mohammed, Ali, Fatima, Hassan and Hussain. He bore the name with pride, and while his father grew his family with his second wife, he is said on occasion to have proudly exclaimed: 'There is one God, and there is one Panjatan!' Ghulam Panjatan, too, was a lawyer, educated at Aligarh University and soon became a wealthy man, quite probably aided by his mother, an aristocratic lady from Tonk, who had brought gold bars into her marriage. He owned vast lands and estates, but was in no hurry to find a wife. One day, so my father tells me, he heard of a girl in a village of which he was the landlord, the third daughter of farmers, without either a dowry or particular beauty. Her prospects were dire, and in casual conversation she was pitied. Upon hearing this, my grandfather decided to change her fate and marry her. She was a slender and delicately built woman, small and plain looking, with thick round glasses, and judging from the few photographs that remain, a somewhat stern expression. Seeing my grandfather, an imposing man of six foot two, for the first time at their wedding, she reportedly thought her end was near – being about to be married off to a giant. However, her fears did not materialise and she soon became the mistress of a house that was to be a centre of Hyderabadi society. She had only one request for her husband, that he prayed five times a day. And so he did to his final day, the mighty high court judge, out of respect for his wife who had come from the village and could hardly read and write.

Their house was a splendid white pillared bungalow, laid out in a big garden, and the location of many great parties and festivities. My grandfather liked to keep an open house, and one could be sure to be served the finest scotch out of crystal whisky glasses. Never, so my father assures me, was a voice or a hand raised in anger. One anecdote goes thus. At one of the splendid gatherings a small boy was running cheerfully among the guests, undoubtedly encouraged by the loving winks of the diverse group of attendees. Maybe while taking a daring turn, he bumped into a table on which the shimmering whisky glasses where placed and knocked one down, which promptly shattered into pieces. His mother, embarrassed by her son's misbehaviour, gave him a slap. As the boy started crying, my grandfather came to console him. 'What matters more' he asked, 'the joy of a child, or those inanimate glasses?' And together with the surprised boy and in front of the flabbergasted mother he proceeded to smash every single one of them, undoubtedly enjoying the cheekiness of the situation.

My grandfather's first child was his only daughter, six sons followed. Her authority over the brothers was never questioned, and she was the only one of his children who was sent abroad to study, returning after a few years with a degree in Anthropology from the University of Edinburgh. After her return she lived in her own house, unmarried, and by all descriptions forming around her a salon of women who included the Nizam's daughter-in-law, the Turkish princess Niloufer, Sarojini Naidu, who was a leader of India's independence movement and confidante of Mahatma Gandhi, as well as simple craftswomen from the opposite end of the social hierarchy. Her interests lay in lively exchanges, her mind not stifled by limitations of class, continuing the spirit of her parents who through their marriage had bridged social divides.

If today I look at my female cousins with admiration, some of them being dedicated scientists, lawyers and educators, all of us tied together by a strong bond of mutual love and respect, then I see them as fruits coming from a tree that was always watered with a healthy dose of female empowerment. It was never a question that women could and would achieve as highly as men. Today, forty days after my father's last brother has passed on, it is his daughter who is a north star to us, who from our origins in Hyderabad now live dispersed across the globe. Herself a doctor of genetics, researcher and professor, she is an institution in the city. I often heard her being compared to our aunt, the same wit, comprised of a sharp intelligence and a warm, encompassing and lovingly mocking humour that expresses itself in a repertoire ranging from a low raspy chuckle to full open-throated laughter.

It might have been this social flexibility and modern outlook that carried the family through the end of the Raj and into the Indian republic. When the old rule collapsed, many formerly grand families went down with it, holding on to their pride, and mourning the loss of their old ways of living. It was those whose focus was on learning, on education and on open mindedness who made a home within the new social order. And so, while the wealth diminished, the spirit stayed high. It is said that my grandfather in order to avoid conflict amongst his sons (my aunt had already passed away before her time), deliberately left nothing behind. And his prediction was right. As there was nothing left to inherit but intelligence and joi-de-vivre, there was nothing to squabble about, no perceived injustices that would drive wedges between the brothers and their children. When my uncles and my father were made aware of highly valuable lands and buildings that were found to be in my grandfather's name in the land title registry, they all rejected them. Decades after my grandfather had died, their lack of interest in material possessions had become so ingrained that no notion of claiming them was made. Questions by me and my cousins were dismissed with the same retorts: 'Why are you interested in this? Is it yours, did you earn it?' And so we accepted, some of us grudgingly. Without doubt their refusal spared us the price of family disunity.

Few old photographs remain to provide a window into a bygone world of riches. In one I see the six young brothers standing on the veranda of their home, some teenagers, some about seven or eight, the little ones wearing the short white trousers of schoolboys, the older ones clad in *sherwanis* with fezs on their heads, the Turkish caps popularised by the Nizam. They look proudly into the camera (judging by my father's age, the picture would have been taken around 1938), my father playfully pointing a stick as it if was a rifle. In another, earlier one, two young boys with little embellished hats and light brocaded *sherwanis* are holding the hands of a tall young man with a fez, himself dressed in long dark embroidered *sherwani*, looking straight into the camera. 'Two little boys with some prince', I thought when I first chanced upon this. 'My brothers with our driver Abdullah on their way to a wedding', my father explained. There are other, separate photos of the six boys, staged in pairs of similar age, all carrying the same proud, almost defiant expression. They reflect a habitus that is rarely found these days, a pride so non-deliberately intended that it was easy to let go of the lived reality of it. My father soon trailed off to Bombay and Delhi to try his luck on the stage and in films with some success. There he lived the life of a bohemian, at times eating at the Oberoi Hotel with Mohan Singh Oberoi himself, at other times sleeping on pavements and going without food for days, too proud to ask his father for money. When I look at him today, after decades in Germany, an artist to the bone, I can still see that pride which the images of his eight-year-old self display.

Hyderabad today is a bustling city, where the relics of the past try to hold their own besides newer and now shinier hubs like the new IT city district aptly named 'Cyberabad'. The Nizams' old palaces have turned into ultra luxurious hotels, are used as glamorous event venues for weddings that out-dazzle any imagination, are museums, or are simply crumbling and decaying. Some of the old private mansions are well maintained, but many buckle under the stress of the upkeep, having become impractical homes. The lovely white bungalows that dotted Banjara Hills are being replaced by multi-storey homes, one by one. The erstwhile lakes, built by the Nizams as fresh water reservoirs, have over time turned into stagnant water sewers.

Driving by the Musi river, in which the memory of the great flood is being enveloped by the stench of wastage pumped into it by nearby factories, I cover my airways with a shawl, a gesture I learned early in life as an imperfect way to ward off the worst of pollution. I see huge advertisements displaying seemingly improbable wedding jewellery, beautiful models with aloof faces turned out in heavy gold embroidered dark red *khada duppatas*, the traditional Hyderabadi bridal wear. There are gold and gemstone studded pendants over their foreheads, ears and noses, and heavy diamond encrusted chokers draped tightly around their necks, with pearls dripping down their chests. The wealth has moved on to a new generation, one that wants to impress on Instagram and takes a fusion of the luxury of the past and the trappings of Bollywood as a benchmark of aesthetic validity.

We arrive once more at my uncle's house. Sheikh Ahmed is long gone, the apartment on the top long deserted. My memories of what used to be are interrupted by the sounds of a new generation. My geneticist cousin's sons are bustling about, and coming out to say hello. My uncle, now old but still lively, follows and greets us excitedly. His wonderful wife who holds it all together, sits on the sofa in the living room that has seen so many stories unfold, and welcomes us with her own brand of loving bemusement. My father soon sits down next to her, and they exchange stories and poetry, she being an acclaimed writer and poet, and my father a great lover of Urdu literature. Soon others join in and we have a small gathering. The doors of the house, just as back in the 1930s, are still wide open.

One night I get up to use the bathroom. It is painted in the typical blue that any traveller to the Indian subcontinent would recognise. The toilet sits at the far end, opposite double swing doors that close together with a long horizontal bolt. Pyjama pants down I get somewhat nervous being so exposed, fearing mosquito attacks on my bottom. Suddenly something else catches my attention. Looking down at the floor, I notice black patches that seem to disintegrate into small streaks. I notice, two, three then more. As if in a dream I look up. From cracks in the ceiling it looks as if thick liquid bundles are forming. To my horror I recognise that these are formations of small ants hanging down, resembling stalactites before dropping onto the floor, where they quickly disperse in all directions with great coordination. Coming out of my shock, I jump up, trying to pull up my bottoms while at the same time protecting my head from the invasion. I wrestle with the bolted door and finally stand outside looking back at the efficiency with which the ants claim the space where three generations of my family have lived.

My uncle has now passed away, as have all my father's brothers. The grandchildren have flown the nest, studying abroad. My cousin and my aunt remain, but the house has become quieter now, the ants waiting to take over and devour the limestone out of which it is built. It is hard to imagine not just my family without it, but Hyderabad itself. And yet, the young generation seems determined to keep the light shining and the spirit alive that so much reflects the story of the city itself.

For many years my family was the only tangible connection I had to any notion of being Muslim, and so my association with Islam is foremost one of fostering a culture of learning and open-mindedness. I know now that as in any cultural conglomerate the lived expressions are too many to count, and mine captured but a sliver of a privileged experience. And yet, it serves as a reminder that the chorus of voices that makes up the song which we call religion and culture is polyphonous and complex. If we listen closely, we can hear the melody of a city called Hyderabad, which sits between the North and South, between Hinduism and Islam, spirituality and humanism. And if we are wise, we may join in.

DEATH AND BURIAL

Andrew Petersen

There are three keys events in a person's life when their otherwise invisible practise of religion suddenly becomes visible. Traditionally these occasions are birth, marriage and death although there are also other social events where religion may be prominent such as circumcisions, rites associated with coming of age and some pivotal moments in their education. Each of these stages is associated with some form of ritual which can involve members of the wider religious community as well as family members. In contemporary society and probably on occasions in the past, some of the religious rites associated with stages of life are omitted either because of expense or because of an increasing secularisation of society. However the religious aspects of the final rite of passage are the least likely to be abandoned both because of the conservative nature of funerary rites and because death is implicitly linked to a religiously inspired afterlife.

There are many examples where friends and colleagues are unaware of a person's religion until an untimely death when they are confronted with the full range of funerary rituals associated with the religion and sect of the deceased. Of course the extent to which such rituals are perceived to help the relatives rather than provide intercession for the deceased varies depending on religious observance, beliefs, and community priorities. Whatever the motivation, funerals and their material manifestations are a significant component of both anthropological and archaeological investigation.

Archaeology and death has a particularly strong relationship as few other rites of passage leave such a strong and durable imprint on the material record. In fact a brief review of archaeological literature will demonstrate that a large proportion of reports, monographs and museum exhibitions are concerned with aspects of death and burial. One of the first archaeological textbooks was *A Handbook of Egyptian Funerary Archaeology* written by Wallis Budge, a Keeper of Egyptian Antiquities at the British Museum and published in 1898. In any case burials are certainly one of the most durable expressions of human culture providing a physical expression of beliefs about death and the afterlife. We just have to look to the excavation of graves at Shanidar caves in northern Iraq to provide some of the earliest evidence of ritual burial 35,000-65,000 years ago, and a fascinating insight into the civilisation that existed at that time. Another famous early example of burial is the so called Red Lady of Paviland, who is actually a man, dated to 26,000 years before the present and comprising skeletal remains covered in red ochre and accompanied by a sea shell necklace and jewellery made of mammoth ivory.

Mortuary archaeology is a well established branch of scientific enquiry, yet its application to the Islamic world is less well developed than for most other periods and regions. The reasons for this are complex but in general there is a tendency in Muslims societies to prefer to leave the dead to rest, and a feeling that archaeological excavation of a Muslim grave is undesirable. A more specific objection to the archaeological excavation of graves may have developed because many of the important ancient sites in the Middle East are partially covered with Muslim cemeteries and there is a feeling that these should not be disturbed by archaeologists, often from abroad, looking for earlier remains. As a result the archaeology of death and burial in the Islamic world has become increasingly significant in recent years, reflecting both an increased interest in Muslim material culture and a practical need to deal with Muslim remains when they are discovered.

A factor of particular importance is the increasing rate of development in the Islamic world, which has meant that archaeologists are often employed to remove graves prior to the commencement of construction projects. One can add to this a growing politicisation of Islamic identity throughout the world, making any questions involving the treatment of Muslim remains particularly significant. The fact that Muslims now constitute the world's second largest religious group obviously adds to the necessity for developing ideas on how to record, process, analyse, and discuss Muslim burials.

The archaeological excavation of human remains is anathema within Islamic tradition. As Palestinian historian, Walid Khalidi, notes: 'according to the unanimous opinion of Muslim scholars, disinterment of the dead is strictly forbidden, and the sanctity of cemeteries is considered eternal.' Although Khalidi's statement is inaccurate, and there are many examples of cemeteries in the Islamic world being removed under the licence of religious authorities, the sentiment it expresses is popular and has meant that there are relatively few published reports on the archaeological excavation of Muslim graves. This view is based on a number of factors, though the tradition that the corpse interred in a grave was capable of feeling pain and was also the actual body, which would return to life on the Day of Judgement, may play a part. This view also exists in Judaism where religious authorities often go to extreme lengths to protect the integrity of the body of the deceased and also to prevent human remains being moved. In the 1980s, Jewish religious leaders called for an end to the archaeological excavation and removal of human remains and issued a curse on all archaeologists working in the 'Land of Israel'. According to Israeli law any discovery of human bones should be reported to the Ministry of Religious Affairs and reburied without academic study of the remains. This law is enforced strictly when it is known that the remains are those of Jews although for Muslims and Christians and prehistoric remains there is less interest as Jewish ultra-Orthodox groups will be unlikely to object. However, the Jewish religious ban and its uneven application in Israel has politicised the issue, prompting Muslims groups to also now object to the removal of human remains in protest at the perceived lack of sanctity offered to their dead.

The recent excavation of part of the Mamilla Cemetery in Jerusalem for a new Israeli museum is one of the most contentious examples of the excavation of Islamic burials. The cemetery, which lies in west Jerusalem, dates back to the eleventh century and contains the graves of thousands of Muslims, some of whom died fighting in the Crusades. Although much of this large cemetery had been neglected and in some cases paved over since the 1960s the burials themselves remained undisturbed until the early 2000s when planning permission was granted for 'The Simon Wiesenthal Museum of Tolerance' on part of the site. As part of the planning process, an archaeological investigation was carried out which involved the excavation of more than 400 Muslim graves, representing a small proportion of those estimated to be on the proposed museum site. Despite objections from the chief archaeologist responsible, the planning authorities gave the go ahead for the construction of the museum. Immediately prior to the construction, thousands of graves were excavated and human remains removed to an undisclosed location. The results of this phase of the 'archaeological' excavation have remained unpublished and the director of the Israel Antiquities Authority who authorised the removal of the graves subsequently stated his regret at the decision to destroy the cemetery.

At this point, it is worth stating that, whilst Islam is a worldwide religion with a strong sense of unity and cohesion in practice, there are multiple forms of the faith, based on factors such as ethnicity, occupation, education, local tradition, affiliation to particular sects, political outlook, and relationship to non-Muslim communities. All of these factors, and more, have an impact on burial customs, so that in many cases the variation in Muslim burials is greater than between a Muslim and a non-Muslim burial. Despite this difficulty of characterisation, there are sets of practices which are generally associated with Islamic burials and as such have relevance over diverse regions and extensive time periods.

The special status of Arabic as the language of the Qur'an has given Arabic traditions a somewhat privileged position. Most of the literature and legal discussions concerning burial refer back either to the time of Muhammad or to the period immediately after his death and are explained within an Arabian context. The Qur'an is the starting point for any consideration of Islamic practices and customs, however, it is interesting to note that burial is barely mentioned in the Qur'an or only referred to obliquely. The main source for Muslim laws and customs are actually the *hadith*, collections of sayings attributed to the Prophet Muhammad collected and committed to writing during the first three centuries of Islam. Neither the Qur'an nor the hadith provide detailed instructions on how to deal with particular situations, so a method of interpretation based on deductive logic known as *ijtihad* was developed, and it is from this that the principles of Muslim religious law, or *fiqh,* are derived. These laws form the basis for a series of funeral manuals, produced during the medieval period and later, which discuss the various legal and religious issues involved in burial. The funeral manuals are of particular importance because they mediate between the religious ideal and current practice. It is noticeable that sectarian differences are not reflected in the burial laws and traditions; thus, there is not much difference between Shia and Sunni laws governing death and burial. In addition to the religious laws, there are a variety of traditions, of either local or ethnic origin, which have considerable influence on how the dead are buried and commemorated. In many cases, such as the construction of memorials above the grave, local custom takes priority over religious law.

Despite regional variations and disagreements about the application of the religious laws, there is broad consensus on how the dead should be treated. There is a preference for dying at home, and to die away from home is sometimes considered a calamity. This may be a reflection of pre-Islamic Arabian beliefs, where the place of dying and hence burial needed to be easily located and accessible to the tribe or community. In pre-Islamic Arabia, although there was no belief in the afterlife of an individual, the requirements of tribal solidarity demanded that the dead were properly buried at a recognised place. If this requirement was ignored, then the souls of the dead were detached from the tribe and afflicted with an unquenchable thirst. The other components of a correct burial involved the washing of the corpse, a shroud, and interment, all of which were later incorporated as part of Islamic burial practice.

Some aspects of pre-Islamic pagan burials, such as offerings and lamentations, were replaced with prayers for the dead person. One of the most interesting aspects of pre-Islamic burial in Arabia is the practice of *baliya*, whereby the deceased is buried with an animal, usually a camel. Although this practice is not condoned in Islamic traditions, archaeological evidence indicates that it may have continued during the first few decades after the adoption of Islam by Arab tribes.

When a Muslim is near death, it is customary to ask for forgiveness for offences against others before praying for forgiveness from God. Also it is usual for a dying person to receive many visitors, because visiting a dying person confers blessings on the visitor. Usually verses from the Qur'an are read out and often the dying person is given *zamzam* water, which originates from the sacred spring in Mecca, to drink. Unlike their pagan predecessors, Muslim Arabs believed in an afterlife – death was not the end of life but rather the end of the period of testing, after which each individual would be assessed on the Day of Judgment. The date, time, and place of death were predetermined, though the fate of the deceased was dependent on their faith and actions, which could only be known by God. An idealised account of the death of a Muslim is provided by Baha al-Din Ibn Shadad, who described the death and funeral of the twelfth-century Muslim leader Saladin. The precise moment of death is recorded as follows:

> He [Saladin] breathed his last after the hour of morning prayer on Wednesday 27th Safar 589 [4 March 1193]. The qadi al-Fadil came into his room just after dawn at the precise moment of his death, and when I arrived he had already passed into the bosom of divine grace. I was told that when Shaykh Abu Jafar reached the words of the Qur'an, "there is no God except Allah, and in him I trust", the Sultan smiled, his face illumined, and he gave up his spirit to the lord.

Traditionally the point of death is when breathing and heart functions cease, based on the idea that breath and blood form the vital spirit. However, recent developments have led to definitions closer to that of modern medical science, based on brain function.

The short interval between a death and a Muslim funeral meant that graves were often dug very rapidly, which in pre-modern times usually meant a communal effort by relatives and friends. Many customs and traditions are associated with the construction of the grave, though there are wide regional and chronological variations. There are two main forms of grave: the first is a deep rectangular pit with a smaller human-sized trench at the bottom, known as a *shiqq* or *shaqq*; the second type of grave or *lahd* is similar to the first but has a rectangular niche cut into the side into which the deceased may be placed. In the first type, when a body is laid to rest in the trench at the bottom of the pit, wooden planks, reeds, or similar material are placed over the corpse, resting on the sides of the trench. In the other case, the sides of the niche were blocked with a wall, usually made of non-fired mud bricks. It is possible that both forms of grave derive from pre-Islamic Arabia, though there are no archaeological or contemporary textual records to confirm this. It is not clear whether choice of one or other form of grave was dictated by custom, region, or both, though it is clear that those built with a niche in the side could only be built where ground conditions permitted and would probably not be viable in sandy or loose soil. The idea behind both forms of grave was that the upper part of the corpse and in particular the face should not be in direct contact with the earth. In a *shaqq* grave the face was protected from the earth by a slab covering the trench and in a *lahd* grave the niche is designed like a shelf. Conversely, it was important that the bottom of the shroud should lie in direct contact with the ground, which explains why coffins are generally avoided in Muslim burials.

Although the archaeological excavation of Muslim graves and cemeteries is not universally prohibited, cultural norms and perceived religious taboos have meant that excavation of Muslim cemeteries is either avoided, or where they are carried out, the results are often not published. It is also noticeable that whilst the archaeological information about the graves may be published, more detailed analysis of the human remains are rarely carried out. However in cases where Muslim burials are analysed and fully published they can provide crucial information for reconstructing many aspects of Islamic society and culture. Two areas where the excavation of Muslim burials can provide important information not available from other sources are the question of grave goods and anthropological studies of the deceased. Like many other aspects of Muslim burial, grave goods are a feature which is either not mentioned or specifically forbidden in religious literature. Whilst ritual inclusion of grave goods is rare in Islamic contexts, an analysis of excavated finds from late Islamic sites in the Near East indicates that small objects such as beads, bangles, mirrors, and coins are surprisingly common. Excavations of a large Muslim cemetery at Tell el-Hesi in the Negev provided quantifiable data of this and indicates that some form of personal ornamentation or prized object is present in 40 per cent of the graves.

There have been fewer anthropological or palaeo-pathological studies of Muslim graves, though notable examples include studies on remains from the cemetery at Kom el-Dikka in Egypt as well as the investigation of a number of Muslim cemeteries in Iberia (Spain and Portugal). Kom el-Dikka is an ancient Muslim cemetery used between the ninth and fifteenth centuries. Two basic phases were uncovered: a ninth-century phase and a Mamluk (1260–1516) phase. In the Mamluk phase, there was evidence of mass burials and disturbance by animals, which led the excavators to suggest this was a plague cemetery; this was supported by the anthropology, where mortality age was consistent with an epidemic of bubonic plague.

In the Iberian peninsula the main focus of research on medieval human remains has been around the question of identity – either religious (Muslim, Jewish or Christian) or ethnic (Arab, Berber, Visigoth, Roman or indigenous Iberian). This question has particular significance as it relates both to questions of national identity and also has relevance for current political debates around refugees and migrants. In scientific terms the question is interesting because at the beginning of the period the region was predominantly Christian before being incorporated into the Islamic world and finally returning to Christian rule during the later middle ages. Whilst the political history of the Muslim conquest and Christian Reconquista is well known, the process and its effect on actual populations is less well understood. For example, did the Muslim conquest mean that a few Muslim Arabs ruled over a Christian peasantry or did it lead to the mass conversion of Christians or the immigration of large numbers of Arabs and Berbers who replaced an indigenous Christian population? Each of these theories has their proponents and each theory has significant problems. On a practical level archaeology can start to provide some definitive evidence although until there are larger scale studies the results are indicative rather than conclusive. Two recent studies of human remains have provided interesting results which, for the first time, provide hard evidence of the Muslim presence in early medieval Europe.

The first is the study of graves from the site of a Christian basilica (church) in Mertola, Portugal and published in 1999. Archaeologists were able to excavate two well dated groups of graves one set from beneath the basilica which were contemporary with its use as a church from fifth to seventh centuries, and another from the period after the church had fallen out of use, between eight and thirteenth centuries. The earliest group of burials were clearly Christian, based on their orientation and the discovery of more than forty tombstones. The latter group were identified as Muslims based on their orientation and position of the bodies lying on their sides with their heads turned to face Mecca. The anthropological study aimed to identify the ethnic origin of the deceased based on measurements of specific features of the cranium. The results of the analysis indicate that the two sets of burials are from different populations and are unlikely to originate from the same gene pool. The researchers suggested that the Muslim burials might be of Arab or Berber origin but were unable to confirm this without examining material from known Arab and Berber cemeteries of similar date.

The second study was more recent and able to draw on a range of innovative interdisciplinary techniques including DNA analysis. The research was based on the discovery and analysis of three graves from the city of Nimes in southern France. Although the Arab conquest of Spain in 711 is well known from historical sources, little information exists regarding its northern extension into France, apart from the famous battle of Poitiers in 732. According to local chronicles, the Visigoth territory of Septimania which extended from the Pyrenees to the river Rhone is known to have included a Muslim presence in the eighth century, possibly representing an alliance against their common enemy the Franks from the North. Although a few examples of ceramics from the Islamic world have been identified in excavations from the regions these are sparse and do not confirm a Muslim presence there. This made the discovery of three Muslim graves on the outskirts of Nimes particularly fascinating. The graves were identified as Muslim from their orientation and positioning. Two of the graves included lateral niches, which corresponds to the *al-lahd* type whilst the third grave had a single narrow slit at the bottom containing the body and corresponding to *al-shaqq* burial. All three of the skeletons were identified as adult males. Samples of bone from the graves were dated using Carbon-14 which when calibrated gave dates in the eighth and ninth centuries, corresponding with the presence of Muslims in the area cited in medieval chronicles. The DNA analysis indicates that all three of the burials were of North African Berber origin which led the researchers to suggest that they were part of a Muslim garrison present in the region between 720 and 752. The presence of one Christian grave in near proximity to the Muslim graves and the lack of trauma from battle wounds provides further evidence that Muslims were living amongst a resident Christian Visigoth community.

Whilst the Muslim ideal is to die and be buried at or near home, following the example of Prophet Muhammad, this is not always compatible with the tradition of burial within 24 hours. In practice this has meant that people are often buried hundreds of miles from their homes. During the fifteenth century the Sufi spiritual leader Abu al-Awn built a mosque and funerary complex for himself in his native village of Jaljuliyya but died in the city of Ramla. Despite the short distance between the two locations his body remained in Ramla and was buried within the Friday mosque he had built in the city. When death occurs at sea and there is no option of returning home within a few hours the traditional practice was to bury the deceased at the nearest landfall and when this was not possible people could be buried in the ocean. The practice of Muslim burial at sea has been highlighted by the US treatment of the remains of the al-Qaida leader Osama bin Laden and more recently the ISIS leader al-Baghdadi. In both cases the sea burials were conducted with a religious service conforming to Muslim practice to avoid the possibility of their graves becoming a focus for followers.

In some cases, however, people wish to be buried at specific locations, far from their place of residence. Amongst the Shia community of Iraq there is a long-standing desire to be buried near the tomb of 'Ali at Najaf, which traditionally involves a journey of several days, with the corpse being strapped to a horse or camel, although today the journey is more likely made by taxi, with a coffin tied to the roof rack. A more difficult situation arises when people die while performing Hajj, as they are usually far away from home and relatives. In pre-modern times, most pilgrims who died on the Hajj route were buried where they lay. However, occasionally wealthy travellers, sensing the imminence of death, or expecting the eventuality, would pay to have their bodies conveyed to Mecca or Medina for burial. In practice, this sometimes meant odd ad hoc arrangements, which become mythologised such as the story of the rotting body of a wealthy Persian lady who had died at Ma'an, being conveyed to Mecca inside a camel skin, carried on poles set between two camels.

In Central Asia, it was common practice for the dead to be transported in large numbers to distant ancestral burial grounds. The strong affinity to the idea of a specific place of rest continues to prompt generations of a family to be buried in the same family plot. Although there is a tendency to avoid ostentatious graves so they do not become shrine-like or a focus for the bereaved, the link between death, identity and place is resolute. Contemporary challenges such as finding more environmentally-friendly methods of burial that remain compatible with Islamic jurisprudence, will no doubt preoccupy forthcoming generations, and marvel future archaeologists.

MINARET TO MINARET

Leyla Jagiella

What comes to mind when the history of Islam in Europe is evoked? One thinks of the *mezquita* in Cordoba and the Alhambra in Granada. Or Sicily under Arab and Norman rule. And the long Ottoman presence in the Balkans and of the beauty of Bosnia and Albania. But Poland? Will Poland come to your mind? Probably not. Poland, a country that nowadays appears almost monoethnic and overwhelmingly Catholic, is usually not associated much with Islamic history. Apart, maybe, from the fact that in the seventeenth century the Polish King Jan III Sobieski defeated the Ottoman forces on the doorsteps of Vienna and thus rescued 'Europe' (Western Europe, that is) from an Islamic takeover. A fact that is often pompously remembered by right wing populists all over Europe nowadays and that has been celebrated by white supremacist terrorists such as Anders Breivik or the Christchurch mosque shooter. Contemporary Polish conservatives and nationalists, most of them decidedly racist and Islamophobic, also make much out of this piece of history and believe in an eternal holy mission of Poland as 'Europe's bulwark against Islam'.

A closer look at this piece of history, however, reveals shattering breaks in the convenient narrative sold both by international extreme right and Polish Catholic nationalists. Jan Sobieski was made an enemy of the Ottomans out of political necessity. He was certainly very Polish and very Catholic. But he was actually also a great admirer of Ottoman culture at the same time. He preferred Ottoman cuisine over any other cuisine and spoke Turkish fluently. As a young man he had once spent a few years in the Ottoman capital Istanbul, an experience that had influenced him deeply. Furthermore, he dressed exclusively in a style called 'Sarmatian', a type of fashion that was popular amongst the Polish aristocracy from the sixteenth to the early nineteenth centuries and that took inspiration from Ottoman, Tatar, Persian and even Mughal Indian fashion. As a Polish gentleman of the seventeenth century, Sobieski would have looked less out of place in Istanbul, Isfahan or Delhi than in Paris or Vienna. 'Sarmatian' fashion was inspired by the romantic ideology of 'Sarmatism' which made Polish aristocrats believe that they were descendants of the Sarmatians. An ancient horse-riding people of the Eurasian steppes they actually spoke an Iranian language related to modern Ossetian, Yaghnobi and (more distantly) Pashtu but which Polish aristocrats of those times considered close relatives of Turks and Tatars. As such, the Polish nobility considered itself a perfect mix of East and West: Catholic and educated in Latin, but descended from Asian horseriding warriors. A legend says that during the battle of Vienna the Polish forces were asked by their other Christian allies to distinguish themselves by a little straw worn on their helmets, since otherwise they could not be distinguished in look from Ottoman soldiers.

Scholars of South Asian art and history have sometimes wondered whether the South Indian Kingdom of Vijayanagar could be called an 'Islamicate kingdom', because, even though it was ruled by Hindu kings and presided over a largely Hindu population, its kings and elites had adopted fashion and other cultural idioms from its northern Muslim neighbours. In that same vein one could suggest that the early modern Kingdom of Poland was actually an Islamicate kingdom as well.

An even closer look at King Jan Sobieski and the 1683 battle of Vienna that he was involved in reveals even more confusing breaks with modern Polish and European narratives. The battle was not between uniform Christian and Muslim forces at all. There were plenty of Christian forces voluntarily fighting on the Ottoman side. Hungarian and Transylvanian Protestants in particular often preferred to fight for the Ottoman side. On the other hand, there also were Muslim forces fighting on the 'Christian' side. In particular, a number of several thousand Muslim Tatars under the command of King Jan Sobieski himself.

Indeed, the ancestors of these Muslim Tatars had been an integral part of Polish society for several centuries at that point. They had been in the country since Tokhtamysh, the Khan of the Golden Horde, had fallen out with his former friend and ally Amir Timur (the same Timur who is remembered as Tamerlane in European historiography and who, through his great-grandson Babur, was to become the ancestor of the South Asian Mughal dynasty), and had with several of his men sought refuge in the realm of another more reliable friend, King Jagiełło of Poland. Tokhtamysh`s son Jalaluddin Khan would later in the year 1410 fight at the side of King Jagiełło against invading Teutonic Knights and the Polish victory at this 'Battle of Grunwald' has often been specifically attributed to the help of Jalaluddin Khan and his Tatar Muslim troops. Since then, Tatar Muslims have settled in Poland, have served the Polish crown and have also played an important part in enabling cultural transmissions between Poland, Tatar Khanates further east and the Ottoman Empire, thereby contributing to Sarmatism and Sarmatian fashion.

Throughout the centuries a large part of the Polish Tatar Muslim community has converted to Catholicism and assimilated to the Polish majority. Historically changing borders have led several thousand other members of the community to be located not within the current borders of Poland, but in Lithuania, Belarus or Ukraine. A number of Polish Tatar Muslims also emigrated to the US in the early twentieth century, where in Brooklyn they founded one of the earliest mosques in North America. Around the same time, others emigrated to Turkey, Crimea or Azerbaijan. Centuries earlier, some Polish Tatars had already relocated to the Ottoman empire at a time when the Kingdom of Poland became more consciously Catholic and religious freedom was tightened. Through assimilation, changing borders, and waves of emigration the community has become a small and dwindling one. But several thousand Tatar Muslims still exist in Poland today and hold on to their Islamic faith. Their older Polish Islamic identity and practices often clash with the ideas and customs of more recent Muslim immigrants.

I am of Polish origin on my father's side and, incidentally, I am also Muslim. I did not grow up in a Tatar Muslim family though, my immediate Polish ancestors were good Catholics. There has been a legend in my family alleging distant Tatar ancestry. This legend has fascinated me since my early childhood but I have never been able to confirm its veracity completely. As an adult I have come to take it more as a cypher, a mythic expression of a cultural memory that remembers and acknowledged the importance that Tatar Muslims and their influence have once held in Polish history, though often forgotten or suppressed today. Closer to historical reality is the fact that my family actually owes its name to the same Polish king Jagiełło who fought with Tokhtamysh and Jalaluddin Khan. And that my great-grandfather once lived for several years in Ottoman Istanbul and, like King Jan Sobieski, took a liking to Ottoman dress and culture there. In that way, I have always felt connected to the history of both Polish Sarmatism and of the Polish Tatar Muslim community.

If you know where to look, the Islamic history of Poland and neighbouring countries can be easily excavated. I have gone on my own little pilgrimage exploring historical sights and visiting Muslim communities – a journey that took me to the old Polish-Lithuanian Kingdom, almost from the Baltic to the Black Sea.

I began on the shores of the Baltic Sea, the city with three names: Polish Gdańsk, Kashubian Gdańsk, German Danzig. Gdańsk is often considered the most 'Western' of all Polish cities, it has always remained open to the Baltic Sea and the Scandinavian countries beyond and it has remained under a strong German influence for a long time. Nevertheless, it was also the starting point for many journeys to the Muslim World. In medieval times, Arab authors wrote about the huge trading centres on these shores. From here the Muslim world purchased Baltic amber, furs and slaves. Large wads of dirhams and dinars from Central Asia found at Polish archaeological sites confirm the importance of these trade relations. In the seventeenth century the French traveller Jean-Baptiste Tavernier met a number of Armenians from Gdańsk who traded with Baltic amber in Mughal India. On their long way back these Armenians would probably have taken with them the priced North Indian, Kashmiri and Iranian textiles favoured so much by the Polish nobility of the time.

The seventeenth century Ottoman traveller, Evliyâ Çeleb, reported that the St. Nicholas church in Gdańsk was considered a place of pilgrimage by Polish Tatars who believed that the Turkish Sufi saint Sary Saltuq was buried there. Modern-day Polish Tatars don`t consider the church a place of pilgrimage anymore but they still consider Gdańsk a place of religious significance. A vibrant Tatar Muslim community started to emerge in the city in the 1920s and early 1930s when Gdańsk was a 'free city', independent from both a newly founded Poland and the German Empire and under League of Nations protection. The members of this community had moved here from eastern Poland in search of work and economic stability but they also found the city a place of fresh and free air, removed from their sticky conservative home villages. The small Tatar community of Gdańsk became a hub of 'Jadidism', a modernist reform movement that had started amongst Tatar Muslims in Russia.

After the Second World War, the German speaking part of the city's population had to flee west, At the same time the city received a huge number of Polish refugees from territories of the country that now had to be ceded to the Soviet Union. Amongst them were a significant number of Polish-speaking Tatar Muslims from what is today Lithuania and Belarus. The newly enlivened Muslim community of the city was planning the construction of a mosque. The new arrivals helped; and the construction of the new Gdańsk mosque was started in 1984. The mosque finally opened its doors to believers and visitors in June 1990.

The mosque was built in white in a style supposed to signify modernity and globality. The minaret seems inspired by Ottoman examples, the dome seems vaguely South Asian, the frontal entrance as ambiguously Andalusian. It looks very different from the traditional Polish village mosques. During its opening one of the most active female members of Gdańsk's Tatar Muslim community, Dżemila Smajkiewicz-Murman, gave a speech that evoked a world very far away from this pristine modern mosque. She remembered the old wooden mosque of her birth town Vilnius:

> Now after so many years reaching back to my childhood, I see a little girl wandering to the mosque with my grandfather, to the mosque in Vilnius which no longer exists. I see the Vilnius Imam, my grandfather, Ibrahim Smajkiewicz explaining to me the principles of Islam, and every morning I hear his voice commencing the prayer. And I pray together with my grandpa, who explains that the 'rug for prayer' (*namaziyk*) must be highly esteemed, because, within it, is sewn one piece of the cloth covering the Ka'ba and brought by Mufti Szynkiewicz. Now, this little piece of cloth, still present in my mind, seems to lead me to Mecca where I shall see it whole.

From Gdańsk I travelled east and entered lands that were once called 'Prussia'. What an irony that this name is associated nowadays, first and foremost, with Germanness and especially so with the most disciplined and militaristic Germanness. The original Prussians were actually a Baltic tribe that spoke a language akin to Latvian and Lithuanian. It was conquered by German Teutonic Knights who set up their own state in this land after less successful ventures in the Holy Land.

I passed a place that Germans call Tannenberg and Poles call Grunwald. It was here that King Jagiełło and Jalaluddin Khan once defeated the Teutonic Knights in 1410. How strange that here the Teutonic Knights must have heard the same call *Allahu Akbar* that their forebears would have heard in Palestine a few generations earlier. The independent state of the Teutonic Order survived for a century more, until the last Grand Master of the Knights converted to Protestantism, secularised the state, declared it a duchy, and placed it under the sovereignty of the Kingdom of Poland. Until the late seventeenth century this Protestant duchy, in which German, Prussian, Lithuanian and Polish was spoken, and where Armenian merchants gathered Baltic amber destined for the Indian market as much as they did in Gdańsk, remained a part of a multi-ethnic and multireligious Poland.

Political tides turned when the Duchy of Prussia fell into the hands of the Electorate of Brandenburg. In 1701 Elector Frederick III finally crowned himself 'King in Prussia' and became Frederick I. From then on Prussia would increasingly be identified with Brandenburg and subsequently with Germany, even though a large part of its population continued to speak Polish and Lithuanian even up to the twentieth century. At the end of the eighteenth century, Prussia, Austria and Russia assaulted Polish sovereignty and annexed the land of the kingdom. Now an even larger part of Polish territory fell into the hands of Frederick II, a string of Tatar Muslim villages. Frederick II recruited all the able male inhabitants of these villages into his army.

After crossing Prussian lands , I reached a place called Gołdap, close to the border of the Russian Kaliningrad region and not too far away from Lithuania. Near this city, on a quiet island in the middle of a river also called Gołdap, there once was a *mizar*, a Polish Muslim cemetery. King Frederick II had given this burial place to the Tatar Muslim soldiers serving in his army. In the 1920s Muslim tombstones could still be found on this island and nearby Christian villagers feared the 'unholy' ghosts of these 'unbaptised dead'. Nothing of them can be found since the end of World War II. Only reeds cover the island. Most probably the cemetery was destroyed by the advancing Red Army when traces of everything 'German' were eradicated from the region.

From Goldap I followed the curving line of the Polish border to the south-east. First the Polish-Russian border. Then the Polish-Lithuanian border and the Polish-Belorussian borders. On the other side of the last two borders I was able to find some old Tatar Muslim villages and mosques. But to find similar villages still existing on the Polish side of the border I had to travel still a little bit further.

Here, in the Podlachia region, roughly between the city of Bialystock and the Belorussian border, I discovered the heartland of the Polish Tatar community. Only a few hundred Muslims still live here, in the two villages of Kruszyniany and Bohoniki. Many of them are of a quite advanced age. All of these Muslims are descendants of Tatars who fought at the side of King Jan III Sobieski in the battle of Vienna. After the historic victory the king had gifted their ancestors land in these villages. During Ramadan and Eid, Muslims from all over Poland come to visit the cemeteries and the mosques in these two villages. The mosques of Bohoniki and Kruszyniany are famous as the last traditional wooden village mosques of Poland. At first sight these mosques look like the wooden orthodox churches also found in the landscape here. But their green paint and the crescents on top of their short towers soon betray their true belonging. Their interiors are heavy with colourful carpets and calligraphies on the walls. Combined with the wood these exude an earthy and homely vibe reminiscent of small mosques in the Balkans or the Caucasus. In earlier centuries many more of these kind of mosques used to dot the Kingdom of Poland. Many of them can be found in Lithuania or Belorussia now. Many more have been destroyed.

In the heart of Kruszyniany is a famous restaurant, Tatarska Jurta, which serves traditional Polish Tatar specialities, most of them very meat heavy. Located next to the historic mosques, the restaurant is run by a couple: Dzenneta and Miroslaw Bogdanowicz, who are renowned for their cooking skills. Prince Charles of England visited the restaurant in 2010 and seemed quite impressed both with the food and the peace and quiet of the environment. When, in 2018, the restaurant, as wooden as the mosques close by, burned down due to an accident, the prince is rumoured to have donated a sum of money to help the Bogdanowiczs rebuild their restaurant.

From Kruszyniany, I travelled far to the South and crossed into Ukraine. Into lands that were once considered 'Poland' as well, before they were annexed by the Soviet Union. I passed through Lviv, a city known as Lwów in Polish and Lemberg in German. It was the most important trading city on the *via tartarica*, the trade road that once connected Poland with the Crimean Khanate , the Ottoman Empire and beyond. Polish Armenians made it their cultural centre, something of which an Armenian Catholic cathedral bears witness until today. In the thirteenth century a mosque existed in the city as well but it was later deserted. Today the city has a new Tatar Muslim community, refugees from the Russian occupation of Crimea.

The region around Lviv has a complicated history of engagements with Tatar Muslims. Local Tatars settled in many of the surrounding villages and were usually considered loyal subjects of the Polish crown. For centuries, neither the borders of the Crimean Khanate nor of the Ottoman Empire (of which the Khanate later became a vassal) were very far from here either. For most of its history, Poland actually had peaceful and cordial political relationships with both the Ottomans and the Crimean Tatars. But there were significant times of conflict; and during those times Crimean Tatars often raided the Polish and Ruthenian villages of the region and abducted young people to sell them into slavery in the Ottoman Empire. In current day Polish nationalist memory usually these times of conflict are remembered. The times of peaceful and cordial relationships are often forgotten.

Not too far away from Lviv is the town of Rohatyn where around the year 1500 a woman was born who would have an enormous influence on the political landscape of her time. Her original name is not known. Europeans later gave her the name Roxolane, reminiscent of Roxane, the Bactrian wife of Alexander the Great. Some historians have speculated that she was once baptised as Anastasia or Alexandra and that she had been the daughter of an Orthodox priest of Ruthenian ethnicity. When she was about fifteen years old she was kidnapped during a Crimean Tatar raid. She was taken to Crimea and from there sold to the harem of the Ottoman Sultan Süleyman, where she had to convert to Islam and received the Persian name 'Khurram' (in modern Turkish 'Hürrem'). Her beauty and intelligence impressed Sultan Süleyman so much that he freed her and made her his only legal wife, a position never bestowed on any Ottoman harem slave before. 'Hürrem Sultan' was probably the most powerful woman of her times, holding political influence both during the reign of her husband Sultan Süleyman and of her son, Sultan Selim II. Throughout her life she fostered close diplomatic ties between the Ottoman Empire and the Kingdom of Poland. Not surprisingly, Polish-Ottoman relationships remained largely peaceful during her lifetime. A monument to her memory can be found today in Rohatyn, a city located in western Ukraine. The Turkish soap opera, *Magnificent Century*, one of the biggest Turkish television export hits of all times that has delighted audiences from Pakistan to Latin America, commemorates her life.

Rohatyn is also the place where Polish writer, activist and public intellectual, Olga Tokarczuk begins the story of her monumental work, *The Book of Jacob*. Tokarczuk, who won the Man Booker International Prize for her novel *Flights*, and was awarded the Noble Prize for Literature, in 2018, is one of the few Polish writers who keep fighting against the tides of nationalism and racism flooding her native country and who consciously tries to keep the memory of a very different multi-ethnic and multi-religious Poland alive. In *The Books of Jacob*, she retells the story of Jacob Frank, a Jewish messiah considered a heretic by mainstream Judaism. Frank was a border crosser on several levels. In his teachings he crossed the limits of common morals. Throughout his life he traversed the Polish-Ottoman border several times in both directions. Even more significantly, he and his Jewish followers once converted to Islam, only to convert to Catholicism later. Tokarczuk captures the world of this border crosser vividly and shows us that here, in the lands that once used to be Eastern Poland and that is now Western Ukraine, the border between the 'Muslim World' and 'Christian Europe' has never been a sharp one. It was constantly shifting and connected people more than it divided them. And there were many people inhabiting the in-between spaces.

Southeast from Rohatyn, there is a place close to the river Dniester. It was once called Kamieniec-Podolski in Polish but is now known as Kamianets-Podilskiy in Ukrainian. Tokarczuk sets an interesting scene of *The Books of Jacob* in this city: a Polish bishop observing how a golden statue of the Catholic Madonna is placed on top of an Ottoman minaret. Tokarczuk did not invent this scene. The minaret with the Madonna on its top can still be seen in Kamienic Podolski today. For centuries the

Dniester river had been the border between the Kingdom of Poland and the Ottoman Empire. An often porous border that facilitated much exchange. But the Ottoman forces crossed the river and Kamieniec came under Ottoman control for a few years during the seventeenth century. Under Ottoman rule the local Catholic cathedral was turned into a mosque. The minaret was built to signify this act of conversion. When the Polish Kingdom gained control over the city again, the cathedral was again turned into a Catholic place of worship. But the Poles had started to like the minaret and found no need to destroy it. Only the Madonna was added to it later.

The Ottoman-style minaret of Gdańsk connects with an actual Ottoman minaret in Kamienic Podolski. There is a wealth of Islamic history and Polish Muslim relics between those two minarets.

THREE FAITHS CITY

Hafeez Burhan Khan

A year ago I found myself outside a Jett bus office in Amman, Jordan. At six o'clock in the morning! It was cold and wet and the wind cut through me. A kiosk was open so I grabbed a tea and went into the office to wait for the coach, which arrived 40 minutes later. My destination was Jerusalem and I had been told it would take a good three hours to cross the border. I was feeling a little nervous at the prospect of a protracted ordeal, particularly as waiting and queuing are in the top five of my least favourite pastimes. But with Israeli border security watching your every move, I knew I had to make sure I showed no outward sign of frustration.

There were six of us and I immediately fell asleep only to be woken when we reached the Jordanian side of the border an hour later. We traipsed into a room, filled in our details and handed our passports to a border officer. We then returned to the bus and waited for about 20 minutes before being given back our passports. The bus travelled a further three miles before stopping again. We paid our departure tax to a soldier, then off again, this time crossing the tiny King Hussein Bridge, which marked the border between Jordan and Israel. I noticed a man in civilian clothes with a machine gun, then more men, all with guns.

We all got off and had to go through security. I was resigned to the inevitable long wait. We presented our passports. The woman looked at mine and asked me to sit on a chair. Everyone else had got through except me. I remained calm, I expected this given the number of times I'd been stopped at borders because I never look like my photo. Several minutes later, a man appeared, he asked me my name and asked if I'd assume the pose. I was nothing but civil and all smiles. They searched me. The soldier asked if I wanted a glass of water, I declined. Then he walked me to my bag and thanked me for my cooperation. I got my visa, which was not stamped on my passport but on a slip of paper. I was asked questions about where my family was from. In an effort not to look shifty I made sure to fix my most idiotic smile and that's probably what helped get me through the process relatively quickly.

That was it! I was out after 15 minutes, I expected to be hauled over the coals and interrogated but nothing happened. There was a minibus, I went towards it only to be told all the seats had been filled. It was 9.15. Another minibus came, I sat in it. Ten minutes later, two Brazilian women boarded. Then for an hour, nothing. I got out and paced impatiently. Please go to Jerusalem I thought to myself. No more tourists from Jordan were due. We had to wait for the Palestinians who exited from a different terminal. They had their own coaches and every couple of minutes buses would drop and pick them up. Nearly all were headed for the West Bank. A few did get on the bus but the expectant wait for more passengers was endless and it was 11 when we eventually set off. Forty minutes later, the bus plonked us down outside Damascus Gate, gateway to the old city. The first thing I did was change my Jordanian money into shekels. I realised I'd been cheated by the money-changer because 20 minutes later as I entered the old city I read the rates. I was down £50.

The city of Jerusalem, known as al-Quds in Arabic and Yerushalayim in Hebrew is, arguably, one of the holiest places in the world. Unlike other sacred cities, which tend to hold meaning for a singular faith, Jerusalem exerts a religious and almost mythic pull to followers of Christianity, Islam and Judaism combined. For millennia, it has played a pivotal role in global affairs, built by the Prophet David 3,000 years ago for the Israelites, it is where his son Solomon built Solomon's Temple. The temple was then destroyed in 586 BC by the Babylonians, who sent the Jews into exile for two thousand years. Imbued with relics, the city has been repeatedly destroyed and rebuilt by invaders who became rulers. The Persians, Greeks, Romans, Arabs, Crusaders, Ottomans and British, form a venerable who's who of civilisations that have made their mark on this dusty corner of the Middle East. Marks that can be found everywhere, reminders of the passage of history, that have become a focal point for worship.

More recently, it has been fought over by the Israelis and Palestinians with the Israelis occupying East Jerusalem in 1967. The significance of Jerusalem to geopolitics is as strong now as it was thousands of years ago, emphasising the concept upon which it was founded, for what Jerusalem really is, is a statement of intent. This statement achieved through religion, nationalism, history or archaeology, is an expression of a people or people's yearning for the land upon which it is built and the ties that go back thousands of years. Each yearn to claim that they are the ones that Jerusalem belongs to. This is the Jerusalem of the mind, a symbolic platonic ideal which has sowed division and discord, that is still being felt today. Most people think the term holy war or jihad is an Islamic phrase coined in the last forty years but it was Pope Urban the second who believed in holy war as a means of taking back Jerusalem. A statement of intent to Christian Europe, he demanded that Jerusalem be purged of the infidel and rightly regain its place as a Christian city. In 1099, the Crusaders sought to carry out his wishes and stormed the city walls, massacring the Muslim and Jewish communities with a savagery that even in those days of wanton massacres by all sides, was considered extreme. Eyewitnesses described the Temple Mount area as knee deep in the blood of Muslims and Jews. Manifestations of this statement of intent appear all over Jerusalem and cast a heavy shadow today.

This is a fractured city. The Palestinians of East Jerusalem face a ring of Israeli settlements, which, like a slowly clenching fist have exerted increasing control over past decades. A recent influx of evangelical Christians from America illustrates their bloated power as they revel in the belief in a Greater Israel as a prelude to the end of times, when Jesus will descend from heaven into Jerusalem and Christ will rule the Earth for a thousand years. Israel's biggest cheerleaders, they believe Israel must be protected at all costs. This is the statement of intent of Christian Zionists, which has seen right wing Jews and right wing Christians, unlikely allies, dedicated to an alliance to empower Israel for starkly different reasons. But there is another Jerusalem, one that belongs to Muslim, Christian, Jew, people of other faiths and those of no faith. A city with mesmerising stories to tell, from which a multitude of lessons can be learned. Interwoven in the city's fabric is a shared wealth of history and archaeological treasures, in which the statement of intent is universal. A platonic ideal again?

The rain was torrential with no let up in sight as I entered from the north by Damascus Gate which leads into the Muslim Quarter. It occurred to me that maybe these buildings, that have borne witness to so much, should not stop us in our attempt to pursue the realisation that Jerusalem may one day become a city of peace.

The narrow alleys were full of fruit and vegetable stalls and vendors selling trinkets. At the side of the alley Israeli soldiers hovered, a common occurrence in the Muslim Quarter. I noticed they always had their finger on the trigger. If this was supposed to make me feel secure, it only made me feel anxious, however finely trained the Israeli army boasts itself as being, an errant trigger finger is all it would take to cause carnage. Old Jerusalem is like any old Middle Eastern city with winding little lanes, some of which are covered and others partially covered. There is the constant noise of street hawkers calling out tourists of which there are many. I heard the relentless twang of American accents as well as languages from across the globe as I navigated my way around, stopping intermittently to seek shelter from the rain and unsuccessfully avoiding the large puddles of water that peppered my path.

My first stop was the Church of the Holy Sepulchre on Golgotha or the hill of Calvary, where Jesus is said to have been crucified. The smell of incense was overpowering. People were bowing and prostrating themselves over a cracked stone slab and kissing the structure, as well as placing pictures of Jesus and incense sticks in a sincere act of devotion. I could grasp in their faces and movements what it meant to them to be standing over the place where it is believed Christ was anointed before burial. I turned right and went up some stairs to be confronted with the site where Christ was thought to have been crucified. There are conflicting opinions as to the veracity of the location but I was willing to be awed by the idea of it all. It struck me how ostentatious the Greek Orthodox Church was, a reflection of the tradition in which it emerged. I walked around the corner and stood in a long queue of people waiting to enter the tomb of the Holy Sepulchre, where Jesus is said to have been resurrected. Famously, for many generations the caretaker of this tiny space has been chosen from one of the oldest Muslim families in Jerusalem, in an effort to show even-handedness to the several different and oftentimes conflicting Christian denominations that all hold this place in deep reverence.

From the Christian Quarter, I meandered into the Muslim Quarter, eventually arriving at the Dome of the Rock or the Haram al-Sharif, which is the third most sacred site in Islam. The call to mid-afternoon prayer echoed all around the old city and I felt moved to offer prayers. A group of Israeli soldiers stationed outside asked me if I was Muslim, I nodded and they let me pass. I entered and once inside another man asked me to recite the Shahada to prove I was actually Muslim. The rain was heavy and my feet were wet. My supposedly waterproof boots were leaking but they were nine years old. My feet were cold. I should have listened to my wife when she told me, before I left, to get some footwear that was actually waterproof. I entered Al Aqsa mosque and prayed. For a while afterwards, I sat quietly, enthralled by the intricacy of the interior and soaking in the feelings that this moment inspired. Calm descended over me, despite all the chaos around. In that moment I understood why this place evoked such strong emotions and why people fought so bitterly to protect the meaning it held for them. I made my way to the Dome of the Rock where I was shaken out of my reverie upon once again being challenged on my Muslim identity. It would be a feature of my time in Jerusalem, to be constantly asked to prove that I am Muslim by reciting a Qur'anic verse. It was annoying, but also symbolic, that a piety test dictates entrance to places of worship. The statement of intent once again emphasises how interwoven identity is to the ownership of this piece of land. It sometimes made me feel like an outsider, even though I should be used to it, as all the time I'm the one dragged out of the line wherever I am in the world. I have one of those faces that doesn't quite fit, that you can't quite place. I could be from almost anywhere. From nowhere.

Such thoughts were whirling around in my head as I set eyes on the rock where the Prophet Muhammad is believed to have ascended on his night journey to heaven, where he met the prophets of the Abrahamic faiths and led them in prayer. Muslims see the Dome of the Rock as a continuation of the Abrahamic faith, which began with Solomon's Temple. Next to that was the Prophet's footprint. Some Muslims touched the footprint then kissed their hands. I could hear Brummie accents and noted a group from England parading around the footprint taking selfies. A very contemporary method of devotion these days: 'like' my display of piety on Facebook or Instagram to confirm your own piety. Too harsh? What was clear to me was that there was a similarity in how Christians and Muslims approached their devotion. The sentiment was indistinguishable. The Haram Al-Sharif complex is where Solomon's Temple is situated and is regarded as deeply meaningful for followers of Judaism. For Christians, this is where Jesus will return to usher in a new Kingdom after Armageddon. So, one can only imagine what this shrine embodies to the three religions who share so many affinities, yet you would be led to believe that the religions exist in hostility to each other. After all I have witnessed at these shrines it seems this can't be true? Certainly, there is tension enough but I counsel to myself that we view this holy city through the lens of the present political situation, which has undoubtedly been exacerbated over centuries by maleficence.

At the western lower end of the complex is the Western Wall, better known as the Wailing Wall, Judaism's most revered place. The wall is a remnant of Solomon's Temple, though nothing remains of the original Solomon's wall. Some of the limestone blocks are from King Herod's time and some were added during the Ummyyad Period. Despite the heavy rain, Jewish worshippers were standing by the wall and praying. Again, what I noticed was the quiet and intent devotion that characterised such commitment to faith. I then wandered through tapering streets of the Muslim, Christian, Armenian and Jewish quarters. I must have walked for several hours in the rain driven along by some innate curiosity despite my sodden feet. I was transfixed by my surroundings. Everywhere I looked, I saw the hand of history directing events and Jerusalem was its stage as actors came and went over millennia. The old city is probably only one square mile but is dripping in the jewels of a sacred history. It was a powerful experience to behold such sights.

The Armenian quarter was well maintained yet virtually empty, the Jewish Quarter was also smart with many places of worship and sparkling new structures or recently renovated monuments. I later learned that the spacious plaza which acts as an entrance to the Western Wall was the old Moroccan Quarter, which was demolished in 1967 to make access to the wall easier. The Christian Quarter was bustling with churches and bazaars, and curiously most of the shopkeepers were Muslim. The Muslim Quarter was quite ramshackle in comparison. It was undeniably gritty but bursting with bazaars and restaurants that offered a glimpse into the vibrancy and resilience of the people. However, as I ventured off the beaten track, the alleys become more litter strewn and the neighbourhood run down. Few tourists ventured here, I noticed graffiti and occasionally barbed wire while ever-present Israeli soldiers kept a close watch on the mundane minutiae of life such as children playing in the street or groups of elderly men sat on a doorstep chatting. The wet and cold had finally taken the edge off the heady euphoria that had compelled me to roam for hours. I was tired, my boots were squelching and my toes were numb. I headed back to my hotel.

The next morning I woke early and had a pastry at one of the excellent bakeries in East Jerusalem. For a pound you can choose from an array of fillings and satiate your belly to keep you going for a good number of hours. I wandered again through the old city and chanced upon an inconsequential garden, which was surrounded by tourists. To my surprise, this was the Garden of Gethsemane, where Jesus had been betrayed. Located at the base of the Mount of Olives, Jesus is believed to have prayed here after the last supper, before he was arrested. Despite being small and fenced it was beautiful with olive trees, which have been carbon dated to nine hundred years old. Once again, I was deeply moved by the significance of my surroundings. I began the walk up to the Mount of Olives, the long way round, where dozens of coaches were dropping off tourists to enter the old city. I walked up the hill from where I could see settlements on several hills, which I believe were illegal Israeli settlements, strategically located to overlook the Palestinian areas. A menacing statement of intent.

For once it was not raining, the sun was out and I could feel the warmth on my face and body. I walked through a Palestinian area, which was quiet and neat. Looking out over Jerusalem, there were many five or six-storey apartments made from sandstone that glowed during the day. Jerusalem looked extraordinarily beautiful. At the top of the Mount, I sat and admired the view of the Old City while having my own picnic for one. This is where you get that classic photo of the Dome of the Rock. There were so many tourists milling around. I heard American Bible scholars, so many of them were in their twenties. I can't give the view the justice it deserves but it was incredibly tranquil.

After an hour, I walked down and then back up to Lions Gate to Via Dolorosa or Way of the Sorrow, where Jesus was forced to carry his cross to the crucifixion. Along the way are the Stations of the Cross, comprising a series of images depicting the scene. There are fourteen stations,

designed to help Christians make a spiritual pilgrimage by contemplating
The Passion of the Christ, which is the time of Jesus's triumphal entry into
Jerusalem, and eventually to his resurrection. The walk at a normal pace
would take around twenty minutes but it took me nearly an hour as I kept
stopping to look at the stations and the surrounding area as I passed. I was
particularly immersed in the second station, which depicts the moment a
crown of thorns was placed on the head of Jesus. The thought of him
stumbling, getting up and stumbling, by the third station I felt very
emotional. Like the Christian pilgrims, I contemplated what this story
meant to me. What it meant to me as a Muslim. Suffering, such an
intrinsic part of the human condition, faith, trust and belief. It captivated
my imagination. Choking back tears, I walked on. At each station, there
was a chapel of one of the various denominations, Polish, Armenian,
Franciscan and Greek Orthodox. The route passed through the Muslim
souks and then uphill to station nine, to the Church of the Holy Sepulchre
all the way inside to station fourteen, which is where Christ's tomb is
situated in The Aedicule, a cube like structure. A long queue snaked all
the way inside the church, and ever-impatient when it comes to waiting
and queuing, I didn't make it into the tomb.

It was mid-afternoon by now. I headed downtown into west Jerusalem
which looks like any European city centre. For some reason, it reminded
me of Manchester. There was a sizeable Ethiopian Jewish community,
many of whom were sporting army fatigues, with the young men also
wearing Kippahs. Prominent religious attire and imagery on display
characterised this part of the city. Unlike Tel Aviv, which is a more
secular city, Jerusalem is steeped in religious symbolism. I wandered
around for a while before settling in a coffee shop. By now, it was dark,
so after spending some time drinking tea and listening to the conversations
around me, mostly conducted in Hebrew, and observing my
surroundings, I headed to East Jerusalem, not as tidy as West but there
were malls and shops open. Families were out and about but it wasn't
packed. Seeing that everything was beginning to close, I headed back into
the old city to Jaffa Gate in the Christian Quarter, where there are many
upmarket bars and restaurants. I found myself wandering through dark
alleys where children were playing football and women chatting, then
turning a corner, I was suddenly back among throngs of tourists. I'd been

walking since 9 am, it had been nearly twelve hours. I headed back to the hotel, totally exhausted.

The next day was Friday. I decided to pray Jumma at Al Aqsa. Around 11 o'clock, huge numbers of Muslims converged on the old city, making their way into the mosque. Hordes of Israeli security were milling about - fingers on triggers. I tried not to dwell on that. By 11.30, thousands of people were wandering around the vast courtyard. The women prayed at the Dome of the Rock, the Men at Al Aqsa. I made my way in, it was almost full and I managed to squeeze in at the back. I sat and contemplated the great questions of life, telling myself that no answers were demanded any time soon. I looked behind and saw a sea of people sitting in the huge open space outside. I was relieved it was a warm day. The call to prayer sounded at noon, we went through the congregational rituals and it was all over 30 minutes later. I didn't feel emotional or experience the euphoria of the recent couple of days. Just a quiet calm and acceptance. I was painfully aware yet strangely detached from the knowledge that I was praying in the most hotly disputed place on Earth. I wandered about for a bit more taking photos, even some selfies, although I don't have Facebook or Instagram accounts, watched families having their photos taken, people sitting around, some having picnics, and detected a vibrancy and positivity I'd not seen in East Jerusalem before.

Around dusk, hanging around Damascus Gate, I saw hundreds of Haredi Jews marching into the old city for Shabbat. I followed them, at a discreet distance along with several other tourists, to the Wailing Wall, which was packed. Segregated by a partition for males and females. I could hear melodic singing by a group of girls moving in a circle. I took out my phone to film but a lady told me to put it away. No photos on Shabbat. Almost every tourist was being told to put their phones away. After a while, I left to wander the old city attempting to make sense of what I'd witnessed the past few days.

I travelled to Ramallah for a week and returned on the Shabbat, so there was very little traffic. My hotel was downtown in West Jerusalem, which was deserted. Once I'd checked in I went to taste the finest hummus (allegedly) at Abu Shukri in the old city. It certainly was fine and pleasantly spicy. Contentedly I headed off to the Haram al Sharif. *Assalamalailkum* says an Israeli soldier. *Walaikumasalaam*, I reply back. He asks where I am from and checks my passport then lets me go. *Assalamalaikum* says another soldier, stopping me just a few metres from the first. I smile back at him. He begins reciting 'Surah Fatiha'. I'm not sure whether I'm supposed to listen or join in. I grin back at him. He repeats the beginning again. I'm smiling insanely but I'm in my head, thinking about the three faiths city, trying to work out if he is an Israeli Arab as his pronunciation is perfect. He pauses, looks at me, or is he looking through me, and repeats the beginning of the surah again. I look at him, he looks at me impassively, all I can focus on now is whether his finger is itching at the trigger ... it comes to me. I blurt out the surah and he lets me go. Yes! I'm in.

No. The entrance is now blocked by a Palestinian policeman, I show him my passport and smile. Keep smiling, I'm thinking to myself, it opens hitherto locked doors. Muslim? he asks. Yes, I say. He looks at my photo. This is not you. It is, I say, my hair is longer now. He looks at the photo again. Oh yes. Keep smiling, don't get frustrated ... I'm sure both the Israelis and the Palestinians don't believe I'm Muslim. I head for the Dome of the Rock.

Muslim? I'm stopped again! It's only happening to me no one else, what the ... try to be patient. I show my passport and my Oscar-winning smile which has been perfected to an insanely moronic level. He stares at me, my passport photo, at me. My hair is long now, that's why I look different. He looks at me and at my passport. Ok. He lets me go. I've made it! I try to dissociate myself and lose myself in thought and prayer. I stare up at the dome. It's breathtaking, I haven't seen complex geometric patterns like this before. Truly, it is a blessing to be here. I realise how fortunate I am. After a while I walk to Al Aqsa which is 100 metres away. Are you Muslim? No, I'm stopped again but this time I open my passport and shove it in the man's face. Look my name, it's Muslim. I'm trying to be patient. *Alhamdulillah*, he replies. I shake my head at the absurdity of it all. He is confused as to why I am shaking my head. But before he has a chance to speak again I stride on. I pray mid-afternoon prayer then do some extra prayers as I'm feeling a surge of spiritual uplift after exercising such patience. I wander around the huge courtyard and sit down by a wall. The sun's rays are beaming down on me. This three faith city has me humbled and contemplative. With a history dominated by such statement of intent, I understand why.

RECLAIMING MANUSCRIPTS

Nur Sobers-Khan

When I was asked to write about manuscripts, or manuscript-as-relic, I have to admit I was somewhat stumped. This is surprising, as the only job I have ever had in my adult life, other than attempting to teach about Islamic manuscripts and history, is as a manuscript curator. In fact, it's the only job I've ever wanted, and manuscripts are the only objects I've ever been interested in. I was recently offered a wonderful curatorial job working with astrolabes, but astrolabes aren't flat enough, or papery or codex-y enough, so I turned it down (admittedly, those weren't the real reasons, but they suffice for our purposes here). You might say this interest is somewhat limiting, but when you consider the range of topics that are contained within the covers of manuscripts, you quickly realise that a lifetime is not enough to master even a tiny fraction of the knowledge therein. And of course, a great deal of that knowledge is considered to be obsolete, or if not obsolete, then certainly effete and rarefied to the point that someone who cares about earning a living in the modern world would avoid entangling themselves with it.

My own specialisation in this topic, if it can be called that, began with Arabic and Persian, both of which have ancient manuscript traditions. Although not many Islamic manuscripts pre-date the Mongol invasion of 1258, a plethora of re-copied texts survive that date and flourish in the early modern period with commentaries and super-commentaries. After Arabic and Persian, my work turned to Ottoman Turkish, and I experienced the dubious pleasure of learning the various forms of Ottoman palaeography, which is famous for being painfully illegible to the uninitiated. And now I attempt to work with Urdu, a much younger manuscript tradition that is intertwined with Indo-Persian culture and material production and is rather under researched compared with manuscripts in the other major languages of Islamic knowledge production.

So that's me and my interest in manuscripts, which might help to explain why I had such difficulty approaching this essay - when you are too close to a topic, it becomes impossible to narrow down what to communicate about it to an audience who may not share your obsession. In my case, after my first few codicology workshops, which provide instruction in how to study the materiality of the manuscript – its paper, the type of binding, the many scripts, inks, etc. – in order to date it, to understand more about the context of its production, I was hooked. It was a gateway drug, I suppose, to my present state. Strangely, I am not interested in the illustrations, or let's say minimally interested – and this is what most manuscripts are famous for – but rather in the epistemic and cosmological worlds that can be reconstructed from the contents of the manuscripts, and the physical presence of the manuscript itself as an object.

I am not, I think, the only one to ascribe an almost animistic meaning to man-made relics that survive from the past, especially objects of cultural or religious production that attempted to create meaning. That every manuscript had to pass through human hands, probably numerous human hands – from paper makers, to binders, to the ink-makers, to the author of the text, its scribe, and all of the invisible past labour that went into planting and harvesting the cotton for the paper, skinning the animals and tanning the leather for the binding. Or the myths that tell us that the black ink used for the text was made by combining soot collected from the candles that burn in mosques, with gum arabic, a fixant to make the soot adhere together to form a liquid; these jars were then tied to animals' saddles travelling to the *hajj*, and the motion of the travel over this distance then mixed the materials together, inscribing the holy journey into the ink itself. Although this might be pure hyperbolic mythology and also rather orientalist as an image (caravans, mosque lamps, pilgrimage, etc.), it gives a sense of the intensity of labour that went into the act of making and writing a manuscript. Beyond the labour, the pages and words themselves have been read by numerous human eyes, commented upon, studied, and travelled great distances. Although colleagues who insist that the fetishising of manuscripts needs to come an end, (and I in part agree about the current state of field, since these works represent an almost entirely male, elite form of historical knowledge production, and the construction of scholarship around these objects is at the moment deeply flawed – more on this later) will mock me for these words, it can be argued that the manuscript does – or can – attain the status, or at least of the aura, of a relic over the course of its long life. So while we might critique the construction of scholarship around manuscripts, there is something worth retaining about the objects themselves and the aura they acquire, and the meaning this might carry not just for believers but for anyone interested in the history of Islamic knowledge production.

At the risk of ascribing an animist agency to the manuscript, I am reminded of Michael Taussig's meditation on the way that objects acquire their auratic poetry that gives them special meaning. I am thinking not just of the manuscript copied by the scholar, but the saint's robe or slippers, the prophet's (or the Buddha's for that matter) footprint, the places where a famous Sufi meditated, such as the numerous *chillahgah*s, tiny spaces carved into rock for a forty-day retreat from the world, that have acquired their own numinous aura because of the figures who occupied them. In *What Colour is the Sacred?*, Taussig explores the resonance of this aura and ponders how it comes about:

> Proust invokes what he calls the Celtic belief that the souls of dead persons who were emotionally close to us pass into an animal, plant, or inanimate object, where they lie imprisoned until, perhaps, one day, by chance, they will be resurrected if we recognize them. "It is the same with our past," he continues, locked in things that no amount of conscious effort can restore to us until, by chance, we encounter that memory and have it restored to us. Surely he had himself in mind when he remarked elsewhere that certain people like to believe that "objects retain something of the eyes which have looked at them"? But what gives this magic its force, as I read him, what makes the aura auratic, is the poetry—I can think of no other word—intrinsic to the "edge sensations" that linger like dust and cling like moss to the situations that one day may be recalled and hence restore Time Lost. "A name read long ago in a book," writes Proust, "contains within its syllables the strong wind and brilliant sunshine that prevailed while we were reading it".

Once we open this numinous relic, whose very ink is supposedly inscribed with pilgrimages, whose pages have absorbed the eyes of long-dead readers over centuries, what do we find? A short stroll through the average manuscript catalogue or handlist illuminates the variety of topics, branches of knowledge, historical periods, and geographies contained in a small collection. At random, a sampling from the pages of the Meredith-Owens' *Handlist of Persian Manuscripts in the British Museum 1895-1966* reveals manuscripts containing the letters of Sufi masters to their disciples, dictionaries of mystical terminology translated from Arabic to Persian and Turkish, works on magic, administration, ethics, historical chronicles, biographies of poets, memoirs of kings, astronomy and astrology, explanations of how an astrolabe works, treatises on smallpox, on geometry, music and singing, archery, on precious stones and aromatic substances, falconry, horses, pigeon-fancying. Translations of Sanskrit treatises and epics into Persian, letters written in the hand of Bahai religious figures, versified dictionaries, poetry, fables, stories, proverbs, works on cosmology, geographical accounts, Judaeo-Persian religious works, stories and poems, which are written in Persian language but in Hebrew characters, a Zoroastrian work on divination and prophecy, a catechism in Persian, a Persian translation of the Harivamsa, with the history of Vishnu and his avatars. Among this wealth of topics, we can get a sense of the shared worlds of cosmology, aesthetics, religious belief and languages that these manuscripts encapsulate, much of which shakes the foundations of modern ethno-nationalism as well as blurring the line of a puritanical understanding of what constitutes 'Islamic' knowledge production. Let me briefly touch upon some of my favourite genres of manuscript and the thought worlds that they allow us access to, before moving on to a discussion of the colonial foundations of the disciple of Islamic studies and the need to reclaim the study of manuscripts.

If you have had the pleasure of examining a catalogue of Islamic manuscripts, you will have found a sub-section labelled 'Occult Arts' or 'Divination', under which a surprising range of topics are subsumed. What might these manuscripts contain, and how are the forms of historic knowledge production contained within their pages relevant? The occult sciences, which formerly were not considered serious topics of academic enquiry and research, have started to receive the scholarly attention that they deserve in the past few years, due primarily to the pathbreaking scholarship of Liana Saif, Matt Melvin-Koushky, Noah Gardiner and Jean-Charles Coulonne, who have all completed their PhDs on topics within the occult sciences and published extensively on genres from lettrism (*ilm al-huruf*) to astrology (*ilm al-nujum* or *ahkam al-nujum*), physiognomy (*'ilm* al-firasa) and magic (sihr). Research into these previously neglected areas of Islamic intellectual production open new possibilities for engaging with epistemologies that have been marginalised or misinterpreted under post-Enlightenment notions of what constitutes science.

There is some disagreement in the wider field about the exact definition, ontologically and methodologically, of what al-'ulum al-gharibah, the occult sciences or esoteric sciences are, and how to contextualise them historically. A definition that does not delve too far into the scholarly debates and will suit our purposes here is that al-'ulum al-gharibah, or the 'strange' or 'hidden' sciences, are those that attempt to explain, harness, or predict unseen phenomena, although as Liana Saif elucidates, her recent publication, 'What is Islamic Esotericism', in a special edition of the journal Correspondences dedicated to this very topic, that this definition can also be expanded to include observable phenomena within the natural world. Saif proposes the analysis and identification of Islamic esotericism as 'intellectual or revelatory approaches' to understanding the meaning of phenomena that are otherwise hidden, including the 'natural, celestial, and divine'. This definition is sensitive to the many historical modes of enquiry into the unseen, and capacious enough to include a range of objects of enquiry that are otherwise difficult to categorise as belonging to the same set of concerns. She also makes a valuable argument against the reduction of esotericism to a Perennialist construct, in which the Islamic esoteric sciences and method become a vehicle for the 'eternal truth' only accessible to an elect few – a much later construction stemming from nineteenth century European theosophical trends and writings.

So what are the historical al-'ulum al-gharibah, or the al-'ulum al-khafiyya, or 'ilm al-ghayb, all genres of intellectual production which remain largely unread between the covers of manuscripts? To understand what the occult sciences were historically, and how they are situated in a larger landscape of Islamic knowledge production, it might be helpful to divide the areas of knowledge along what are considered to be traditional classifications: al-'ulum al-aqliyya are the rational sciences – logic, mathematics, areas of knowledge which can be deduced rationally – and al-'ulum al-naqliyya are the transmitted sciences, namely hadith, 'aqidah (doctrine), balaghah (rhetoric), which are transmitted from master to pupil by memorisation. Sciences that neither measure nor analyse what can be seen nor are transmitted through memorisation and tradition, are the 'strange' or 'occult' sciences, which include, among others, astrology (*ahkam al-nujum*), alchemy (*kimiya*), various forms of divination such as lettrism ('*ilm al-huruf*), and dream interpretation (*ta'bir al-ruya*).

Another way of looking at the 'occult' or 'hidden sciences' is that it is not the sciences themselves that are hidden, but that they allow one to access what is hidden or unseen, which is especially true for the science of divination. In the same way that the transmitted sciences give access to knowledge such as *hadith*, passed down from teacher to student, and the rational sciences give access to knowledge derived through human reasoning, such as logic or mathematics, the arts of divination, called the *al-'ulum al-khafiyya* (hidden sciences), *al-'ulum al-ghamida* (dark or murky sciences), or '*ilm al-ghayb* (knowledge of the unseen) hint at the same – these sciences give access to knowledge of the unseen, or *ghayb*. The *ghayb* itself is defined as what is hidden, inaccessible to the senses and to reason, which means that is also absent from human knowledge - or human powers of deduction –- and is found only in the metaphysical. In the Qur'an, the term itself is often understood to mean 'the mystery.' So how do we access the *ghayb*, which lies beyond human knowledge, through the occult sciences, and how has the idea of the *ghayb* been conceptualised by different groups of Muslim thinkers?

The common denominator in the many conceptualisations of the *ghayb* is the notion of mystery, divine or otherwise, at times not revealed and unattainable, at other times revealed in part as an essential element of humankind's spiritual development. In the *tafsir* literature on the Qur'an and in other religious literature, the term *ghayb* is applied at times to the absolute mystery of God, but more often it is the invisible world taken as a whole. Certain strands of Sufism interpret the *ghayb* as the unseen realms of cosmology, namely the three worlds that exist beyond the terrestrial: the '*alam al-jabarut* (the highest stratum of Sufi cosmology of archangels, paradise, and the afterlife), the *alam al-malakut* (the invisible realm where the non-material beings, such as jinn, demons, and lesser angels, dwell, which also contains both the realms of hell, the *barzakh* and the lower levels of paradise, and is often elided with the *alam al-mithal*), and *alam al-lahut* (the realm of pure spirit). Another interpretation of the *ghayb* is the hidden essence of all that is, whether visible or invisible. It is then the *ghayb al-huwiyya* ('mystery of selfhood' or ipseity) or absolute *ghayb* (*al-ghayb al-mutlaq*). This *ghayb* is not a physical cosmological location but is interspersed throughout everything, as particles can be dispersed in a solution. This can also be understood as the *ghayb* of the self, the inner unseen cosmos to which we have as little access as the macrocosmic *ghayb* of the layered unseen worlds described in Sufi cosmologies. All of these cumulatively are the *ghayb*, to which humans can only gain insight through recourse to the *'ulum al-ghariba* or *'ulum al-ghayb*.

Although the occult sciences (often mislabelled as 'pseudo-sciences' in modern literature; a scholarly error that I have fallen prey to in my own previous work to as well) and an interest in them today is considered the preserve of crackpots and lunatics, and until recently scholarly research did not take these aspects of historical knowledge production as a serious topic of enquiry, these areas of knowledge were not always as marginalised in intellectual history as they are today. Rather, the occult sciences were at one point considered to be the pinnacle of knowledge. For instance, as Matt Melvin-Koushki explains in his article on the historical importance of divination in intellectual and court history of the Islamic world, entitled, 'Persianate Geomancy from Ṭūsī to the Millennium: A Preliminary Survey,' in the writings of the Ikhwan al-Saffa, the tenth century group of Neopythagorean encyclopaedists and philosophers, there is an epistemological hierarchy of the mathematical, natural, psychological and metaphysical sciences, which culminated in the sciences of divination: astrology, alchemy and magic, demonstrating the value placed on these modes of attempting to know and understand the world.

As for the sciences themselves, there are roughly forty different forms of divinatory practice outlined in Toufic Fahd's magisterial work *La Divination Arabe*, published in 1966 and considered to be the authoritative study of Islamic divination practices. Although Toufic Fahd describes forty specific divination practices, I would argue probably countless more existed at the level of popular practice that have not been documented in manuscripts or other forms of textual or material record. Among Fahd's scholarly investigations are included: *ta'bir al-ahlam* or oneiromancy (dreams – the highest form of divination, and considered to be an element of prophecy); *'ilm al-firasa* or physiognomy (also a prophetic quality); *fa'l al-Quran* or bibliomancy; *'ilm al-nujum / ahkam al-nujum* or astronomy / astrology; *'ilm al-huruf* or lettrism (divination through the letters of the alphabet); and many other forms of divination, such as predicting the future from throbbings in parts of the body, flight of birds, intestines of sheep, cloud formations, and palmistry. Divination is today often viewed as a cultural practice, somehow divorced from, or not informed by, the mainstream of Islamic philosophy and religious belief. This is, however, not the case. By exploring the link with the *ghayb*, methods of divination, and accessing the unseen worlds and spiritual knowledge, it becomes clear how the occult sciences are central to certain aspects of religious belief and practice, including Qur'anic *tafsir* and Sufi conceptualisations of cosmology. In addition, the theories of divination and how it works are also central to the development of Islamic philosophy and intellectual history.

Recent scholarship illustrates how theories of divination were central to the development of Islamic philosophy using the example of astrology as a form of divination and occult science. Astrology at its essence deals with how celestial bodies influence terrestrial ones, how the stars and planets act upon us, and how we can influence or at least read and attempt to predict the stars to then influence the world. The premodern (and pre-Copernican) cosmological vision of the celestial plane placed the earth at the centre of the concentric spheres (*aflak*) each occupied by a planet. As explained by the art historian Stefano Carboni, in his work *Following the Stars: Images of the Zodiac in Islamic Art*, premodern Islamic cosmology was defined by the concentric rotation of eight planets, in order of their nearness to earth: the Moon, Mercury, Venus, the Sun, Mars, Jupiter, Saturn, and an eight invisible planet, Jawzahar, that was responsible for eclipses and was often represented in astrological symbolism as a dragon who would swallow the sun or moon, thus bringing about an eclipse. The celestial world, containing these planets, in tandem with the zodiac and lunar mansions, were thought to act on the terrestrial world in manifold ways. As the recent and path-breaking work of Liana Saif in her 2015 monograph *The Arabic Influences on Early Modern Occult Philosophy* has demonstrated, there were two theories of how divination by astrology funtioned: hermeneutic versus causal theories. The hermeneutic approach held that celestial bodies serve as signs indicating resemblances, sympathies, or correspondences to be read and interpreted by cosmographers and astronomers. This approach gave rise to the 'two books' theory, by which nature becomes a second scripture to be read and interpreted using the same methods as the exegete of the Hebrew

Bible of Arabic Qur'an. This approach also later become common in early modern Europe, when Isaac Newton, for instance, engaged in numerology and lettrism to try to understand the cosmos through the text of the Bible. Such practices were also considered standard in Islamic courts from the Mamluk and Timurid periods of fourteenth-fifteenth centuries as well as the courts of the Ottomans, Safavids, Qajars and Mughals in sixteenth-nineteenth centuries, through to the advent of modernity. In contrast, the causal approach adopts an Aristotelian framework, in which the occult forces become naturalised: the celestial bodies are causes of generation and corruption – the stars bring about change and transform the natural, terrestrial world, including human activities. Early Arabic philosophers theorised that the stars functioned both causally and hermeneutically – they were a system of signs, as well as natural and spiritual causes that acted on the terrestrial realm. This process of synthesis of the Neoplatonic and the Aristotelian was essential to the development of philosophy itself in the Islamic world, demonstrating the astrology or other 'occult sciences' and their attempts to understand the seen and the unseen or *ghayb* were not marginal areas of thought limited to crackpots, but central to the intellectual projects of their time.

As recent scholarship on Islamicate occultism has pointed out, researchers consider the occult sciences integral to Western intellectual history; however, those studying the development of Islamicate intellectual history, especially the history of science, do not yet place occultism at the centre of their re-construction of Islamic knowledge production in the past. And of course, the false dichotomy that 'Western' and 'Islamic' intellectual history are somehow separate areas of enquiry has yet to be overcome, it goes without saying, despite the best efforts of excellent scholars in the field. What is the reason for this unwillingness to acknowledge the centrality of the occult sciences to Islamicate knowledge cultures of the past, and arguably, the present? As Melvin-Koushki explains in his introduction to a recent special edition of the journal *Arabica* 64 (2017), which he has edited with Noah Gardiner on the occult sciences, 'Introduction: De-orienting the Study of Islamicate Occultism':

> Reacting to the depredations of European colonialism, orientalism's wellspring, the well-intentioned scholarly compulsion has been to exorcize

Islamicate history and culture of "superstition" and "magic" in an effort to banish orientalist stereotypes of cultural and scientific stagnation.

As scholars, he argues, we need to reclaim and re-examine the role of the occult sciences within the formation of Islamic intellectual traditions, and recognise the role that colonialist scholarship has played in shaping the scientistic narrative of Islamic intellectual history, wherein only the disciplines that conform to what is recognised as 'science' by Western modernity are granted the status of legitimate objects of study. While Melvin-Koushki argues for a re-enchantment of history, I would argue for a re-enchantment of the present as well, with the *ghayb* as a foundational analytical category. The reformism that has gripped the understanding of the aesthetic, theological and social formation of the Islamic world, especially rampant in the diaspora, requires a process of re-enchantment and a de-Wahhabitising that allows us to reclaim an intellectual past that is deeply relevant to the present, and should be allowed to shape it in creative and enchanted ways that the current reformist, scientistic default conceptual framework does not permit. Studying the history of esoteric sciences in Islamic intellectual history can cast a great deal of light on the intricacies of how philosophy, Sufism, and the natural and occult sciences were interwoven in premodern Islamic knowledge production, and how much of this effort hinged on a desire to engage not with what can be observed and known, but what will remain beyond our grasp in the *ghayb*.

The premodern forms of thought inscribed in the manuscripts, such as astrology and other sciences of divination, were not marginalised sciences or areas of thought, but were central to religious, social, intellectual and political life in both the premodern Islamic world and many other areas of the world. They can be re-harnessed to create autonomous epistemic worlds that are situated beyond the rupture of modernity. Their creativity permits us to imagine something that is not as reductive as literal interpretations of scripture, or of natural laws and science, and to access a way of thinking that permits a sense of wonder or perplexity at the range of sciences and methods of attempting to understand the unseen, as there is an infinite variety of conceptualisation of cosmology and eschatology. Shahab Ahmed's *What Is Islam?*, suggests a similar valorisation of thought that does not enforce a reduction or homogenisation of a rich and often conflicting intellectual history. Perplexity is an attempt to understand that divine knowledge manifests itself in an overwhelming variety of opposing forms and statements, he argues. Pursuit of the *'ilm al-ghayb* can be considered an epistemological and hermeneutic method that allows rediscovering and valuing perplexity through a contemplation of the unseen. It permits us to cultivate a sense of wonder, humility at knowing that much is unknown, unknowable, unseen, and beyond the reach of our human machinations, although we may, through various occult sciences, attempt some insight into worlds – conceptual or otherwise – that lie beyond our grasp.

I am of course not instructing you, the reader, to actually believe that the cosmology of the world involves only eight planets, one of which is an invisible dragon, circling the earth in perfect concentric circles, or that the occult sciences can actually give you access to divine knowledge through de-coding throbbings in your bodily extremities. But rather, I argue that we should engage with the manuscripts that contain these epistemic worlds, for the creative images, the worlds of thought, the surprising concepts, and their ability to restore some imagination, ambiguity and creativity to what we understand as 'Islamic'. You do not have to believe in alchemy, or astrology, for these ideas and thought systems to give rise to a poem, an artwork, a short story, a narrative or even just an anecdote shared between friends, or for the content of these manuscripts to enrich the lived experience of what it is to engage with Islamic intellectual and cultural heritage either as a believer or not. In a previous article for *Critical Muslim*, I spoke about the term that Leyla Jagiella originated to describe the visually and spiritually impoverished state of Islamic cultural and intellectual production and lived experience, namely, the wahhabitus. A portmanteau of 'Wahhabi' and Bourdieu's sociological notion of the 'habitus', namely, the set of beliefs, practices, mannerisms that our surroundings inculcate in us and that we come to reproduce and embody, this word sums up the problem of reductively defining what is 'Islam' within a puritanical and visually and intellectually impoverished literalist paradigm. What Islamic manuscripts do, sitting silently in repositories in their hundreds of thousands, is remind us that we have other options, other histories and other, richer narratives to draw on when constructing our own understanding of what Islamic cultural and intellectual production was in the past, and what it can be today.

We have so far contemplated the numinous aura of the manuscript, whose text allows us to converse with the dead through the many comments and marginalia that accompany it, that gives us access to lost epistemes and cosmologies, visions and landscapes – but now we should ask, do these uncanny relics have any revolutionary potential or relevance to our lived reality? This rhetorical flourish would suggest that yes, manuscripts have the potential to give us access to cosmological and epistemic worlds that were trampled upon and reduced by colonial modernity; taking ownership of this area of scholarship is however itself fraught with problems in terms of how the discipline is framed, and who is given access to these texts and their interpretation. I am not arguing that we resurrect a nostalgic premodern utopia where all the brown people lived in harmony and that all of the Islamic knowledge systems that existed were somehow perfect and did not embody or reinforce any form of violence, patriarchy, or social inequality (because they most certainly did), but rather that the texts contained in these works give us access to philosophical and cultural worlds, and possibilities, whose richness – and strangeness, and sense of wonder – has been largely lost, or if not lost, reduced in meaning and hollowed out. The very questions we ask of these texts as scholars needs to be re-imagined, as well as our orientation toward them within the discipline of Islamic Studies.

The problem of course is that access to, and scholarship on, Islamic manuscripts in Europe and North America has been limited largely to white male academics whose writings on these works have been defined by the very specific parameters of the disciplines they are operating within, and these disciplines themselves have emerged out of histories of colonialism, Enlightenment rationalism, patriarchy and white supremacy. While many talented female scholars of colour exist in the field, it is a struggle to get recognition, much less jobs and pay-cheques in a relevant profession that would allow us to continue our work; my female researcher friends of colour in Islamic studies are often excellent, ask questions that challenge the field and cause it to grow, yet have to work twice as hard, and put up with twice as many micro-aggressions, or just sometimes aggressions, in order to just get recognised, much less achieve renown or success. Until space is permitted in the field for a range of approaches, stemming from one's own orientation toward the material, I am afraid the study and use of manuscripts in Islamic Studies will remain the staid preserve of a limited, privileged few.

Just as an example, as recently as 2018, I attended a conference in London on Shii studies and philosophy with a focus on medieval texts, manuscripts and philosophy, which over the course of two and half days of panels and maybe twenty to thirty presenters, only featured two female scholars, both of whom were white. In the same conference, the (white, male) senior scholar delivering the keynote openly criticised the #MeToo movement in his speech as promoting a narcissistic focus on the self, having, I hope, completely missed the point that the movement is about calling out and redressing sexual harassment and violence so that others won't suffer the same fate – clearly the opposite of narcissism. I'm still puzzled about the relevance of his comments to Shii studies, except on a meta level, where they perhaps served to shore up the barrier of the field against female scholars. I say that 'I hope' he fundamentally misunderstood the hashtag, because if he understood it and still insisted that it was a narcissistic movement in a keynote speech in front of a large audience of, mostly male, academics of Islamic studies, then that is a much bigger and more horrifying moral failing. No one, of course, objected verbally or otherwise to these goings-on. How, as a woman of colour attempting to be part of the same academic field, can you be expected to innovate, to posit your own theories, or work outside of the reigning conceptual framework when you cannot even be expected to raise your voice in such an openly hostile environment, much less succeed as a scholar?

Beyond obtaining a job as professor, even professions in cultural heritage institutions that house Islamic(ate) artefacts and manuscripts are limited to the same group who dominate scholarship in Islamic Studies. Outside of Muslim-majority countries, I do not know many Muslim manuscript curators employed in public institutions, or beyond religion, many manuscript curators of colour, in large institutions in the West; while the number of art curators of colour is growing, the world of the medieval Islamic text is still largely a white male preserve. The few manuscript curators of colour who do exist suffer institutional racism and bullying that make it extremely difficult to do their jobs; this I can say from personal experience and first-hand observation. If you even look at the instructors

of Islamic codicology workshops in North America and Europe, it is rare
to find any names that reflect any religious or ethnic diversity. It is clear,
then, that Islamic manuscript studies and institutional work with these
collections is not the preserve of those who have specialised in this
scholarly area because they consider it their intellectual and cultural
heritage, but rather just a privilege for those who have escaped the
racialised category of 'Muslim.'

As Ayesha Chaudhry identified in her article, 'Islamic Legal Studies: A
Critical Historiography' in *The Oxford Handbook of Islamic Law*, the scholarly
focus on medieval Islamic texts written by men emerges out of a history of
colonialism that has yet to be seriously challenged in the institutions of North
American and European academia. She elaborates with great clarity that:

> Islamic Studies in the western academy finds its roots in the colonialist project,
> which was, at its core, a white supremacist project. Colonialism championed
> the ideology that whites ought to rule the world and in the hierarchy of human
> races, whites ranked above all other colours. In this ideology, they are the
> chosen people. God (and/or 'nature', and/or social Darwinism, and/or
> whomever) chose them and made them better. This thinking privileges whites
> above all other races, is white supremacist without regard to its intentionality.
> In the same way that patriarchal thinking privileges men over women; it does
> not matter if a patriarchal thinker means to be patriarchal or not. Similarly, it
> does not matter if white supremacist thinking means to be white supremacist,
> if it privileges whites and whiteness de facto, then it is white supremacist. The
> French and German colonialists studied Muslims in the lands they colonised,
> along with the animals, and vegetation, and architecture. There is a reason that
> Islamic Studies doctoral programmes require language competency in German
> and French, rather than other living Muslim languages.

While we can acknowledge that this is indeed where the foundations of
our discipline lie, I cannot see, from my vantage point, much effort on the
part of the academy to shift the discourse away from these foundations.
The study of manuscripts, for instance, is still almost entirely dominated
by approaches that claim to be 'empirical,' 'objective', 'scientific', based
on 'philology' and 'historical context,' without querying how the
conceptualisation of these terms and methods has developed over decades
if not centuries, and how these notions shape what constitutes legitimate
research, and more importantly, *who* is qualified to undertake this

research. I am trained in exactly these sorts of research methods — philology, archival and manuscript research, carefully constructing a positivist account of 'what actually happened' in the past, through empirical and material evidence, either textual or visual. I can see from the inside of a discipline how this entirely false notion of objectivity is a powerful tool of exclusion that refuses to let certain groups such as women of colour, or really anyone who cannot afford to spend decades mastering medieval texts and the supposed methods needed to interpret them within a narrowly defined discipline, to take part. This exclusion prevents certain important questions from being asked, not least of which is the relevance of these medieval texts to the living breathing Muslims who have a cultural and religious stake in their contents.

At one conference in 2011, I recall a European male philologist from the same department as me in Cambridge, saying that he only studied these texts as a hobby or pastime, and that is all it was to him. If studying medieval Islamic texts is just a fun little hobby — interesting but ultimately an amusing make-believe game — then why is he allowed to do it, and paid to do it, when the people to whom it would be meaningful are largely excluded, or have to struggle to play a role? As Ayesha Chaudhry very trenchantly points out in her article:

> Colonialist Islamic studies, which is to say, white supremacist Islam Studies designates above all else, pre-colonial, medieval male Muslim voices, as captured in pre-colonial texts as the most important, and authentic expression of Islam and Muslims eternally. So, a small, male, Muslim elite comes to speak for Muslims universally and eternally. Thus, a living religion — an evolving and vibrant religion — is treated like a dead religion, captured only in medieval texts. Even when discussing urgent contemporary debates, the standards of excellence in the field demand that we ignore contemporary Muslim voices, that we confine ourselves to historical, textual study, because that is what 'good' scholarship looks like.

While these words will come as no surprise to any student of post-colonial theory, critical race studies or gender studies, such seemingly obvious claims remain anathema to the mainstream of Islamic Studies, which still holds that the 'objective' study of Islamic manuscripts or history must not be 'anachronistic' and discuss the bearing that medieval texts can possibly hold over our lives. While Chaudhry argues for a turning away from this form of scholarship to embrace intersectional feminist scholarship in Islamic Studies that emphasises the voices of living Muslims and makes space for women of colour, I would argue not to throw the medieval baby out with the bath water. While I agree with her premise that the undue focus on textual history of the Qur'an and *fiqh* has made Islamic studies (both the questions asked as well as the resulting answers) an often stilted and stultifying field, I would argue that there is much contained with the rich premodern epistemological world of the manuscript that has yet to be explored. The right questions have not yet been asked of this material, because those who are able to ask those questions have rarely been given the tools to engage with manuscripts and medieval texts, and in the rare cases when they have been given the tools, it is an uphill battle to have one's voice heard in the wider field.

So I conclude with a plea for reclaiming the manuscript, and the complex worlds it embodies – from its numinous aura, to the forms of knowledge it contains, to the insights and inspirations those forms of knowledge can provide us – from the suffocating privilege of the academy.

TOUBA

Yovanka Paquete Perdigao

Senegal's late poet-president, Léopold Sédar Senghor, first proposed the establishment of a Museum of Black Civilisations over fifty years ago. It wasn't until 2018 that his dream came to posthumous fruition in the form of a proud and confident circular building in Dakar, a design inspired by traditional homes in Southern Senegal. In the same year a report commissioned by French president Emmanuel Macron recommended that artefacts and treasures looted from Africa during the colonial era should be returned to their country of origin. This was particularly poignant for Senegal, which has suffered the indignity of seeing many of its most important relics on display in museums abroad.

Despite continued intellectual pillaging, there are some relics in Senegal that cannot be ripped out and carried off. The mystic beauty of Senegal is the hidden treasure of this breathtaking part of West Africa and growing up in its capital Dakar, I was always enchanted by the various tales one would encounter wandering through the rumbling busy city. Fom the islands of Gorée known for their important role in the slave trade, the almost untouched islands of the Madeleine where a powerful Djinn ruled, and the holy site of Popenguine, where Senegalese Catholics flock, Dakar is steeped in history. However, it is one yearly event celebrating the rich cultural history of the region, that remains etched in my memory.

The pilgrimage of Senegalese Muslims to West Africa's largest mosque, Touba, fascinated me during my childhood. I was twelve years old when I moved to Senegal, and was quickly adopted by my sprawling Senegalese family, descendants of my grandfather's Saotomean cousins that had moved to Dakar in search of better opportunities. Over the years they had married amongst Senegalese and Beninese people and had maintained their strong Christian roots while espousing Islamic influences. In some of the smaller families, children were given both a Bible and Qur'an, raised knowing Christian values and Islamic pillars and celebrating Christmas and Tabaski. Every year I would excitedly anticipate some of my cousins setting off with the adults in the family to undertake the much talked about Grand Magal of Touba.

Islam has been a fixture of the history and landscape of Senegal for nearly a millennium, beginning with the King of Takrur, War Jabi, in 1040. He set about introducing Sharia law and was the first regent to officially pronounce orthodoxy in the Sahel, establishing Islam in the region for centuries to come. The Takru kingdom grew to be an extremely powerful state going as far as challenging the Ghanaian empire and capturing its capital, Kumbi Saleh. After converting to Islam, War Jabi's subjects, who are commonly known today as the Toucouleur people, followed suit. However, before long the empire began to crumble with the Susu people breaking away and the first Wolof empire, Waalo, was established. When the Madinka tribes allied themselves to the Mali empire, the Takrur empire was finally condemned to a slow death. The Emperor Sabajoura of Mali and later the Jolof empire captured the remaining Takrur in the thirteenth and fifteenth centuries. However the spirit of Takrur would re-emerge when a Fula rebel returned to reclaim the empire of Takrur and named it Fouta Toro and eventually established the Denianke Dynasty. That dynasty also had its days numbered. In 1776, a Fouta revolution led by Muslim clerics brought it down and established a theocratic oligarchy. Influenced by other Islamic movements, the Toucouleur used military force to capture traditional religious states where they could establish Muslim theocratic states. Their conquest was hard fought, and they ran into the Serer who fiercely opposed any plans of expansion of Islamic influence, before defeating them at the Battle of Fandane-Thiouthioune.

Four Islamic Sufi orders known as tariqas, eventually emerged in Senegal and it is this mystical form of Islam that came to dominate. An estimated 95 per cent of Senegalese Muslims belong to a Sufi brotherhood. The two largest orders are the Tijaniyyah and the Muridiyyah, more commonly known as Mourides, followed by the pan-Islamic and oldest brotherhood, the Qadiriyyah and the smaller Layene. The city of Touba is a focal point for the Sufi order of the Mourides founded by Cheikh Amadou Bamba in 1883. Anyone who has visited Senegal will easily recognise Amadou

Bamba's image which is a constant fixture on city walls, buses and taxis. For years I saw his benevolent eyes follow me everywhere, standing tall and elegantly dressed in a white kaftan and wearing a large scarf. Amadou Bamba was the son of a marabout belonging to the Sufi order Qadiriyya. Born in 1853 in the village of Mbacké in Baol, Senegal, by the age of thirteen he was famed as an ascetic marabout who wrote exquisite poems and mystical texts emphasising work and industriousness. He firmly believed salvation came to those who worked and studied hard, famously advocating the motto: 'Pray to God but plow your fields'.

Whilst studying Islam in Sudan, he experienced racism as his teachers treated his Arab peers preferentially. This led him to quit his studies and he declined to take over his father's former position as counsel to a Wolof king. But he would relent when King Lat Dior, who was embroiled in a bitter war with the French, came to him asking for advice. Cheikh Amadou Bamba famously responded: 'to control the world, turn your back on it. Devote yourself to studies. Depose your arms. Liberate your soldiers and horses. In return you will find something greater – inner peace and tranquility.'

Bamba was considered by those who revered him as a renewer of Islam, a *mujaddid*, sent by God every hundred years to bring hope. One day whilst fasting during Ramadan, Amadou said that the prophet Muhammed and his companions appeared to him in a dream in Touba, and it was this vision that confirmed Amadou's destiny as a Servant of the Prophet. Before long his fame and influence spread across the country and the French, who had significant colonial interests in the country, became frightened by his growing power and potential to inspire anti-colonial sentiments. Of concern to them was the number of traditional kings and followers with strength in military numbers, who had converted under Bamba, making the threat of an uprising a possibility. He was arrested in Diéwol and transferred to the office of the Governor of the colonial administration in Saint-Louis. Just before he was due to appear before the Privy Council of Saint-Louis, he prayed two *rakats* in the Governor's office and declared his firm intention to be subjected not to the Council but to God alone. As a result of this defiance, the Privy Council deported him, condemning Bamba to remain in exile in Gabon. This only made him even more influential as he came to embody a new form of nonviolent resistance against colonial powers. Amadou Bamba would spend almost eight years in Gabon, five years in Mauritania, then finally under house arrest in Diourbel, Senegal, for fifteen years composing poems and songs such as this one:

Hide yourselves, you who search for knowledge, this will save you from trials and sorrows,
have determination, thus you will surpass your generation.
Do not grieve for the trials which come upon you,
be courageous, so that people believe you want for nothing.
For the Science is never granted to one who fears hunger,
God raises his servant who shows patience.
You who wish to acquire knowledge, review your studies constantly,
every time, my sympathy is with them.
You who seek knowledge, do not at the same time go after money,
for the Creator provides for the needs of those on the quest for knowledge.
Fear God and follow his religion which is Islam,
for he who disobeys God or does harm to others will never hold knowledge.
Keep yourself separate from the opposite sex, young or old,
for approaching them will only lead you to contempt, disobedience, and destruction.
Do not sacrifice the hereafter for this world, O Son of Adam!
It is clear whoever trades light for darkness will regret it.

Bamba remained a figure of influence, particularly in the field of politics, as well as a man to whom his followers were devoted. He led a pacifist and spiritual struggle against French colonialism, unlike several prominent Tijaan marabouts, who had aligned themselves with colonial subjugators. He taught what he called the *jihad al-'akbar* or 'greater struggle', which fought not through weapons but through learning and fear of God or *taqwa*. Since one of the fundamentals of mouridism was hard work, the Sufi order quickly developed into a complex and well organised economic organisation that mobilised many aspects of the country's economy such as groundnut cultivation. Young followers were given marginal lands in eastern Senegal with the task to form communities and farm the land with supplies provided by the Brotherhood. A portion of the proceeds were then returned to Touba, and through this system, after a period of years, ownership over the plantations and towns was acquired.

With the Mouride Brotherhood growing, the French found themselves at a loss as to what to do with Cheikh Amadou Bamba. They allowed him to establish his community in Touba after realising that his desire was to be free to practise his religion and they decided that his emphasis on hard work and productivity seemed to align with French economic interests. Their attempts to win his cooperation did not succeed however, and in 1918, when the French rewarded Bamba with the French Legion of Honour for enlisting his followers in the First World War, he pointedly refused it, which won him even greater admiration among his devotees.

In 1926, Cheikh Amadou Bamba began work to create the great mosque at Touba, a site that would become a holy relic for Mourides in West Africa and across the world. At the time he wrote: 'My lord has blessed me with a place that rid me with all obstacles the minute I entered it.' Mouridism depends fiercely on the relationship between a *talibee* or follower, to his marabout, or spiritual leader. Marabouts are organised according to a hierarchy based on their relation to Cheikh Ahmadou Bamba and located in specific geographic regions within Senegal. They are powerful spiritual guides in the Senegalese community and are seen as being able to understand and interpret the Divine: 'O you who believe, obey God, obey the messenger and those in authority.'

The City of Touba is a two hour drive from Dakar, Senegal's capital. It has rapidly grown since becoming a sacred destination, becoming the second largest urban area outside the capital. The mosque lies at the epicentre of the city with all major roads converging to it. Construction began in 1926 but was only completed in 1963. The result of the painstaking work is an impressive 87-metre-high central minaret with marble façade and jade domes shimmering in the distance. A guide is always at hand among the local men, women and children one encounters on arriving at the mosque's main entrances found in the west and eastern parts. They navigate visitors through the maze of rooms, dishing out historical facts about the mosque and its founder, relaying local tales and the gossip of the city and outlining the rules and etiquette of behaviour expected of visitors to the holy place.

This auspicious building is the main attraction of those undertaking the annual Grand Magal. Magal is a Wolof word derived from the verb 'mag', which means 'to be important' or 'to be old', and the noun form is translated as celebration or anniversary. Grand Magal refers to the pilgrimage to Touba, but there are other annual Mouride magal such as the Magal of Saint Louis, which commemorates Cheikh Amadou Bamba's defiance of the French. However, the Grand Magal is the most important and widely attended of the Mouride magals and remains the largest celebration in Senegal, religious or secular to this day.

The Grand Magal began when Cheikh Amadou Bamba asked his followers to celebrate the anniversary of his exile to Gabon. However, it morphed into the revered tradition we witness today when his son and successor Serigne Moustapha Mbacke organised the first Mouride gathering on the anniversary of his death rather than his exile. This was later changed by the next successor, Falilou Mbacke, who altered the date of the celebration back to the anniversary of Cheikh Amadou Bamba's exile. The period spent in Gabon remains significant to many Mourides who regard this as a test of Bamba's spiritual resilience: 'the motive of my departure to exile is the will of God to elevate my rank and to make me the mediator between my people and the Prophet.'

The date of the Grand Magal is determined by the Hijri calendar, the events of the pilgrimage begin on 18th of Safar and last for two days. It can best be described as an intricate ceremony featuring religious rituals and a festival with a dizzying array of entertainment. It is greatly anticipated by all religious as well as non-religious communities in Senegal and is a tremendous fixture in any Senegalese person's calendar. Every year and sometimes twice, depending on the lunar calendar, followers of Cheikh Amadou Bamba come from across the world to perform the Grand Magal. Traffic mayhem is inevitable as worshippers and enthusiasts make their way into the city. Excitement reaches a fever pitch and it is common to hear people remonstrating in Wolof. Just as there have been tragic accidents in Mecca during Hajj as authorities struggle to manage crowds of devotees, incidents have occurred in Touba, the worst occurring in November 2016 Magal when sixteen people were killed and 572 injured while making their way to Touba.

The large number of pilgrims demands a sophisticated logistical system, which came under scrutiny and re-evaluation after the accident of 2016. The city of Touba devotes itself completely to welcoming pilgrims, with the Mouride Baye Fall a subsect of Mouridism, established by a disciple of

Bamba, Ibrahim Fall, providing most of the logistical support. Local associations called *da'iras* maintain the pilgrimage sites whilst residents feed the pilgrims. All those involved are expected to carry out their duties with a high degree of discipline, solidarity, and single-mindedness. Preparations begin officially on 1 Safar each year, seventeen days prior to the pilgrimage, and are led by the Committee of Organization of the Grand Magal of Touba.

Two central events of the Magal take place during the pilgrimage. These are a visit to the Great Mosque of Touba, and to the mausoleum of Cheikh Amadou Bamba to offer respects, where devotees wait hours to snatch a few minutes of prayer and comfort. Many other Mouride leaders are traditionally buried in Touba near the mosque, so often form part of the itinerary. In addition, visitors will offer thanks at the Well of Mercy, said to have been created by God to flow for Cheikh Amadou Bamba, and will spend time reading and reflecting at the central library of Touba, which contains the many writings of the Cheikh and other influential Mourides. The final ritual in the annual celebration is a personal meeting with one of the Mouride spiritual guides or Mourides followed by a night of singing Bamba's poetry.

There are particularities that distinguish Touba from other Muslim pilgrimages, such as the journey to Mecca. Women in Touba have no restrictions on where they may or may not go. However this does not indicate a utopian equality of the sexes as illustrated by the occasion a gender parity law was passed designed to introduce Shariah Law in Touba. The Khalif of Touba refused to submit to the new law, with no consequences or sanctions for his defiance. Another exception are the Baye Fall, who can appear quite peculiar to untrained eyes, sometimes sporting dreadlocks and adorned in silver and multiple earrings. They wear colourful pieces of cloth made into what seems a patchwork of vibrancy, and humble leather sandals. They are excused from prayer and are allowed to drink and smoke. Anyone who visits Senegal will often recognise their fervent singing that can go well into the night. Their uniqueness rhymes well with their motto: *On ne naît pas Baye Fall*, which translates as 'No one is born Baye Fall, you become Baye Fall'.

What is clear is that the Grand Magal is not just a simple pilgrimage. For political elites and government officials the Grand Magal is an opportunity to shore up political power and religious influence, with Mouride leaders often nudging voters towards certain candidates, before this was outlawed in 1988. Interestingly, this tradition goes back to the colonial period where it was created to garner peace between French and Mouride leaders. In contemporary times, however, as Cheikh Abdou Bali Mbacké explains 'one cannot aspire to run Senegal and have Touba against them'.

For us children, the most interesting part of the Grand Magal was Touba's renowned marketplace, one of the biggest in the country, with a phenomenal range of objects that could be purchased at prices lower than the inflated cost of things in Dakar. We learn to haggle and bargain in Wolof:

'*Nyatta La?* How much is it?'
'*Daffa seerr*! It's too expensive!'
'*Wanyi Ko*. Reduce the Price'

The spread and endurance of Mouridisme is strongly connected to Touba's economic success.

Since the seventeenth century, Mouride marabouts were able to create large sources of revenues through land and cultivation which went untaxed by the state. Furthermore, the community received payment for schooling, healthcare, municipal expenses and, until recently, even water and electricity – all of which play a significant role in sustaining the city. An estimated one million visitors every year also means it is an excellent opportunity for business deals to be struck.

Money is only an achievement when seen through the lens of solidarity and not through the enrichment of the individual. Success is seen as the result of God's Mercy and reward for following His will. Marabouts preach that static wealth has no value, so money is to be shared and used within the community. This thinking can be credited with the success of Touba, which has fostered a tightly knit and independent community ensuring basic necessities for its members and a sense of family. Even for those living outside of Touba, community remains central, with purposeful religious communities called dahiras built for worship and to facilitate economic solidarity. Mouride businesses abroad also contribute significantly to the

Senegalese economy. Followers send money home and enrich the communities they live in. For example, the Senegalese have numerous enterprises in Harlem, New York. Their presence is so strong that parts of Harlem are known as 'petit Senegal'. The communities meet weekly for *dhikrs*, prayers, recitation of Amadou Bamba's religious poems, and conversation. Through these *dhikrs,* Marabouts foster solidarity and remind their followers of mouride values of humility, endurance, and sharing. Community and solidarity, particularly when it results in economic empowerment, offers a major attraction to followers of Mouridism.

Cheikh Amadou Bamba died in 1927 and was buried in Touba. However his impact continues to extend beyond the grave. In Senegal alone it is estimated that four million people are followers of Mouridisme. Across the world parades are organised to celebrate his life and legacy with thousands regularly in attendance. In 2017, his contributions were acknowledged at the United Nations General Assembly as Senegalese leaders and intellectuals were invited to speak and celebrate his contribution to Senegalese society. By the roadside in Senegal, people converge morning and night as they drink copious amounts of Cafe Touba inspired by Bamba. I always admired how these rituals evoked the well-known Senegalese spirit of *teranga,* which has the combined meaning of hospitality, respect, community, solidarity, sharing, warmth, friendliness, and selflessness. From Dakar to Touba, one is infused with that spirit and the joy of pilgrims. It is truly a celebration of culture and religion, a festival bringing together believers for prayer and devotion.

The grand mosque, overlooking Touba, remains an eminent embodiment of Senegalese history, a symbol of the perseverance of one man and his determination to be a student of Islam through hard work and devotion to prayer. But it is also a symbol of anti-colonial spirit, a feat of architecture that stands proudly defiant against French colonialism, which, despite its best efforts, never managed to break the Senegalese spirit. The mosque shows its timeless elegance: as the years pass it remains a permanent relic adored by followers and admired by non-believers, finally a vestige of greatness. Now all that remains is for the rest of Africa's stolen relics to be returned to the land from which they were looted under the protective gaze of their rightful heirs.

I, RELIC

Tam Hussein

Whenever I walk towards Brick Lane Mosque in the east end of London I always look at it as a continuation of a Dickens novel; from the Artful Dodger picking pockets, cockneys selling jellied eels, Jack the Ripper spying his next victim in the prolific bawdy houses of the area, to three Bengali Lascars with cutlasses entering said house to reclaim what the prostitutes had taken from them, to Bengalis worshipping in that very building. It is an intrinsic part of the East End where the poor huddling masses have always congregated.

Before its manifestation as a mosque that very building used to minister to the Huguenot community as it fled Catholic persecution in France in the mid-eighteenth century. For sixty years it stood thus until it was turned into a Wesleyan chapel with an eye to convert the local Jews of the area. But the Jews to no avail clung on to the law of Moses, and so it evolved into a methodist chapel 1809. By 1880 a series of Russian pogroms brought Lithuanian Jews to the area filling it with tailors, bagels, fish and chips and handy boxers, who transformed the church into a synagogue. It remained thus until the area saw an influx of Bengalis and the building became a mosque in 1976 – a few years before I was born.

But don't think for one second that Bengalis are newcomers to the area, far from it, they have been there since the 1600s. Perhaps the most notable being a secretary to the East India company, I'tisaam Uddin who wrote the first Persian work on Blighty and helped develop the country's understanding of the Persian language. But what is curious is that it was mostly Sylhetis who came as Lascars or sailors even though that part of the country is landlocked with little access to the sea. Some have posited the idea that the hills so favourable for growing tea and the presence of navigable river meant that the local populace developed a close relationship to the sea. Bengal after all has always been a stopping off point for ships on the way to the Far East. It was no wonder that Islam came to Bengal within a hundred years of its inception. The area was famous for its shipwrights and would have no doubt remained so had it not been decimated by the arrival of the East India company. Others point to the local populace's foreign stock coming as it did from the saint Hazrat Shah Jalal and his followers whose offspring configured their character to look outwards and be like the Irishmen of the South, voyaging and settling in many parts of the world. This includes my Nana, my maternal grandfather who established Brick Lane Mosque.

If truth be told never before have I felt compelled to write his story down, as a journalist I am usually concerned with other people's stories and not my own. I have as of yet, not figured out why I have this sudden impulse to put pen to paper so to speak. Maybe because I am approaching my fortieth year, and I don't know yet whether my place is in heaven or hell. Or maybe it's simply a mid-life crisis when men become particularly vulnerable to nostalgia knowing that one's youth is no more and one is on the way to becoming a relic. I am after all entering the autumn of my life and the grave does not seem so remote. After all I can no longer walk down Brick Lane thinking that I shall live forever or that beautiful women who grace those pavements are within my grasp, if indeed they ever were! And yet those things that satiated me once, satiate me no more.

I increasingly feel the need to tell my children about this place when I am no more. Perhaps I have seen so much now or am bewildered by the changes around me, that I have a need to return to that idyll of my ancestors which, if not told, will most certainly be forgotten in the saw dust of eternity. I worry that my children will forget who they are and their past becomes mere grist to the ever consuming city that needs a constant flow of the throng to stay alive, erasing their pasts in the process of moulding them into Londoners. After all does the young banker who enters the City of London's plush offices, remember that poor slave who was thrown overboard in order for the merchant to claim for loss or damage to goods at Lloyds of London? There be no statue for that poor soul. And so perhaps it is now important to put down the story of my Nana, his brother and these Bengali seaman who came to the East End, before they too are forgotten and perhaps even more importantly, the teachings they brought with them are swallowed up in the Londoner's swagger.

As much as I love London there are things that our grandfathers taught us that London values less. If the truth be told, what use is honour in London? But that's what they instilled in us; honour, filial piety, loyalty to kith and kin, honouring the old, respecting wisdom, being a man and looking after one's own come what may. Love God and be true. Those things don't seem to matter as much in the city that doesn't love you back. And should you mention these things to the Bengali youngsters, they laugh, 'what you on about bruv?'

Perhaps I am being melodramatic, over indulgent infected by the same emptiness and narcissism of the selfie generation that I am railing against. But if that be the case indulge me and let me tell you about my Grandfather and those like him because they made the East End and I am grateful to him as I am to Mrs Winston who came on *HMS Windrush*, Mr Singh, Mrs Jones, Ms Goldstein, Mr Khan, Ms Rashid and Mr Abdullahi as well as Mr Smith and Mr Anderson and all those other people who with their graft and hard earned taxes raised me and educated me. And if the cry is raised that I have become an Uncle Tom then I will retort as my Nana did: *Baba* to show gratefulness to God is to show gratefulness to people who are mere instruments of His will.

I have never really considered Brick Lane Mosque a relic reposing as it does in quiet dignity in Spitalfields between Fournier Street and Brick Lane. The building has a sundial and queer avant garde minaret appended to it. Inside, it is a lofty tranquil place with a crystal chandelier and blue carpet. It is a perfect place to find peace away from the busy goings on outside. The mosque is not as slick as its larger counterpart on the Whitechapel Road, East London Mosque. That mosque is run like a business, full accounts, debts, extensions, trustees and all that. And so it should be, it is a thoroughly modern place for modern times. Brick Lane Mosque still struggles to be transparent about where donations are spent, not due to any hint of corruption but probably due to the old ways of those who run it. They still struggle with the monthly bills.

Unlike the East London mosque with the *Akhis dem,* many of Brick Lane Mosque's worshippers would struggle to outline the religious evidence as to why they perform the rituals the way they do. Their reply runs simply thus: this is what my father taught me, he was a righteous man and closer to the Prophet's time than you. And they would pray to God with such devotion, that discussing such intellectual issues seems almost pointless, almost sacrilegious, for in their hearts there is no doubt about the veracity of the Prophet and God's oneness. They look at you as if you were a strange fellow when you quibble over such things. Why quibble over something that was established by those that came before you, how is it that you in the 60s or 70s aided by Saudi petro-dollars have somehow discovered a flaw, when greater intellects than you could not discover them? Does it not sound a tad bit arrogant young man?

And so, these old timers irrespective of what East London Mosque youngsters think, celebrated the *Milad*, the birth of the Prophet, like they did in Bangladesh and fed the multitudes; and look at you strangely if you hesitate to celebrate it. Is it a sin to remember and celebrate the birth of the Prophet? Is it a sin to remember Ashura and the death of Imam Hussein at Karbala? They don't have many sectarian qualms, after all the Persian saint who brought Islam to them in Sylhet, Hazrat Shah Jalal with his followers, had done so, it is said, having crossed that riverine land on their carpets settled there and busied themselves with good – nothing more, nothing less. There were no stalls, no loud speakers, no shariah patrols, nothing, just love and good conduct to all and sundry, and so my ancestors be they Hindu or Buddhist flocked to them. And later, centuries later, the descendants of these men, stood up to the *Ingrez* when it was needed.

These days youngsters find these old Sufis docile but forget that it was these very people who started India's first rebellion against the East India Company in 1782. One of the descendants of Shah Jalal's followers, Pirzada drew his *talwar* and beat the local governor, Robert Lindsay in a sword fight and the latter in a most ungentlemanly fashion got hold of a pistol and shot him dead. And after that Lindsay met many others who wanted to wreak their revenge on him for that unchivalrous act. In fact, back in London he met a Saeed Ullah a man servant who had sworn to avenge Pirzada and when he discovered that he stood in front of Lindsay himself drew his sword again. But Lindsay somehow managed to deescalate the situation and Saeed Ullah curiously ended up cooking a curry for him and his family which seems like such a thoroughly Bengali thing to do.

These are the descendants who now old and wisened sit underneath the crystal chandelier waiting to meet their Maker, some recite Qur'an hypnotically whilst others snore like brown Santa Clauses warming themselves beside the radiator. Sometimes you might catch one of them reciting a poem to the mawlana in the side room. I watch these old timers and I cannot help but marvel at that generation of men who weren't ever allowed to be offended, even when they were called Pakis, Wogs and chased down the streets by all sorts of thugs and yet achieved so much.

My grandfather Shamsul Haque and my Great uncle, Ayub Ali landed at Tilbury docks in the East End in 1919. The brothers had left their village, Achol in Jagarnathpur in Sylhet in East Bengal, India, and had already done a stint in New York. I say landed, but they had actually jumped ship and swam for it having nothing to lose and everything to gain; in those days, Lascars didn't get paid until the job was complete, and that job contract could go on for years. Many a Bengali sailor died hungry and penniless on the streets of London no doubt yearning to die in Bengal.

My Nana was only twelve when he came to the East End. Sturdily built, he was a grafter and had an extraordinary gift: whatever he touched turned into money. Along with his older brother, Ali, he worked hard shivering in that cold and strange country. He dragged rolls of cloths on his back in Petticoat Lane and saved enough money to open up the Curry Cafe a year later on Commercial Street. The business succeeded and by 1935 he had managed to open up the famous Cafe Shah Jalal, a restaurant and cafe catering for Bengali and Indian Lascars as they were known. He was also a partner to Dilkush Delight in Soho which was run by a compatriot and friend Shah Abdul Majid Qureishi who came to the country in 1934 following the example of the two brothers. The name Dilkush Delight was named after the store that my grandfather had opened in Dhaka, Bengal.

Unlike many of the Bengali sailors in the East End these three men were literate. And so it fell on my grandfather and great uncle and Mr Qureishi to help those who had jumped ship, hunted by the ship companies to fulfil their contract. They sheltered them, fed them and helped those sailors writing letters and sending their remittances to their families. They would register them at India House and the local police station and settled them in their own home, no. 13 Sandy Street, allowing them to live there rent free until they found work and could stand on their own feet.

But whilst my grandfather had the Midas touch, my great uncle was a political animal. Ayub Ali loved the cut and thrust of politics, he seemed to live for it. He wanted Indian independence and demanded Indian sailors' rights and so the cafe they opened in 1935, Shah Jalal Cafe, was filled with the politicking of activists from Calcutta to Delhi where troublesome lawyers and thinkers were agitating.

My great uncle went on to set up the Indian Seaman's Union or league with a view to look after the welfare of Indian sailors. For one shilling a year, the organisation with its office in Christian Street promised to: 'look after the economic, social and cultural interests of Indian seamen, to provide them with recreation in Great Britain and to communicate with their relatives in India in the event of any misfortunes befalling them'. During the Blitz they succeeded in establishing the East London Mosque in a meeting which catered for their spiritual welfare.

But one suspects that there was more to Ayub Ali's political activities than mere welfare. He held meetings in Shah Jalal Cafe where all sorts of Indian activists attended from Khrishna Menon to the Indian radicals Bose. Ali became treasurer to Menon's All India League and hobnobbed with the founders of Pakistan, Mohammed Jinnah and Liaquat Khan who dropped by the cafe. When Pakistan became a political ambition he became treasurer of Jinnah's Muslim League in the UK.

By the time the Bengal famine struck after the British empire had impoverished what was one of the richest provinces in the world, my great uncle returned home to his village, got married and involved himself in local politics. My grandfather remained after independence and set up Orient Travels and other businesses on Brick Lane. And by the time he became a Pakistani national he had opened up branches of the travel agency in Bradford, London, Karachi and Bangladesh. By the sixties he was successful enough to open up cloth businesses in East Pakistan's capital, he returned home married, fathered children and resided there, moving away from his ancestral village.

But as the business prospered my grandfather became increasingly political, and became convinced that East and West Pakistan could not remain as one. They were not only culturally different, but he felt that East Pakistan was being exploited by West Pakistan. He joined the Awami League and set up various associations both in London and East Pakistan that campaigned for Bengali independence and yet although, my grandfather had perhaps the most to lose, he was never a fervent nationalist. When East Pakistan declared its independence in 1971 after

Mujibur Rahman was denied the presidency by Bhutto, he was in Karachi. There the authorities detained him alongside thousands of Bengalis all of whom were unable to leave the country.

One of his Pakistani colleagues, Mr Begg, visited him and advised him to join the Tablighi movement in Pakistan as a way of escaping his detention. My grandfather joined them with a view to escape. But instead of it being merely his get out of jail card, the Tablighi movement this proselytising organisation that spanned all over the world, took hold of him. Though Nana was devout in the ordinary sense, the movement reawakened his devotion to his faith, and for several years or so he abandoned his business interests and travelled the Muslim world preaching the gospel of Islam to lapsed or non-devout Muslims like himself.

My mother received occasional letters saying what a beautiful country Beirut, Tripoli and many other places were. But his desire to awaken Muslims meant that his businesses went to ruin and his young sons were left to run what remained whilst he flitted from London to Dhaka. It was during this time that he established Brick Lane Mosque. But his religious zeal impacted his children to this day. My uncles still have an aversion towards religious movements and imparted a healthy scepticism of religion in us. It has held us in good stead especially with the proliferation of YouTube sheikhs who vie for you to press the like button and donate to their cause.

Things were only halted when my Nano, my grandmother and uncle were murdered over a property dispute leaving the whole family devastated. My uncles held the fort and fought a court case whilst my grandfather somehow trundled on. It was God's will after all, and he had an uncanny way of accepting what has passed, good or bad. And even in that, I now see some of his stoic wisdom. As a journalist it is easy to despair, especially when you see all the horror around you, nothing seems to make sense. And yet I keep despair at bay through the example of my grandfather, he had that unshaken belief that all this madness is in the hands of a loving wise Maker who like a weaver knows the pattern of a beautiful carpet whilst the ant, us, knows it not. And even though the killers were able to bribe their way out of prison and emigrate to the streets of London, at least they and their children still walk, perhaps even pray in that very mosque that my grandfather built and perhaps through it find salvation.

My grandfather's ability to forgive them astounded me. How could he brush shoulders with those murderers? But as my Nana would have it, what has passed is due to God's will. Even if that be the rapaciousness and cruelty of the East India company, for after all perhaps they were the instruments of His will and a manifestation of his divine names. Is one of God's divine attributes not 'The Punisher'? And the real test for him and us is perhaps how we deal with the buffeting of history and fate, for whilst one might reject these organisations and cruel acts of men, the way things are after all is due to the Divine will. And to reject that would be to reject His decree. And so Nana accepted Fate even if it hurt. It allowed him to heal and move forward and not be angry where as many of my uncles never could. And so by not accepting that which passed they could not fully heal and move on. After all, even you or I, would we want to change the fact that we now think in English or walk the streets of London? In order for us to be who we are, certain historical events in a Liebnizian way had to happen. And so whilst many historical events surely anger me, my grandfather taught me how to accept the past and so oneself in order to move on. In order to heal one has to accept the past even if it be the way a son accepts a cruel and neglectful father. For in the end it was still this cruel father who gave the son the most precious gift of all – life. These were the cards one had been dealt and the sooner one accepted the sinner one can move on – this I think is the secret of Dostoyevsky's *Brother's Karamazov*.

After my Nano's passing my grandfather returned to the East End busying himself with raising money for the Tablighi movement helping to set up their headquarters in East London. Only returning to Dhaka to spend his last days there. And though I didn't know him as a young boy growing up finding him often distant and strange, now that mosque of his is one of the places where I find peace. In many ways, I feel his presence, as if I can touch him there, as though I am in communion with him. And I pray that I and my descendants too will bear good fruit.

FOOTPRINTS

Aaftaab Haider

I am one of those people you have heard a lot about in recent years. Those who came to Europe in the middle of the 'migrant crisis'. Or so I have been told. I am not sure why they call it a crisis. Crisis is what I have seen where I grew up, in Pakistani Punjab. With political and social insecurities, the economy offering ever new adventures in survival, prices of vegetables, wheat and rice rising up to the skies. When I was younger I never thought of emigrating. I loved my mother, my siblings, my village, the fields surrounding it. I felt comfortable there. I was always interested in the world. I dreamed of travelling and exploring it. Sometimes my family also got on my nerves and I wanted to breathe fresh air.

As a child I always liked to listen to stories about Alexander the Great. Alexander the Great once travelled from Europe to Punjab. I thought of making the same journey one day, only in the other direction. But I never thought that I would want to leave forever. That thought only came later, when I got older and more mature, more aware of the responsibilities that I carried in life and of the impossibility of fulfilling them with the resources that I had at hand.

I am my mother's oldest son. We are five siblings, two sons and three daughters. Our father deserted us when I was very young. He keeps loose contact with me and my siblings but otherwise lives somewhere else with a second wife and other children. My father owns land and he always supplied us with what he could. But it was never enough and my mother made ends meet by opening a little grocery shop in which me and my brother started working as soon as we were old enough.

I am not the most educated person, in the formal sense. To be honest, my marks from my school days look horrible. It was my own fault because I was mostly just interested in playing cricket at that time and didn't put any value in education. But from my teenage years on I also didn't have much other time to look for tuition or complement my education in other ways because I needed to help my mother in the shop so that we could all live well. I was therefore never able to pursue higher education. But my mother made sure that I got the best education of the heart. She taught me to respect other people and to always listen to them with attention. She taught me to never lie and always speak the truth. And she taught me to care for the people in my life even before I care for myself. I am not a perfect human being. But I have made these values my own and always try to live up to them.

I try to be a good Muslim. I am not, but I try to be. Most of all, I believe that trust in God is the best virtue a human being can have. That virtue has always carried me through all struggles in my life. I know that He will always provide for me when I am in need. And so far, He always has. I love my Prophet and I love to hear stories about his family members. I like the Tablighi Jamaat and listen to the sermons of Maulana Tariq Jameel whenever I get a chance. They give me peace of heart and strengthen my morals. My girlfriend is Shi'a and doesn't like the Maulana too much. She says his ideas are too strict and that most of these bearded guys are hypocrites. She is afraid that I might turn into such a maulvi-type myself one day. But I find that his words just inspire me to be a better human being. He is sharing verses from the Qur'an and traditions from our Prophet that make us work on who we are. To smile at others as a good deed. To remove obstacles from the side paths so that others won't stumble. To seek God's forgiveness every evening and try doing better every morning. What is bad in that? It is not about wearing a beard. My mother always taught us that first of all one needs to purify ones inner life, only then comes the outer life; everything else is hypocrisy. I value those words more than any Maulana's.

My tastes are not very fancy, I guess, and my joys are very simple. I like to listen to Qawwali music. My favourite is Nusrat Fateh Ali Khan, no one better has come after him. I also like Mehdi Hassan and Ghulam Ali. And Punjabi songs. You know, the kind of *mujras* that (film actors) like Saima or Nargis dance to. I like to go to the gym from time to time and build my muscles a bit. When I have free time and am not too exhausted from work and household chores. I enjoy Salman Khan movies and stupid jokes. I don't eat much meat and am always happy with a simple dish of chickpeas and *roti*. When I eat, I prefer it to be one dish alone. I don't like having to choose and I like keeping it humble.

When I was thirty years old my mother arranged my marriage with a distant cousin who was ten years younger than I was. I didn't know much about the world at that time. I was also too shy to even look at girls. I had known my bride as a child and liked her. I was the best cricket player in my village and all the villages around us and the girls talked about me and so my bride was excited to get married to me as well. But this was the first time we had looked at each other or spoken to each other as adults. It was a beautiful time.

Something funny happened during my wedding celebration that I have to mention. My brother had a friend, let me call that friend R. R was known all over the village because he was a little bit feminine. Sometimes people made fun of R and his feminine behaviour, but in a gentle way. R had a very good heart and in fact once saved my brother's life. On the day before my wedding day, R came and congratulated me and brought some presents. Then, later in the evening, my brother had organised a dance performance for me. A group of beautiful made-up women in blinging dresses appeared and started to dance to the newest Punjabi songs. They didn't seem like the women in our village but more like the women you see on TV. My brother encouraged me to enjoy the performance but I could barely look at the ladies. I felt it was wrong to look at them that way. Suddenly one of the ladies approached me and asked, 'But Aaftaab Bhai, don't you like my performance?'. When she spoke I realised that the lady was actually R. I was quite astonished. I had never seen something like that. I replied, 'R Bhai, what has happened to you?'. Now, ten years later, I have to laugh about that, how naive and ignorant I was. Many years after that encounter, R introduced me to my girlfriend with whom I have been for several years now.

My wife gave birth to three children, my two sons and one daughter. I love all three of them dearly. They are the most important human beings to me. The birth was difficult in all three cases and my wife suffered a lot. After my daughter had been born she said that she did not want any more children and told me to make sure that we would not have any more. I respected that. And in hindsight I have to say that I am more than thankful that she made that decision because it would have been so much more difficult to take care of even more children. My wife takes the most sensible decisions. Just like my mother did. My girlfriend does as well. I thank God every day that I have such sensible women in my life who give me strength and who support me.

Ah, you ask about these two women? My wife and my girlfriend? Yes, why should I lie about that. I am not ashamed of anything in my life. As I said, when I was young I never even dared to look at girls. And even long after my marriage I wouldn't even have thought much about other women. I married the woman that my mother chose for me and she chose well. It would have remained like that, had I not been stuck in a cold foreign country, far away from my family, for many years now. And had it not been that R had also thought of a good choice for me. It is good now as it is. My wife knows my girlfriend and my girlfriend knows my wife. I am not cheating on anybody and not hiding anything. And I wouldn't have started with any of this if any of them had told me that it hurts them. It doesn't hurt them. They are like that. Be angry with me over this if you must. I know, there are far too many men in this world who treat women badly and disrespect them. Men who would secretly cheat or secretly marry second wives. And who expect their wives to accept everything they do. My own father acted like that. If you think I am like that as well then that's no surprise. But I assure you that I am not.

In Europe I have met men who are married to other men and women who are married to women. Some people say this is against our religion but I don't judge that either. The most important thing is that people respect each other. And I respect all the important people in my life. I respect all the women in my life. I want to marry my girlfriend as well. But right now the laws in Europe make this impossible. And we are still trying to figure out how to organise this situation in a way that would not do injustice to anyone.

But now I have stepped forward too far. I have already started talking about my life in Europe. But first I need to tell you how I got there. And how God and our Prophet met me on that journey.

My wife and I had a good life in the first years of our marriage. But the more children we had and the older they got the clearer it became that I needed to make more of an effort to provide for them. Added to this came the fact that I was the oldest brother amongst five siblings, my father didn't provide much for us and also became quite old, my mother also became old and sick. I was the one who was responsible for the whole family. My three sisters needed to get married and, as you may know, a marriage in rural Punjab is a very expensive affair for the family of the bride. They say this isn't actually Islamic but the truth is that we do a lot of things that are not Islamic and still consider them parts of our culture. The demands that I needed to fulfil became bigger and bigger. While at the same time the economy in our country became more and more insecure.

As I told you, my school marks have never been too great and I had no higher education, so my options were very limited. For a while I was able to find a job as a policeman in Lahore. I worked for the police for four years but the longer I did it the more I became disillusioned. Here in Europe, whenever I have a problem, I go to the police. I wouldn't do the same in Pakistan, to be honest. I saw a lot of bad human beings around me there. And I also felt myself becoming bad in that job. I eventually quit. Then for a while I became a foreman in a textile factory. Work there was better because I liked the workers there and the workers liked me. But in the end it wasn't enough to make ends meet either. The situation for my family became more and more demanding but the money I earned was never enough. Then I moved to Karachi and tried to find better work there. Already I had moved quite far away from my home village. And still it wasn't enough. What would be my next step? Dubai? Saudi Arabia? But what to do there, with my little qualifications? Work on the construction sites where every day people die?

We are not poor people, mind you. We own some land, we have a house back in our village. My younger brother keeps operating my mother's shop. And still with every year it became more and more impossible to make sure that we would not constantly run into debt. And I wanted to make sure that my children would never have the feeling that they lacked anything and that they had a chance for a better life. If a family like mine already struggles so much, I can not even imagine the plight of people worse off than us. And I do not only want to be able to provide for my family. There should also always be something to share with others as well. I owe that to my God. And to my mother, who passed away a few years ago.

The decision to leave for Europe came quickly and spontaneously. It was in the summer of 2015. Someone told me that there was a group leaving for Europe and that I could join them immediately if I had the money ready. I didn't even have time to think much about it. I thought of my children and my wife and my mother, who was still alive at that time, and how much I would miss them. But I also thought how much better I would be able to provide for them should I be able to reach Europe. I quickly assembled all money I could organise, packed my rucksack with the most necessary things for the journey, and said good bye to my family and left. First we had to go to Quetta where we had to pay an agent who would bring us across the Pakistain–Afghan and the Afghan–Irani borders.

I have later been told that the people who take your money to guide you across the borders are criminals. That they are human traffickers. I don't know. I am sure there are people on this planet who will make a business out of everything and exploit other human beings. I am not saying it does not happen. But the way I see it is this: I see all these people in our world who have the right passport and the right resources and who are able to travel anywhere they want, explore whatever country they want and seek their fortune wherever they want. Maybe with a little hurdle here or there. But not much. They are free on this earth. And then there are people like me who do not have the right passport and the right resources. There is no way for people like me other than paying people to help us to travel in other ways. It is not us who have made those rules nor is it the people who are paid by us. The rules are made by people with the right passports and the right resources. Where is the justice in that? The whole earth belongs to God. If I want to travel on it like Alexander the Great, who has the right to prohibit me from doing so?

The people we pay deserve that money. They go through a lot of troubles to help us. At least those who helped me did. They themselves risk losing their lives by getting shot by border guards. An evil person would not do that. And never at any point on my journey did I feel like I could not trust these people. They always did their best to keep us safe.

The journey through Afghanistan was swift, by bus. I once saw a movie in which two young boys travelled from Afghanistan to Europe. They spent most of the journey in a dark container. I think some people travel like that. But most of us don't. The journey goes step by step. You are handed from one guide to the next. A network of human beings stretching across borders and countries. My girlfriend calls it 'an underground railroad'.

We entered Iran at night. Crossed the border by foot. Then we travelled through the country alternating by foot or car. We were told it was better this way so that we would not get caught. Sometimes our group had to separate, then we were united again. Then a car appeared from somewhere. I didn't have any time to look at the country. All I remember are the date groves that we sometimes hid in at night. We didn't have much to eat, just the dates. I remembered the story of the birth of Jesus in the Qur'an and how Mary was fed with dates. I also remembered how much our Prophet loved dates. This was humble food but it was blessed food. God was with us.

We reached Iranian Azerbaijan where we were handed over to another guide and had to pay more money. I remember this as the most dangerous part of my journey. For several days we walked through the mountains. We had no food at all and the hunger was unbearable. We slept between the rocks at night. It was August and fortunately warm enough. My sneakers tore at that time. I was lucky enough that I still had a pair of *chappals* in my rucksack. I had to continue the rest of my journey in these slippers. All across the mountains. My feet were covered with blood and blisters. In the middle of the night we crossed the border into Turkey. We were caught by border guards and they started shooting. I heard bullets pass right next to my ears. I saw some of my companions being hit and staying behind. Two of them were boys from my own village. Our guide urged us to run and I ran. Through the rocks, through the darkness, under a starlit sky. Suddenly I was in Turkey. There were only two borders between my home country and here and already I was in a country that was partly on the European continent. How strange.

We reached a Kurdish village the next morning. Our guide locked us up in a stable. 'For your own security', he said, and I had no reason to doubt him. The people in the village brought us food and juice and milk. They were poor. Much poorer than my own family. But they shared the few that they had. My girlfriend once asked me whether I would ever visit these countries again or whether I had too many bad memories connected to them. I told her that I didn't remember too much of the bad experiences. But what I always remember is that everywhere we arrived there were people who treated us with kindness.

No border guards came, no police, no military. The next day the guide opened the stable and led us a few miles more through the Kurdish mountains. Then we were put on another car, straight to Istanbul. I had completed the largest part of my journey. It had taken less than a month, can you imagine?

When I reached Istanbul I knew that things would be alright. My journey wasn't over yet. Later I was about to cross the Aegean Sea on a boat. Again I heard the bullets of border guards. I saw corpses lying on the sea shores. I arrived in Greece. I managed to call a friend and ask him to send me some money via Western Union. I managed to call my mother. She had become sick from worrying about me and cursed me when she heard my voice. This was the most painful moment of my journey. It was the time when the German government had opened its borders for the refugees from the Syrian war. I knew that this was my chance as well. I walked. I walked through Macedonia, through Serbia, through Hungary, through Austria ... finally I was in Germany. On that road on which I travelled so freely at that time people are stuck now. They stay in dirty camps on toxic dumping grounds. They die from the cold in winter. They are insulted and beaten up by European policemen, bones broken by batons. I was much more lucky when I arrived.

But Istanbul? That was different. It was here I knew I would be ok. Why did I know that things would be alright? First of all, I had finally crossed over to a new continent. And while I was still far away from entering the EU, I was already on the continent that I wanted to reach. And, additionally, I felt that I was on holy ground. I was told that this was the city that had been the capital of the Muslim Caliphate for centuries. I had no time for real sightseeing but I saw the silhouettes of the Sultan's palace and the grand mosques from afar. I know this was the city that was mentioned in the Qu'ran in Surah ar-Rum. I had been to Data Darbar (the shrine of the eleventh century Sufi Saint and scholar Abul Hassan Ali Hujriri, also known as Data Ganj Baksh – 'the master who bestows treasurers') and to Kasur (where the shrine of seventeenth century Sufi poet and saint Bulleh Shah is located), but I had never been in a city mentioned in the Holy Qu'ran before. One day I will go to Makkah and Madinah. But for the time being, Istanbul was as close to that holiness as I could get.

Someone in our group told me that a companion of our Prophet was buried in this city, Ayyub al-Ansari, who had fallen during the battle predicted in Surah ar-Rum. I hadn't seen any special sight on my journey but I knew that I had to visit this one. We set out to find his grave, asking around. Some people guided us to the right quarter. We found the complex of his mausoleum at the end of a long road with shops selling things like *tasbeehs* (worry beads), headscarves and prayer carpets. In a way this reminded me of home, of our shrines and holy places. But it was also very different. Much more in order. But also much less vibrant. When we reached the entrance to the shrine I was surprised that there was a machine that handed out plastic bags so that we could carry our shoes with us inside after taking them off.

We entered the shrine and were bathed in a dim green light. Here we were. And here was also the body of a man who had known our Prophet, had loved our Prophet, had touched our Prophet, had fought for our Prophet, had died for our Prophet. Tears welled up in my eyes. I thought of the troubles of my journey. The hot August sun. The hunger. The fear. My shoes tearing. My blisters and blood. My companions being hit by bullets. And here I was. As physically close to my Prophet and his companions as never before. There was also, in a niche at the side, bathed in more green light, another relic. A footprint of my Prophet. It was in a glass case. How much I longed to touch it but I couldn't. But setting my eyes on it already felt like a blessing. I remembered my own footprints in the Balochi desert and in the Kurdish mountains. I remembered the pains that my Prophet and his family had gone through. Pains that had been so much more than my own. Around me the voices of men and women saying their salaams, praying, reciting the Qur'an. In the glass in front of the relic I caught a glimpse of my reflection. I looked as if I had become ten years older since I started my journey, I barely recognised myself. I opened my heart and raised my hands and started to pray myself. I remembered my mother, my children, my wife and my siblings. I prayed for all of them. And I asked God that He would give me success so that I would be able to provide for them. When I closed my prayers and touched my face with my hands, I knew that God had heard my prayers and that He will answer them. In the presence of our Prophet and his righteous companions every just desire is fulfilled.

Based on an interview and translated from Urdu

WHAT'S IN A NAME?

Sahil Warsi

In late 2018, the Hindu nationalist government of the Indian state of Uttar Pradesh (UP) renamed Allahabad, the state's judicial capital, Prayagraj. For over two decades the Bhartiya Janta Party (BJP) had promoted the moniker change as a return to the original, ancient name of the city. The alteration was not just an attempt to reclaim a lost heritage, however. It was part of a longer-term right-wing policy to expunge Muslims from the national landscape. This contributed to ongoing discussions around the country's changing identity and the place of minorities in it, most notably Muslims. The act was seen as another step toward making India's Muslim history and Indian Muslim identity a relic of the past. It was welcomed by many, and denounced by those who hold a vision of India at odds with the current nationalist dream.

Hindu texts suggest that at their *sangam*, their confluence, the Ganges and Yamuna rivers are joined by a third mythical river Saraswati. The *sangam* is included among several sacred confluences cited in scriptures, along one of which an ancient city of Prayag is said to have been located. No archaeological evidence exists, however, of a permanent settlement here before the late 1500s when the Mughal emperor Akbar established a new urban centre as the district capital of *Ilahabad*. Meaning 'the place where God lives', the name was an acknowledgement of the *sangam's* religious significance for local people.

For half a century, Allahabad emblematised what would be known as the *ganga-jamuni tehzeeb* of the gangetic plains: a syncretic culture springing from the convergence of Muslim and Hindu traditions, flowing together like the city's two rivers. The city's intellectual and cultural foment produced some of South Asia's most famous figures such as the literary giant Akbar Ilahabadi, the country's first Prime Minister Jawaharlal Nehru, and the 1970s' Bollywood heartthrob Amitabh Bachchan. Allahabad is also where my paternal grandparents settled after my grandfather's forty years of service for the UP central jail system.

My grandfather, whom we all called Papa, married my Daadi when he was eighteen. Originally from Mirzapur, the two were from *pathan* families of lawyers and *'alims*, religious scholars, where men and women were educated in Persian and Urdu as well as English. Compelled by family circumstances, Papa joined the state services at seventeen, eventually moving his extended family across various cities throughout the state. Towards the end of his last posting at Allahabad's historical Naini Central Jail, he and Daadi bought a plot of land in Mahewa, a small fishing village across the Yamuna river. They built a house and moved in with their remaining three unmarried children shortly after I was born.

Mahewa was a mixed village of Shia, Sunni, and Hindu families. Even through the mid 1990s the fields between the houses were planted with mustard or wheat, and from our roof we could still see the Yamuna River and the rows of gigantic palms that provided a livelihood for basket-weavers and most likely a steady supply of sap to be fermented and sold locally. Papa was known in the village as 'Jailer Sahab', as opposed to the other *pathan* 'Khan Sahab' further up the road who was a doctor. While the *pathan* identity was important to my grandparents, what defined them above all else was their devotion and discipleship as members of the Warsi community. Papa's grandfather was one of the first followers of the saint Waris Ali Shah whose shrine is in the town of Dewa, just outside Lucknow, the state capital. The founder of the Warsi branch of Sufism, saint Waris Ali Shah admitted devotees from branches of all faiths. His central instruction was to follow the tenets of one's faith and see God in everything and everywhere.

For Papa and Daadi, all Warsis, in fact all individuals who had 'clutched the hem' of any saints' teachings, were a family. They sought and were sought out by those in need wherever they lived. Through sharing their resources, material or otherwise, they built relationships with people in Mahewa, across Allahabad, and beyond. Consequently, the house in Mahewa was never bereft of visitors and family.

A modern house built with concrete and steel, Daadi and Papa's home was planned on a more traditional layout. Set back from what was then still a dirt road, guests entered the house through a small anteroom where male visitors not intending to stay long were entertained. The room opened onto a large, rectangular formal drawing room. Two sofa sets lined either side, and a raised wooden platform was set out with bolsters and cushions at the far end. The furniture was light and easily removable for when cotton carpets covered with white sheets would be laid to seat larger gatherings.

The door at the far end of the drawing room opened onto the veranda of the first inner courtyard. Cemented, rather than laid in brick or stone, the courtyard was the heart of the inner house. At the opposite end of the veranda was the *nazar ka kamra*: the room under the gaze of the saint. It was effectively a store room for everything from our grandparents' prized and personal items to everyday essentials like incense, soap, or toothpaste. A photograph of saint Waris Ali Shah crowned the doorway on the inside, covered respectfully with a yellow curtain that symbolised the yellow robe he wore in his earthly life.

Children were not allowed unsupervised in the *nazar* room, though that was perhaps more to keep them from digging into the boxes of dried fruit, nuts, and sweets stashed on high shelves inside locked armoires. Sometimes, when the adults would finally fall asleep, those cousins who had not given in to the post-lunch slumber would tiptoe to the courtyard and make their way past the silence of the inner house. Taller cousins could reach the key holder and remove the heavy set of house keys. Some would go and play on the roof, some would raid the *nazar* room, but me and another cousin preferred the box-room.

The journey required courage. Besides the tiny lattice vent above the doorway the small room at the end of a dark corridor was windowless. A constant, still dampness deepened its darkness, and we held our breath in the seconds between prying the door and flicking on the lone bulb, in case the witch from the loft above materialise and snatched us away. But wonderful treasures awaited the end of this expedition.

By all accounts a completely mundane room, the box-room was a museum-like playground of household items not regularly used and stacked with iron chests and suitcases filled with our parents, aunts, and uncles' belongings. Each box contained nested stories of dowries saved and received, photographs, jewellery, mementos and souvenirs from decades past. Rolled straw mats and large cauldrons, which had fed countless guests at weddings and religious ceremonies, served as perfect hiding places. The most magical objects, however, were a shield and two curved swords as tall as us, which had belonged to our paternal great-grandfather.

One sword had already become tarnished from the family's crisscrossed transfers across the state. The other retained a dull glint when removed from its engraved scabbard. It was not till much later that I would be able to read the Arabic inscription on the bifurcated blade engraved amidst a bed of undulating vines and flowers: 'there is none as valiant as Ali, and no blade compares to his sword Zulfiqar'.

Over the years, the swords became a constant in a house being extended, remodelled, reshaped. Every summer, arriving from the railway station, I'd greet my grandparents and anyone else at home and rush to the box room. The sight of the swords, the whiff of rust, the metallic coolness of the grip were an assurance that some things were still the same. Then, in 2012, they were gone. After a good fifteen minutes of searching, I casually asked Papa about the swords. 'Oh, those? We sent them off to Dewa to be displayed in the *astana*. We didn't realise you liked them, otherwise we'd have kept them for you!'

I was surprised at my own feeling of loss as I blurted out: 'Dewa? Why did you send them there? They were your father's!' I knew, of course, why. It made sense. My great-grandfather and his father were buried within the courtyard of the shrine at Dewa. More importantly, as Papa explained patiently, the swords had been given a new lease on life as 'their value was not appreciated here'. Rusting for decades in the box room, they had now been cleaned, polished, and mounted on a wall in the shrine complex, observed and appreciated by countless eyes passing by every day.

Moved by my questions, Papa got up and went to the *nazar* room, returning with a wooden box wrapped in green satin. 'I have something better to show you,' he began, 'these are our *tabarrukat*.' Papa carefully set down the box on his bed, gently unwrapping the satin folds. As he removed each of the *tabarrukat*, the blessed items, he kissed them, handed them to Daadi to kiss, then to me, and then placed them on the unfolded satin. The box contained fragments of saint Waris Ali Shah's robe, a strand of his hair preserved in attar, vials of attar from the holy cities of Mecca and Medina, and a bag of about a dozen *mohr,* a small block of earth Shia Muslims prostrate on during daily prayer, made from the soil of Karbala.

The presence of a bag of *mohr* confused me, given we were Sunnis, but they made sense in the context of the box. 'Your late uncle bought them when he was working in Iraq,' Papa narrated, 'he might not have understood exactly what they were for, but even if we don't use them in prayer, they are a sign of the prophet's grandsons'. Each object in the box created a little universe of what was important to my grandfather. They connected him to the prophet's family, the *ahlul bayt,* through saint Waris Ali Shah, the soil of Karbala, and the smells of the holy cities.

'Who knows what will happen to these after we die,' Papa lamented, 'Who knows if anyone will value them and keep them safe?' The question was rhetorical; the correct response would have been that I would take them. There was a context in which it made sense why Papa would ask me to take care of the *tabarrukat.* However, in that moment I also knew I could not make such a promise.

Some years earlier, my father had taken two Qur'anic manuscripts penned by Papa's mother back to Texas along with the reed pens used to write the manuscripts. The aim was to eventually digitise and preserve this family heirloom and make it available to a wider audience. While nobody objected to this, my claiming of the box would complicate a tense family situation that had developed over the previous several years. Thus, instead of responding as I thought Papa might want me to, I assured him we would collectively preserve the *tabarrukat* as they were valuable to us all. His eyes suggested this was not what he had expected, but he smiled warmly nonetheless, tenderly packing each item back in the box before kissing it and returning it to the *nazar* room.

Eventually, after Papa's death, the box went to my youngest uncle. Ten years my elder, he was the darling of my grandparents and the loss was heavy on him in a way different from the older siblings. I thought about what Papa had said to me about the swords, how in letting go of an object, we may allow it to live on. What made the *tabarrukat* valuable to Papa is perhaps not exactly what makes them valuable to my uncle or relatives who visit him. Yet through their gaze and reverence, the objects live on. The *tabarrukat* immediately evoke the memory of Daadi and Papa's love for their family, for their children, for all of us. This love was, of course not separate from their affection for the prophet's family. With my uncle, the *tabarrukat* keep this love of my grandparents fresh for more people than they would be able to, stowed away on a shelf in a musty London closet.

About a year after Papa had shown me the *tabarrukat,* Daadi passed away somewhat unexpectedly as the result of medical oversight and mismanagement in the wake of an operation. I had arrived the day before to help with things at home while she was still in hospital. When my cousin called and abruptly hung up at three in the morning, Papa woke up saying 'there's only one thing this can mean'. I asked him to go back to sleep, suggesting it was perhaps a mistake. He shook his head and lay back down to sleep saying 'sixty-eight years'.

Preparations for funerary rites and the burial began the next morning after dawn prayers. While other cousins were busy making arrangements, I was to take care of Papa. Papa had a regimen of medicines to be taken at specific times throughout the day before and after food. Within a half hour of the first medicine, in preparation for the second dose that could not be taken on an empty stomach, Papa always had a fried egg with toast and tea. That morning, the kitchen was empty. Assuming people were either sleeping after the night's commotion or busy setting up for the day, I quickly began to make Papa's breakfast.

A flutter of rubber slippers raced down the hallway shortly after I had lit the stove and put the tea to boil. A timid voice reached across the door with a message that my elders were asking why I was in the kitchen? Thinking the objection was that a man should not be in the kitchen, I explained the urgency to prepare breakfast. The same voice returned a few minutes later with another message asking if I didn't know 'stoves should not be lit in the house of death.' I calmly responded that I had indeed heard the saying, but was only ensuring Papa could take his mid-morning medicine.

I did, in fact, remember hearing the saying as a child, though delivered with a different sentiment. When my maternal grandfather passed away sixteen years earlier, there was a similar rush about the house. Aside from burial preparations, arrangements for the waves of relatives and guests also had to be made. Much of the food was bought from shops nearby, but in all the commotion a visitor had brought a simple dish to be shared by immediate family. Politesse required my eldest aunt to say there was no need for such generosity, to which the neighbour replied 'but of course, stoves should not be lit in the house of death'.

This was admittedly not the case in 2016 Mahewa. As Allahabad grew, it spilled over the river into Mahewa. There were no more fields around the house, and from the roof the river was now hidden by a sea of brick and concrete, the palm trees long gone. Many of my grandparents' friends and neighbours had sold their plots to developers, built rental accommodation for students, or passed away. Like Daadi and Papa's own children, neighbours' children and grandchildren had moved to other cities or countries. The way neighbours could come to the aid of grieving households did not seem to hold as it had in the past.

My seeming obstinance in keeping the stove alight prompted one of my aunts' to come to the kitchen. Taking a cup of tea, she suggested a solution would be to ask one of the lodgers in the detached rented portion of the house if we could use their stove. Papa ate his breakfast quietly in his thoughts. Handing me back the plate he quietly asked 'What happens now?'.

As news spread across family networks, relatives started streaming in from Allahabad and nearby cities to attend the burial. The mother-in-law of one of my aunts had hired a car from Banaras as soon as she got the news. A slender and caring lady, I remembered her bright eyes and wit from when I'd seen her over two decades ago. Now weathered and hunched in her white sari, she still exuded the confidence born of surviving life with a sharp intellect and full purse. Relatives swarmed around her, drawn perhaps in equal part by the calm she exuded as well as that particular authority commanded by wealth.

After a teary greeting, she set herself down on Daadi's *takhat,* the raised wooden platform where Daadi slept. Facing Papa, she sincerely assured him '*Arrey bhaisahab*, now you don't worry about a thing. We will take care of everything'. Throughout the day, she would weigh in on how things should be done, or more importantly how they should not be done. A naturally quiet man who often spoke in sayings or poetry appropriate to the situation, Papa was pushed to the fringes as relatives gathered around her, nodding in agreement with her every word.

Her approach to religious practice was markedly different from my grandparents. It was austere and in-step with the contemporary shift to conservative modernism heralded by suited televangelists, sidewalk hecklers, and everyone in between. When she pronounced there was no need to commemorate the *soyem*, the third day after death, by holding a *fateha* ceremony of ritual prayers and almsgiving at home, Papa quietly recited a couplet to the effect of 'Look how the maid servant is sitting like a queen.' The comparison was lost on his children and others present.

Throughout their lives Daadi and Papa faithfully held *fatehas* for different occasions. The house would be cleaned and prepared for visitors. Cauldrons of savoury *pulao* and sweet *zarda* would be prepared for guests participating in the recitation of the Qur'an and prayers and for distribution among the poor. As a child, such events were electric, an occasion to see family friends or relatives, eat good food, and break from routine. In the case of funerals, they also allowed family and community to gather and mourn collectively.

Traditionally, many Muslims in India have commemorated the third day, fortieth day, and one year anniversary of a person's death. Not everyone has always supported the practice, some on religious grounds others for practical reasons. Decades earlier, some of my aunts and uncles had voiced disagreement with holding a *fateha*, suggesting it was a waste of resources where freeloaders with no connection to the family might show up. Papa merely responded that anyone attending was welcome as being *ahle muhabbat*, people related through love.

Opposition to practices like *fatehas* increased over the 1990s. Detractors suggested such events were non-Muslim practices to be expunged in order to purify people's faith. As a supporter of this view, my aunt's mother-in-law glibly dismissed the thought of commemorating the *soyem* as we sat in Papa's room planning the next days' arrangements. She stated, matter-of-factly, 'there's no need to do anything at home for the *soyem*. Better to send money to feed orphans and pay for Qur'an recitation'. My aunts and uncles present nodded enthusiastically, ignoring Papa who sat stone-faced. As the youngest in the room, all I could do was pointedly ask Papa in front of the others about how he wished to proceed. Giving in to politesse, he morosely responded with 'what does my opinion matter when others have made the decision,' which everyone present wilfully misunderstood as his consent.

I could see Papa's deepening grief at potentially being unable to perform the requisite rites for Daadi, the rites in which he believed and which he knew she would have expected. Unable to openly contradict my elders, I appealed to my parents in the US. Over the next day and a half, a silent tussle ensued as my parents, an aunt coming from Bahrain, and an aunt and cousin in Allahabad worked to ensure the *soyem* would be commemorated.

The event did not have the flair of Daadi and Papa's *fatehas*, but we did our best to replicate what we had seen them do. When I started clearing the drawing room, an aunt chided me again, reminding me how 'brooms should not sweep in the house of death'. But, Papa's eyes lit up when he saw the room cleaned, white sheets laid out over the carpet, and chairs arranged in the anteroom and driveway for anyone who might show up. My aunt prepared the *zarda* of sweet rice, and savoury meat *pulao* was cooked for guests in the large cauldrons fetched from the box-room.

The *fateha* was held after mid-day prayers. People dressed in white streamed through the front gates from all over the city and state: people who had known Daadi and Papa for years, people they had never met but whom they had supported in some way, people who were children or grandchildren of those whom Daadi and Papa had helped through hard times. Everyone came, ate, prayed, and sat outside with Papa in the November sun. He was not alone for a moment that day. Sometimes smiling, sometimes laughing, sometimes breaking down in tears, he recounted stories of the saints and memories of his long marriage. A hundred hands were shaken, a hundred glistening eyes held him fast when he would slump from grief. In the end, it did not matter what one thought about commemorating the *soyem*, for Papa was held that day in the embrace of the *ahle muhabbat*.

The last time I was in Allahabad, the Supreme Court had just ruled in favour of the Hindu-nationalists' 1992 demolition of Ayodhya's historical Babri Masjid, about 150 kilometres north of Allahabad. The Parliament was on the eve of enacting the Citizenship Amendment Act that, in conjunction with the upcoming nation-wide implementation of the National Register of Citizens, would specifically render Muslims without citizenship. The UP government was still to unleash the state-wide pogroms in response to protests against the Act by intimidating Muslim communities with targeted killings, destruction of businesses, and confiscation of property.

Driving through Allahabad, I was happy Daadi and Papa could not witness the city today. In preparation for the 2019 *Kumbh mela*, an ancient

Hindu festival celebrated at the *sangam* since the 1800s, the BJP government had undertaken mass urban renovation. Urdu was markedly absent from new road signs, traditionally trilingual, while several other Indian languages were included for potential pilgrims. Large, garish concrete *shivaling*s, symbols of the god Shiva, were erected at prominent streets, and murals of hyper-masculinised or feminised deities were painted across the city. The old British-era wall of Naini jail where freedom-fighters like Nehru, Abul Kalam Azad, and Indira Gandhi had served time, was now hidden from public view by a new, taller wall emblazoned with gaudy renderings of scenes from a Hindu creation story of the churning of the ocean by gods and demons.

Advocates for these changes would argue the government is merely reviving the city's past Hindu identity. For others, the process is an explicit altering of the city's material and social culture through purging any connection to its Muslim past. In either case, one is faced with the question: what does it mean for this North Indian Muslim culture, for the *ganga-jamuni tehzeeb* to become a relic?

This suggests that relics are anything but static. They might be materially finite or serve as specific symbols, but the meanings ascribed to or contained within them are multiple and inconstant. The swords that became, for me, a repository of remembered smells and emotions mixed with childhood imaginings of my great-grandfather were expendable, old metal for others. The *tabarrukat* brought forth emotions connecting Daadi and Papa to their children, though they evoked different feelings for my aunts and uncles than they did for my grandparents.

As containers of meaning and sentiments, relics reflect our relationships to ourselves, to others, and to the world around us. Relics call us to make a decision about what we hold on to through them and what we let fall away, revealing how we locate ourselves in the present. Sometimes letting go can allow things to live on in different ways or permit others to hold on to something they need. The commemoration of a *soyem* by holding a *fateha* is part of the past as much as the custom of not lighting stoves or sweeping in the house of the deceased. In the context of Daadi's *soyem*, neither tradition fits squarely into the present, and the choice to discard one in favour of another was made based on how the decision-makers perceived themselves and related to others in the present. Ultimately, the consideration of continuing the practice revolved around the love for Papa, what it meant for him, and how it gave him what he needed.

While the North Indian Muslim culture of my grandparents, the *ganga-jamni tehzeeb* that felt like home, might be erased from the present, it was perhaps a relic long before India's political swing to the right. The cultural praise for Ali was not just for Shias but was equally important for the Sunnis. The Mahewa where neighbours, Hindus and Muslims, shared food and visited each other during religious festivals, has been replaced by an urban culture of anonymity. This process has, of course, been complex, and has been part of the same changes contributing to the country's political shift over the last three decades. But what now?

One orientation to the cultural relic of the *ganga-jamni tehzeeb* is to extinguish it. This is the position of contemporary purists – Hindu and Muslim alike – whose logic of identity requires a separation. Those of us who hold on to the relic must, however, not only consider how we preserve it, but also why we bring it into our present or future. These are perhaps the questions the protestors in India are asking themselves as they brave the winter smog and police batons. While I am suspicious of states and their symbols, I hope these are in fact the questions they are considering in their defence of the constitution and their rallying cry of '*hum bharat ke log!*', 'We, the people of India!'.

ARTS AND LETTERS

LANGUAGE

David Shariatmadari

Language is different. We shouldn't settle for just knowing how to use it. To understand it is to understand what it means to be human. Speech is deeply entwined in all aspects of our lives. It's not hyperbole to say that linguistics is the universal social science. It intrudes into almost every area of knowledge: psychology, sociology, neuroscience, anthropology, literature, philosophy and computing. If that's not enough, professional linguists must have some knowledge of anatomy (albeit an incomplete slice, from the diaphragm to the brain) and also of physics, which is important in the study of phonetics.

Wherever we are, language is. Most of what we do, we do using language. Ignoring its workings seems foolish. And this isn't just a question of satisfying intellectual curiosity. Listening to people speak a language you can't understand is a strange and maddening experience. It can be more than that. It can be the origin of prejudice and hostility. If you are unable to talk to someone, it's hard to appreciate how much you have in common. When I was nineteen, I arrived at university and took a course in Arabic. I didn't want to. I wanted to learn Farsi, my father's language, but the rules said you couldn't study that on its own from scratch. I had to take another language too, and Arabic was the obvious choice (Farsi borrows around 30 per cent of its vocabulary from Arabic). I may have been a reluctant student, but what happened over the following weeks and months was a revelation – and one I've never told anyone about, because it's embarrassing to admit to prejudice, however vague, and however young you were at the time. My perceptions of the Arab world, insofar as I thought about it at all, had been shaped by news reports of violence in Palestine and in Lebanon, of the Lockerbie bombing, of hijackings and the war waged by Iraq on Iran.

I wasn't alone in this: when baddies in movies weren't English, they were Arabs. If I pictured an Arab in my head, he was an angry man, jabbing his finger and shouting guttural syllables at a news camera. At the same time, I thought the script was beautiful – but then scripts don't have an accent. The sound of a human voice has a unique emotional resonance, and the resonance here was bad. But as I began to chip away at the edifice of Arabic grammar, to learn about its elegance and precision, something changed in my attitude to Arabs and the Arab world. I found myself spellbound by Arabic morphology – the way that words are built up – and I still find it astonishing today.

Every word in Arabic, unless it's been borrowed from another language, is based on a set of three, or more rarely four, consonants. This is the scaffolding around which the word is built. So you have, for example, 'k-t-b', which is the root that has to do with books and writing. *Maktab* means 'offi ce', *kitaab* is 'book', *kataba* is 'to write', *kaatib* is 'a scribe', *aktubu* means 'I write', and so on. The roots can be used to build verbs which take up to ten forms: *kataba* is form I, *kattaba* form II, *kaataba* form III. Skipping ahead, form X is *istaktaba*. Any root can be made into a verb using these patterns: so, form II of the root 'm-l-k', which has to do with owning or possessing, would be *mallaka*, form III *maalaka* and form X *istamlaka*.

Each of these forms has its own 'flavour' of meaning. Form II is often a causative verb: *kattaba* means 'to make someone write something', *mallaka* means 'to make someone the owner of something'. Form III is often about doing the action to or with someone else. So *kaataba* means 'to correspond with someone'. Form III of 'm-l-k', *maalaka*, doesn't actually exist (not all roots take every possible form). Form X often involves asking for something or thinking something should be done. *Istaktaba* is 'to ask someone to write something'. *Istamlaka* is 'to take possession of something'.

This was my first experience of a non-Indo-European language, and it overturned my assumptions about what language was. Everything that had seemed natural and obvious to me – like the way you look up a word in the dictionary – turned out to be a quirk of the languages I was used to. (In Arabic you have to pick out the root consonants and look the word up under that entry. *Istaktaba* doesn't come under 'i' but under 'k'.) The formal kind of Arabic I was studying seemed a lot more sophisticated than English in many ways, and my main feeling was one of respect, awe even.

I'm not saying it was the verbs that did it, but they were a way in. Of course, I was learning much more about the Arab world in general; but in terms of establishing a human connection, there was something fundamental about getting to grips with the language. Arabic was no longer scary sounding. Learning it had offered me a more accurate picture.

People are now more exposed to foreign languages than ever before. Sadly, we're not better linguists – far from it, in many cases. But as we move about modern cities and fly abroad for business or pleasure, we hear foreign accents and incomprehensible words far more often than our ancestors did. There is a risk that we fall back on our instinct to disidentify with these people, to judge them as being not like us, or worse, not quite human. Understanding the mechanics of language – not necessarily understanding the words, but appreciating that here is a complex mode of expression with layers just like our own (phonemes, morphemes, words and syntax) – can help check this instinct. If you are a native English speaker, you're also now more likely to be exposed to more people who speak your language with some degree of difficulty. You may find their speech laborious, or their accents grating. You may fall into the trap of thinking that they are slower or less intelligent than you because they struggle with English prepositions (on, over), phrasal verbs (do up, tie down), or definite and indefinite articles (the, a). Perhaps if you knew what these things were, and how they are not laws of nature but idiosyncrasies of your own language (many others lack articles, don't use phrasal verbs, and the number of prepositions varies hugely), you might not.

Extracted with permission from *Don't Believe a Word: Surprising Truth About Language*, Weidenfeld & Nicolson, London, 2019

AN ARCHITECTURE OF FORGETTING

Alev Adil

Hotel Amnesia

For over a year I took photographs of all the empty beds I slept in, alone. Sliding the electronic key card into its slot, I felt lucky because life afforded me this certainty; I would always find a safe space, anonymous, hygienic, cleared of the traces of previous occupants, of the inevitability of history. Hotels indulge the fantasy that consequence can be cleaned away by the chambermaid. Tomorrow will wipe the slate clean: two glasses by the bathroom sink, miniature bottles of shampoo and bubble bath, a mini bar and price list, the room service menu, dial 9 for an outside line. Every hotel in every city, whatever the view from the window or the décor: from the efficient ugliness of the 70s brutalist Holiday Inn in Niejmegen, to the decaying grandeur of Sarah Bernhardt's room in the Pera Palace in Istanbul, every hotel had the ambience of Hotel Amnesia. I love to watch TV in languages I don't understand. I have learnt to bide my time. Waiting is my newly acquired skill, a talent I value highly - quite an achievement when time is in short supply, is not on my side. I sat in cafes, in Vilnius, Prague, Porto, Seville, writing out fugitive itineraries, although I was never quite certain if I was evading my ghosts or tailing them. The urge to remember and the compulsion to forget are locked in complicity. They are all part of the same haunted clan: the detective, the analyst, the archivist, the academic, the assassin – all searching for clues, tampering with the evidence, hoping for a conclusion that does not come.

My Favourite Dream

Long after your death I'd wander aimlessly, ride buses to their unfamiliar suburban conclusions, abandoning myself to numbers magic. After several centuries of random searches I knew that I'd find you, that finally the living might speak with and not for the dead. Reparations would be made. The mourning could, would, end. The celestial Route Master to armistice would stop for me and everyone I'd ever loved and lost would be there, sailing to oblivion on the upper deck. Sometimes this idea flooded me with a blissful sense of peace, at others it terrified me so completely I'd walk in the rain for miles or hide in the library until the darkness fell. I'd wake up suddenly with the sense of being urgently expected elsewhere. That immobilising panic, a nervous lassitude, you know that feeling that you're too late for a crucial meeting, a vital, forgotten, rendezvous; too late for redemption.

When the dream goes well I finally find you again, we meet in the ruins of a cinema, a grand old Gaumont, a 1920s kitsch medieval folly. Snow filters through the collapsed ceiling, motes melting and dancing in the light of the projector. The red velvet curtains are ripped and charred, rich ragged shrouds from a glamorous past. Everything is as devastated and beautiful, as irretrievably strange and lost as Salamis, or Pergamon. Gorgeous filaments of light, sparkling stars and flakes of snow occlude my vision, and although our private civilisation is long gone the screen is still intact, the projector still whirrs into action. We sit side by side and we speak in the silver nitrate glow.

When I wake up I try desperately to hear your voice again. How I long to hear your voice again. I try to remember what we say to each other but it's gone. All I can remember is the snow and the whirr of the projector. We're talking so intently that the first time I had the dream I paid no attention to the screen at all but in subsequent iterations I try to watch, to remember what the film is, because I know there's no possibility of recalling your words, your voice. But you become upset, you want me to look into your beautiful dark eyes, to listen to you. There's nothing I want more myself and so I abandon myself to your gaze and your scent. I miss your scent. The way I miss your scent breaks my mammal heart.

The Ruined Cinema, the Screen Memory

The ruined cinema is the key to everything; it is the set for the screen that memory is projected upon. The editing strategies of the unconscious provide many technologies of fictionalisation. Events are transferred to a place they didn't occur. Several people are merged into one or one is substituted for another. Separate experiences are combined. Every time we remember we use psychic technologies analogous to those used in fiction or filmmaking.

A psychic suture is inherent in the act of remembering. The screen memory serves to (incompletely or problematically) repress and omit the objectionable. Memory does not emerge it is formed, edited. We create an archive (fragments of memories) to generate screen memories/ narratives; use visual, acoustic, linguistic and melodic metaphors as contiguities to elude closure and allude to indeterminate unarticulations; to explore the processes that determine what we exclude/edit out and what we present as fact or choose to fictionalise. Both the memory and the representation of memory are crafted objects open to interpretation, both have the power to deconstruct and disturb historical and personal narratives as much as to confirm them. The screen is not only a cover but just as it is in the cinema it is a plane of projection. 'You projected two fantasies onto one another and turned them into a childhood memory', Freud tells his double, his imaginary analysand. We are the projectors as well as the directors, editors and audience in the cinema of memory.

Perhaps Freud's concept of screen memory is compelling precisely because his interpretation of the screen memory refuses closure, the secure finality of a definitive interpretation, which he promises. The screen memory is not only a shroud over a hidden object (subject) it is a process of allusion, a stream of metaphors which provide a contiguity to the zone of the inarticulate. The inarticulable shifts: there is no single unsayable; we are cast into a zone of indeterminacy, an imaginary cinema where we are both projector and sole member of the audience.

We are always divided from the self we see in memory, and any detective work around the identity of that alter ego inevitably alters the ego. The analysis is never complete, the 'meaning' of the memory never fixed. There can be no Final Interpretation to uncover; it will have to be read against all the other analyses created by prior, and subsequent, selves. Whereas the promised pleasures of the detective genre in film and fiction (and of psychoanalysis) speak of a fantasy of order, that the criminal will be apprehended; that the Law of the Father will be reinstituted; the mystery will be solved, Freud's detective work here speaks from a more culpable position. Rather than Deleuze and Guattari 's forbidding 'priest of interpretation' who is at hand every time 'desire is betrayed, cursed, uprooted from its field of immanence', in *Screen Memories* Freud presents us with the psychoanalyst as far more ambiguous, playful, figure. For while Freud as analyst/detective 'solves' the murder (that which has been exiled from articulation), he is also his own analysand/criminal covering his tracks. The detective is closely related to the assassin. The urge to remember and the compulsion to forget are locked in complicity.

A Small Forgotten War

Mine is a small, forgotten war, a modest war even, nothing on a grand scale, some squalid atrocities but no Srebrenicas, more of a sour extended sulk, a long-term corrosion of the soul. I was born into a time of war. I am as old as the Cyprus Problem. I am thousands of years old. The street I was born in has aged centuries in the decades since I left. The memory of the place and the place itself are just so much rubble. That narrow winding back street close to the border in the old walled city is now a trashed slum. The border, that abject septic scar, serves as a monument to War. On both sides of the city we look away, there is a move outwards, towards Kyrenia in the north and Limassol in the South, to dreary new build suburbs, barbeques in the yard, satellite TV. At the heart of the city there is this wound. Perhaps the Forbidden Zone is almost beautiful in the way it speaks to all of us of our failures, our culpability – unless we choose to forget our own responsibilities for this, our own bloody, tired legacies and see ourselves as only and always the victims of others. Mine is a small forgettable war but all wars give birth to ruins. Ruin eternalises and naturalises destruction, as though it has always been this way, and always will be.

And yet I am not repelled by the festering spaces of the Forbidden Zone. The rust, the stench of rubbish, and the bored conscript soldier boys all shimmer with perverse seduction in the August heat. I am drawn to the dead end streets that mark the border. I follow the fault line from both sides of the city, hungrily photographing the lines of barbed wire, the observation towers, the bricked up windows, the bullet-pocked walls. I film my walks until the border guards order me not to. Soldiers are familiar to me, especially the tall impassive Canadian UN soldiers I remember from the 70s. Crossing the Green Line was something I did every day as a child. I was born into memories of UN blue, of military convoys, checkpoints, rumours of impending war. When the checkpoint opened again I came back after years away. I kept crossing and re-crossing; the journey was cosy and nostalgic. I liked that walk, my footsteps invisibly scribbling along the scar of the Green Line, past the bus stuck in no man's land for thirty years, past the Ledra Palace Hotel, once the glamorous haunt of visiting ballerinas and spies. The swimming pool I swam in every day in the summer is sandbagged, the hotel now announces itself as a UN exchange point. I like crossing from one side to the other, and back. It doesn't disturb me. War has been home to me. And the sea. Like K says, you can never get tired of watching the sea.

The words 'I don't forget' are emblazoned across Greek Cypriot children's school exercise books. The phrase 'We will not forget' is used in official propaganda on the Turkish Cypriot side. Yet I can make no sense of what is to be remembered or how. All memories become controversial and contested. How to remember? Perhaps more crucially, I ask myself what did I choose forget? How are we to unstitch the sense we made of it, to wear the scars with equanimity?

The Names of All Her Dolls

All the names of her dolls. She remembered all the names of all her dolls. Their blind faces lined up, a silent jury in the nursery bearing witness to the blue blurred busyness in the feral shadows of infancy. Memories of childhood are determined by what preoccupied us then. A little girl in Freud's *Screen Memories* remembers all the names of her dolls but no significant family events from that time. Freud contends that these happenstance 'trace-memories' are often contemporaneous with, and speak of, events that profoundly affected us at that time and are also edited and narrativised to make connections with, and metaphorise later events.

There is only the memory of all the names, her dolls; the rest is a blanket of forgetting, something clean and cold, soft like snow. But she remembered all the names of all her dolls. Memories are important because there is a constant correlation, as Freud puts it 'between the psychical significance of an experience and its persistence in the memory.' What are we to make of the elliptical and elusive 'indelible traces' left from our childhoods, 'the relatively small number of isolated recollections of questioning or perplexing significance' that we remember from our earliest years, of the 'banal' fragments that assert an hallucinatory visual insistence? All our earliest memories are sensorial and fragmentary. These shattered pre-narrative vignettes, Freud contends, are not simply unmediated random 'trace memories' but are screen memories that try to articulate the inarticulable, to breach the borders and mark the lineaments of contested territory in the war between the urge to remember and the compulsion to forget.

She remembered all the names of all her dolls, of the blind jury in the nursery. The significance of the screen memory resides precisely in that which is not seen, that which is not shown, but is alluded to. The memory both refers to and suppresses what is significant. The urge to remember and the force of resistance, which wants to forget, do not cancel each other out but reach a compromise.

Memory and the Impossibility of Fidelity

On the last day of his life, in the afternoon Lysandros whispered his last poem about Apollo, the gleaming warrior now disguised as a thousand reeling birds, and slipped irretrievably from the spoken to the written word. His funeral was as theatrical, dignified and unconventional as he was: the gilt splendour of the Greek Orthodox Church in Camden, with all its traditional incense and ritual but also with, controversially, unbelievers, heathens, Turkish Cypriots reading elegies. I'm not sure who persuaded the Greek Orthodox priest to allow such a heresy. Mustafa made sure that Lysandros was buried in Highgate cemetery as he'd wished. The flowers were white. He'd written: 'Anoint me with white flowers when I lose my blessed breath' although there was no 'crown of white flowers, jasmine, held by a golden thread'.

I can't quite capture the grain of his voice, the cadences of his speech, the swoop of a downward inflection at the end of each line but I can still hear the sound of the handful of earth each mourner flung on the coffin. Years later, when Mustafa opened the tidy little suitcase that held Lysandros' work, poems spilled out, yellow pages like doves, jaundiced with age, or bleached ravens. Silence flocked and filled the room; the air was heavy, as if rippled by invisible moths. His words are a challenge to that silence, if not a refutation of it, while I am putting words on a dead man's eyes. In whose shiny currency are my words minted? Where is the most unjust betrayal? Mourning erases the lost ones, translates them always and only as absence.

A Minute Taker at the Conference of Birds

Something that Aamer wrote reminded me of a time I haven't lived, a place I haven't seen, under an open slate grey sky. I came to the tower (the blue plaque read 'Rapunzel cried here') at dusk, in the autumn. Don't ask me when, I can't remember whether we wore our trousers tight or flared that year, whether we dressed like gypsies, soldiers or porn stars, whose song played everywhere, leaked out in every café and bar. It was in the time of forty days – the measure of time they mark you out with when you are born, when you give birth, when you are lost in the wilderness, after you die. It was that kind of time, which is all the time in world; is no time: the time you measure when everything no longer makes sense.

I could see all the world from the tower. All the world I could see was empty. There was no one but me. I sang and the echoes orchestrated me, the wind carried me across the desert. No one heard me. I waited. I waited for the one who tracks my invisible footprints. I waited for the one who knows my name, who comes to find me. Whoever you are, I kept watch for you, a tiny figure on the horizon. Believe me it was a cinematic moment. No one filmed it. No one disturbed the elegant line of the horizon but the great flocks of birds that filled the sky. That winter they flew south at a distance: geese, flamingos, little birds whose names I didn't know. I'd come well prepared for solitude and lots of walking but my knowledge of ornithology was, still is, nil.

I shared the tower with birds. My room was filled with ravens and doves. They cooed. They clawed. They crowded me. I remembered what Aamer wrote, that the Sufi sage had said the doves were our nobler feelings, the ravens our anger, our fear, our doubt. The Sufi said I must free the doves, let them fly free; but should keep the ravens locked in or they'd only return with their malevolence redoubled, to shatter the windows, demolish the tower.

In truth I wanted them all gone. They blurred my vision, got caught in my hair. They deafened me. I tried. I did as he said. But the doves (oh, in my darker moments I see only albino pigeons) kept coming back to roost, breeding in the eaves enthusiastically, back in the overcrowded room again. The ravens grew thin, grew restive, they pecked at me, ate the doves' eggs, hatched conspiracies in the darker corners of the room. I lived in a flurry of feathers: birds battering to get out, birds battering to get back in. And a lot of shit.

Let them all fly. I gave up. I left the tower, climbed down Rapunzel's dead plait, avoiding the thorns that blinded her lover. I set out across the sand. The horizon was a shifting curve ahead, the tower an inky black landmark behind me. I walked my words across the desert, letting the wind delete each phrase easefully with sibilant breaths before a sentence could reach any conclusion. I did not mind. It was a kind of mercy. I walked to find a story, to draw a line and mark a path to the sea. It was a journey. It was a map, a map of forgetting.

The birds were my compass. I knew I'd smell the salt, scent the open sea long before I reached the shore. I'd hear the scream of seagulls. I'd know I had arrived. A vulture kept me company. We shared the same dry sense of humour (useful in a desert). When I despaired he'd reassure me that he'd always stick with me until the end. Then further. When the time came he'd polish my bones, make them pretty. I was grateful. We must strive to keep up appearances, to maintain certain aesthetic standards. We must look our best irrespective of circumstance, despite the puzzling absence of a camera crew or paparazzi. After weeks of waiting we doubted we'd ever find the coast and he tried to comfort me. 'Maybe you should give up on the ocean thing. Maybe that's too excessive an ambition for the season. Why don't we see if we can make it to the Salt Lake for the annual Conference of Birds?' A good idea, surely someone in that mirage of flamingos and nightingales, of eagles and swans, surely one of the delegates would have news? They'd know if there was Someone, the Someone who was waiting not knowing I'd been delayed and lost my way, the One who had set out to find me.

Back in the tower the ravens and the doves flourished and mated. A new species, a sleek grey ghost raven was born. Invisible at dusk and dawn, on a grey winter's afternoon, nameless equivocal creatures, they sang all of happiness, all of sadness, violence and tenderness; all of it and all at once. What is there to say of these mercury spun creatures with the habitual stealth of London's December afternoons, who steal the day from you before you are properly awake, who invade your dreams masquerading as presentiments and omens? They cannot be caged. They cannot be trained and tamed. They'll only sing when they feel like it.

Put your hands on this cage of bone. Feel them beating to escape from my ribs, a burst of wings, of feathered wildness, a beautiful terrible song. Send for the hawk to hunt them. Let it swoop and circle its prey mercilessly: a gorgeous symmetry.

WHAT IS SAVED

Aamer Hussein

JUNE

'Will you take me to the rose garden the day after my birthday?'

Sara had rung up while Murad was struggling to finish a story about a pet pigeon that he'd been told by a friend, but the screen in front of him looked like a puzzle of disconnected words and phrases. The doctor at the fractures clinic had told him that he needed some sunlight; his bones were suffering from staying at home for so long.

'Yes, mercifully I'm free of the crutch as of yesterday. Let's meet at 5 on Saturday then,' Murad replied.

The park was lushly green and festive with floral colours and lightly clad picnicking youngsters in June. Swans and all kinds of ducks and geese were solemnly making their way across the lake, or occasionally soliciting some passer-by for a bit of bread.

After forty minutes, Sara and Murad sat on a bench to catch up with their news of the last few weeks. Three laughing boys went by in a battered yellow canoe. Spotting a cigarette in Murad's hand, one of them waded ashore to ask him for a light. Murad pulled out his lighter from a pocket. The lad lit up, cheerfully thanked him, and splashed off to join his friends in the yellow canoe.

After two months on his back with a broken leg and another month of hobbling around in a boot and with a crutch, Murad was lazily breathing in the flower scents and the sunshine.

'I wish I could spend my entire life in parks and gardens,' Sara was flushed in the evening sunlight.

'But you have such a beautiful garden!'

'We tire easily at this age! And then this leg of yours...'

They crossed over to the nearby restaurant and joined the queue to buy themselves coffee, which they took to a bench in a leafy corner of the café's courtyard. When they rose, the first shadows of evening were falling on the grass.

'Oh, I nearly forgot the cats! (Sara had two pet cats; once there were four.) 'They must be famished. Time to go home.'

When Murad rose, his good right leg was stiffer than the left. Sara stretched out both hands; Murad took one of them lightly, and, resting the other firmly on the arm of the bench, heaved himself up.

'Remember LM's paintings are on show next month at the Serpentine,' Sara said: 'the first in twenty-five years! Everyone's forgotten her. And my book about her is being reissued, too.'

Murad saw Sara onto her bus by Madame Tussaud's and, humming a folk tune and dragging his bad leg a little, walked to Baker Street station. He put his hand in his trouser pocket to retrieve his pass and found his wallet was missing. He checked the other pocket and then both back pockets too.

But no, it was gone.

JULY

'Let's go to the opening of the LM show at the Serpentine,' Sara had said last week.

Sara had once been a very talented painter, but had tired of the art world at the height of her career, and taken to growing flowers and planting trees instead. She still taught art twice a week, and reviewed exhibitions for a left wing weekly.

But this morning she called to say that she had broken her wrist and couldn't make it. 'What happened?'

'Oh, I came home to find Cicero running around with a dead sparrow in his bloody teeth. I chased after him and after a few minutes' struggle I managed to make him let go of the sparrow but he'd broken the poor bird's neck'....

'So you broke your arm...'

'No, listen! I decided to bury the poor bird. If not my cats, some other animal would get at the poor thing. There's a family of foxes just beyond the edge of my garden these days, and at night they make such a noise that the cats start caterwauling too and I lock the kitchen door so they won't get out. I dug a grave under the apple tree and buried the sparrow, wrapped up in a silk scarf, but as I knelt down to put a stone on the grave so none of the animals would dig it up I slipped, I don't know how, and I fell backwards and put out my right arm to break the fall. I fractured my wrist in several places... My daughter's brought me to Oxford, I'm going to stay here and let her look after me for a few days.'

There's a text from a friend in Cyprus, on Murad's phone: *Johnson's our new PM! He's going to chase out all the Europeans.... next, it's going to be the turn of us Muslims. But when?'...*

Murad's homesickness becomes more acute; he's been away from Karachi six months, and misses the sea and the sand and the bougainvillea and the camels, and most of all his friends. They complain about taxes and rising prices and camel bones and blood in the lanes after ritual sacrifices, and the flooding after unexpected rainfall... and yet they get on with their lives and relish whatever each day has to give them.

He puts on his shoes and steps out to take some photographs of trees and water on his phone. The water in the canal mirrors leaves which are different shades of gold in the sunny haze. But the rose on their bushes, in full bloom two days ago, have withered today. Their yellowed petals are scattered on piles of trash and withered leaves.

Hey BoJo, twin of Trump and Modi's shadow brother, you've turned July into autumn, now even the summer roses rot in your reign....

Dust and pollen, like ash, makes his eyes itch. He makes his way home.

AUGUST

'I went to the eye doctor yesterday,' Murad told Sara. He said I needed surgery on both eyes. 14 hours on the right eye, under general anaesthesia.'

'And then?'

'I woke up. Rubbing my eyes. Thinking I wouldn't be able to see, and I really couldn't. Maybe it was dark, or maybe the sky was still overcast after yesterday's storm. I slept for a while, a restless sleep, and woke up to lightning and thunder and heavy rain...'

'The after-effects of LM's show!' Sara laughed.

Murad had finally gone with Sara to the LM exhibition at the Serpentine Gallery yesterday. It was Friday, and their last chance to see the paintings together. The gallery was crowded, but Murad was so taken by the artworks on display that he was barely conscious of other presences around him.

Several of the canvases in the first room took up an entire wall: blurred images in powerful shades of purple, red, yellow, midnight blue. They had titles like 'Exile', 'Anomie', and 'Devastation'.

'These were painted during the Vietnam war, I think,' Sara said. Her eyes were pensive; she was stroking her right arm in its sling with her left hand.

Murad had read in Sara's brief monograph that LM was born in Kenya and had abandoned an art degree in England to go and live in the US with her husband. She'd become politicised there and taken part in anti-war demonstrations in the 60s. In 1970, she separated from her husband and went away to travel, teach and paint in south and southeast Asia. In the late 70s she lived in London, where her daughter worked, for three or four years, before moving to a remote seaside village in Sussex, where she stayed alone and was almost forgotten.

'Lucilla came to London to take part in every political protest that mattered to her,' Sara said. 'She was nearly 83 when she told me she'd come to stay with me during the demonstration against the war in Afghanistan. She was walking on two crutches but was determined to march with us. I'd just started working on the book about her... but she died in her sleep two days before she was meant to get here. And then I went to her wake, where we sang and danced, as she would have wanted... nothing solemn or lugubrious.'

They stood in silence in front of an untitled painting which from a distance had appeared to be a river at high tide. But up close Murad saw that what he'd seen as a river was a panel of the piled-up bodies of eighteen or nineteen youths – writhing, jerking bodies with black streams spurting from their lips and from their eyes.

'Painted after the massacres of Sabra and Shateela,' Sara murmured.

That morning Murad had heard from three of his Kashmiri friends. Two of them had left Kashmir after spending the Ramadan holidays and Eid with their families; Asghar was in Qatar, Murtaza in Aligarh. Kamil was in London; he'd asked Murad for a story he'd sent a while ago for Murad to include in the Kashmir issue of a journal he was guest editing. Kamil wanted to read it at a protest gathering at the university where he taught, but he'd lost the file and his copy of the journal. None of them were able to reach their families; telephone lines had been cut off four or five days ago. And as they stood silently in front of the painting, Murad was beleaguered by images of Kashmiri youths with eyes wounded by pellets in the events of 2016.

'Let's go to the next room.' Sara touched his elbow. 'From the last decade of Lucilla's life; what she saved from all paintings she did after the first gulf war. She had macular degeneration by then, but she was still working constantly.'

They seemed to have entered a wood or a wild garden. Trees, the dense green of leaves and ponds, birds on branches, fish in ponds, tropical flowers – patterns of life in the womb of abstraction. The smallest painting was of a very pale green, shrouded in a whitish mist that only appeared when you were so close that you might even take it for a trick of the light. It was titled 'Eyes'.

The last picture in the room was half blue and half white, with a broad yellow ray dividing the blue and white spaces like a doorway to sky or sea. In the bottom left hand corner of the canvas the artist had painted, in lower case letters, the words: 'before life, death.'

And there the exhibition ended. Sara sighed: Murad felt, along with her and all their absent companions, a lifetime's gleanings of disappointments and despair, scattered shards of hope and gathered up fragments of happiness.

'Let's go', Murad said. 'My head's reeling and my leg's stiff from walking around and standing so much.'

It was 6 pm when they left the gallery. The rain had darkened the late summer sky to a November shade of greyish black. They stepped over puddles. Neither of them was carrying an umbrella.

'No point in having a drink in this ghastly weather and it's too early to eat,' Sara said. 'But the cats must be hungry. When do you plan to leave for Karachi?'

'Oh, another three weeks', Murad said. 'Shall we meet before I go?'

They left the park. Sara turned left to catch her bus to East London. Murad crossed over to Exhibition Road and limped down the pavement that would take him straight down to the entrance of South Kensington Station.

Translated and abridged by the author from his original Urdu story,
'Zindagi se pehle'

For Mary Flanagan

THE SLAP

Shahbano Alvi

We got out of the taxi and looked around. A profusion of colour hit us through the drizzle. There was a yellow building, a blue building and next to it an ancient little house of bricks. It had a colourful boundary wall, half the size of a tall man. It comprised hundreds of broken ceramic pottery pieces stuck on the white plaster, spreading colour and bringing smiles to the people walking on the pavement. The wall next to the staircase going up was also beaming through its broken, coloured pieces of what were once beautiful pieces of clay shaped by capable and dexterous hands – with centuries of experience – into tiles and vases and bowls and plates; painted in as bright colours as the tulips and azaleas and pansies lined along the avenues and lawns.

A little further at the end of the road I could see the slim and tall minarets of the Blue Mosque and opposite it the massive dome of Hagia Sophia; the Greek Orthodox Christian cathedral, built in 537 AD, later an Ottoman imperial mosque and now a museum.

Centuries of heritage was in the air and scattered around.

We ran towards Hagia Sophia and passed the Basilica Cistern. We had to stop. It pulled us into its cavernous depths. Walking along its raised wooden platforms, I felt water dripping from the vaulted ceiling. Its grandeur was breath-taking.

We stopped at one of its huge columns. It was the weeping column; drops of water sliding down its ancient surface. They say it has been crying for centuries for all the slaves that were killed during the construction of this symmetrical and grand structure in the sixth century during the reign of the Byzantine Empire.

The bases of two last columns are blocks carved with the snake-covered heads of Medusa; one upside down and the other holding the column on its cheek and one side of its head. It is thought that the heads were brought to the cistern from a building of the late Roman period.

I gazed at the face of Medusa carved out of a block of stone. Is it really true that the feeble pay a price for their weakness? And has it been happening across civilisations?

I glanced at Mina and looked away.

In myths Medusa is described as being a beautiful maiden. Her beauty caught the eye of Poseidon, who desired her and proceeded to ravage her in Athena's shrine. When Athena found out she sought vengeance not from Poseidon but Medusa by transforming her hair into snakes, so that anyone who gazed at her directly would be turned into stone. The once beautiful mortal was punished by Athena with a hideous appearance and loathsome snakes for hair for having been raped in Athena's temple by Poseidon.

Poseidon symbolised intense, irrational emotions. Athena was the flag bearer of wisdom, battle, craftsmanship, and justice.

I looked at Mina again. She is gazing at the head of Medusa. Her thin face and hollowed eyes are not frightened anymore, but a tic under one eye gives away her nervous tension; a gift of her pretty and frail mother-in-law's harsh and venomous character.

Mina was neither beautiful nor ugly; neither brainy nor stupid. She was a simple soul happy in her own world. Everyone liked her because she was kind and good and made people laugh with her quirky sense of humour. She married her handsome class fellow, who was madly in love with her and moved into his ancestral house with his widowed mother, Bano Begum. Mina's entry into that sad desolate house brought with it a lot of laughter and happiness. And then stately and acerbic Bano Begum, happy Mina and her handsome husband lived happily; at least that is what Mina believed.

I often visited Mina and we had long leisurely chats in her lounge. Sometimes Bano Begum joined us and did her knitting as she sat in her own specific armchair. Mina couldn't see the veiled hatred in Bano Begum's eyes. Her husband was around at times but she seemed oblivious of his slowly increasing impassive behaviour. She was happy in her Eden.

'I am so happy in my life. I have everything anyone could want', she exclaimed one day.

Bano Begum looked up at her and I was stunned to see the intense loathing in her beautiful dark eyes.

'Do you ever actually see what goes on around you, outside your own world?' She asked sarcastically.

I could see her sarcasm was lost on Mina. She laughed and turned to her as she guided me inside the lounge.

'Of course.'

I saw her glance oddly at Mina sideways and then we continued with our chatter.

Mina was never unhappy! She lived life as it came and adjusted herself accordingly, content with her lot. She didn't see that her laughter and exuberance and happiness jarred on the mordant Bano Begum, who had got used to a certain sad sombreness after her husband passed away and people's attitude had changed towards her. They looked up to her as a quiet and brave widow who had dedicated her life to her only son. She carefully kept her household drab and humourless to feed on people's sympathy and reverence. She had no place for Mina's misplaced sunny disposition.

Life continued with this silent seething energy and happy, sunny disposition. Nobody even acknowledged the gravity of the frustrated handsome man.

Years rolled by and I saw Mina growing quieter and paler and thinner. The laughter was gone through when she smiled her nervous face changed for that instant. She couldn't have children; she kept losing weight although all her medical reports stated that there was nothing wrong with her. Her impassive husband turned into a quarrelsome monster and she couldn't please him howsoever she tried. Bano Begum grew distant and was scathing when at all she spoke to her. Mina dreaded facing her.

She stayed in her room most of the time and stopped even going out of her house. I saw her change into a hysteric and frightened person; doubting everyone's intentions, believing none.

Once when I went to her she mentioned that she keeps finding small feathers in odd places; her neatly ironed clothes inside her wardrobe, between the carefully folded linen in the cupboard, even on the curtains in her room. I consoled her to that odd feathers stuck about are nothing to worry about.

I tried talking to her husband in my concern, but he said he was done with this nervous wreck. He had married her for her carefree happy nature; to bring light into his gloomy house and life. He didn't want anything to do with her. She can live in his house or go; whatever she wants.

And then the day came when Mina found a small doll stuck with pins in its head, underneath her mattress. She sat there stunned for hours forcing herself to get up and get out of that house. She called me and in strange hysterical whispers asked me to take her away from this house.

I did.

We came out of the dark interior into a burst of bright sunshine and colour. It had stopped raining and the sun was out. A little further was a small building with a little garden and we saw huge big pink tulips swaying in the gentle breeze enclosing a lawn.

We crossed the road and walked towards the Blue Mosque. There were long queues and a crowd of people everywhere. A family was walking in front of us and as we watched we saw the husband slap the wife's face in a split second and then continue moving forward. We saw the woman's stunned flushed face, saw her adjust her head scarf self-consciously and then follow her husband.

The pink and yellow tulips provided rows of colour in the bright sunshine. The gentle breeze hummed between rain washed shining green leaves of the trees. The proud dome of Hagia Sophia looked down on the crowd as it had done for centuries. The tall slim minarets of the Blue Mosque stood quietly.

What is civilisation? The dictionary describes it as the process by which a society or place reaches an advanced stage of social and cultural development and organisation.

Across centuries, in myth or reality.

TWO NEIGHBOURHOODS IN TUNIS

Iason Athanasiadis and Dalia De Gondi

Few outsiders get to know Tunis' densely-inhabited, twisting Medina. Those who penetrate to the southern edge of this southern Mediterranean city's cobbled labyrinth — past the UNESCO World Heritage Site scrubbed streets, tourist tat and hipsterish *shisha* cafes — will exit muffled lanes into the sensory overload of a crowded square, still retaining elements of a medieval marketplace, and thickly-carpeted with the organic effluent of several open-air markets. This is Algeria Square. It rests in the valley between two hills: one is a cemetery where the main conditions for entry are death and being Muslim; another a garden suburb developed by French colonisers and inherited by a now-faded or departed Tunisian bourgeoisie. The *jellaz*, Tunis' largest necropolis, is topped by the shrine of Sufi saint Sidi Belhassan Chedli. It was the site in 1911 of the first major Tunisian uprising against the French, following an unpopular bid to pass a tramline through the cemetery. ('Protecting the dead is what finally moved the living', says Tunisian architectural historian Iheb Guermazi. 'It is their past that people refused to see colonised rather than their present. Seizing "space" was temporary and bearable, but erasing the cemetery meant that "time" was being colonised, and that was irremediable'.) Facing the *jellaz* is Montfleury, a verdant garden district full of Art Deco villas and modernist apartment blocks, emerging from bougainvillea and cypresses. A necklace of bazaars, working-class neighbourhoods speckled with saints' tombs and tile-studded internal courtyards, transport hubs, a defunct abattoir and a massive military hospital choke the valley in between the two.

The whole district is a newer extension of the Medina, including later gates like Bab Fella and Bab Alioua (whose names live on despite their demolition). Here we find social housing, the headquarters of one of North Africa's largest football teams, several hammams, a man who practises an African exorcism ritual, Zituna University, rivalling in prestige Cairo's al-Azhar, and an Ottoman fort that went from French military base during colonial times to counter-terrorism headquarters today. It has been home to Arab-Moorish nobles, Jews and Greeks, French colonists, White Russians fleeing the Communist Revolution, an Italian middle class, and windmill-operating Maltese. The founder of modern Tunisia, Habib Bourguiba, lived here. This was the birthplace of Leila Trabelsi, wife of President Zine El Abdidine ben Ali, the autocrat who was brought down by the Arab Spring. These inhabitants conferred a unique distillation that survives to this day in the genes of residents, and in an architectural mélange of traditional Mediterranean courtyard houses with Art Deco and eclectic apartments alike. There's even a neo-Gothic villa beloved by Tunisian horror-filmmakers. But the cinemas, breweries, bars, brothels and theatres that developed in the 1920s and 1930s have almost completely disappeared.

Eight locals, as diverse in their backgrounds as the district itself, recall their histories and talk about their lives. Among them an archivist, members of the district's Sufi and *stambeli* religious communities, descendants of the beylic aristocracy's servants, the post-Independence bourgeois class that occupied Montfleury, and the daughter of an Italian woman-convert to Islam. Their words evoke forgotten memories, still-current superstitions, and the demolished buildings and departed communities that bound the districts together. To live in these neighbourhoods is to shape a portal between yesterday and today.

Mohammed Bennani, 64, an archivist dedicated to the memory of the neighbourhood

I lived in Brussels for many years and moved back to Tunisia twenty-eight years ago. Feeling nostalgic and homesick in Brussels, I developed a passion for collecting old books and photographs about Tunis. When I returned to my family home, I set up an archive containing a lot of rare books and photographs alongside social and architectural information.

Montfleury started being built as of 1910 for the French professional middle class, and for Corsicans specialising in security. From the start it was a mixture of villas and apartment blocks, and it was served by trolley-buses #8 and #9 and a tram. The main street, named today after Tunisia's national poet, Abu Qassem Chabbi, was called Quatrième Zouaves, after the French military body headquartered in the fort at the top of the hill.

The French authorities completed the task of knocking down the Medina's walls, which no longer served a defensive purpose, and built the 9 April highway in their place, acting today as a ring-road.

Between the two world wars the Muslims wouldn't frequent Montfleury much except if they came as itinerant peddlers. There was an unspoken ban on entering it, and an absolute separation between its residents and the Arab Muslims – who were considered to be thieves, bandits and dirty – from adjoining suburbs built around the *sabkha* (lake) such as Mallaseen. If heading to the Medina, locals would circle around Montfleury, which was guarded by discreet security.

After World War Two, everything changed, and Montfleury opened up and became more mixed, with wealthy Tunisians entering the neighbourhood and even buying property. Having benefited from the wartime rationing system, the Jerbians had significant purchasing power after the war.

I live in this house with my wife and it acts as a research centre for anyone interested in the urban history of Tunis.

Mohamed and Turquia, mother and son, who live in a small palace in Bab Jdid, reached by a narrow lane, which they bought from the noble family that used to own it

We've been living in this old palace all our lives. We think it's 800 years old. It used to belong to a family who were generals for the *beys*. We grew up here among French and Italians, hearing these languages spoken alongside *Tunsi* dialect.

Women would only leave their home to go to the *hammam* in horse-drawn carriages. Bab Fella was full of Italians and Maltese, and wealthy Jewish traders lived in the apartment buildings of Bab Jdid.

As of the 1970s they closed up their houses or sold them off, and left. The last Italian woman I remember left in 1990. I had a Jewish woman friend who let her cleaning lady have her apartment when she left. Our neighbour bought his apartment from the monks. I still remember the nuns who maintain a library in Montfleury (they are still alive but getting old).

On hot summer afternoons when I was growing up, twenty years ago, we'd sneak into the mausoleum of the *beys* with a bottle of cold water and a watermelon and slumber off the heat among the tombs. We didn't mind being next to the dead; they can't hurt you.

The *jellaz* is the big national cemetery where our heroes from the battles against the French are buried. In our neighbourhood, the locals were buried close to their homes in the small cemetery of Gorjani. But like many other cemeteries *entre les murs*, it was then moved elsewhere.

I remember when Bourguiba, who lived in our neighbourhood, decided to move the cemetery, he told people to gather there, dig up their relatives' bones, do their traditions for them, gather the bones up and rebury them in the *jellaz*. The only one whose tomb was permitted to remain was Sidi Gorjani (a local saint and disciple of Sidi Belhassan); the neighbourhood insisted on keeping him close to us. Then the resulting empty space was remodelled into the hilltop garden, a municipal swimming pool and a wedding hall that are still there today. A defensive gate that had existed was demolished in the 1890s. Bourguiba continued living in a palace in our neighbourhood with his second wife, Wasila, served by discreet, entirely silent black servants who never spoke to us, however much we'd provoke them.

The neighbourhood is quieter today than it used to be; the Facebook generation has abandoned the old traditions. It's ten years now that we don't do much for the Prophet's birthday, aside from making sweets. There are no longer the brass bands, or the *mezwed* musicians, or those flame-breathing performers, or everyone cooking outside together.

Our palace is listed, but falling apart, and I'm always fixing this or that. All my appeals to the municipality have gone ignored. We've turned away about ten of our neighbours offering us money for the right to dismantle and cart off the hand-painted tiles and marble floor tiles, to take away my childhood memories. I told them 'Get lost while I'm still expressing myself politely'. My dream in life is not to make money to travel and dress well but to fix this palace and rehabilitate it. I'm such good friends with my mother that I never got married; I didn't want to jeopardise our beautiful friendship.

Riadh Ezzawech, 44, an exorcist and the president of the Stambeli Association, lives in Bab Jdid's Sidi Ali Lasmar shrine

I grew up in the Medina and have been at the shrine of Sidi Ali Lasmar for twenty-six years, since a time when I had an eye problem. My parents were Shadhli Sufis. The shrine is in Rue de Persan, colloquially known as Sabbat Ajam (Lane of the Ajemi), that used to host one of the four to five brothels of the Medina catering to different classes and nationalities.

The Nineties were the last good period for this district, before people from the countryside started moving in with their non-urban habits and inappropriate accents, changing everything. The influx pushed out old *Tunisois* families such as the Zmirlī (authors and politicians) and the Chennoufi (tribal dynasty from Kef) who'd lived in Montfleury.

Bourguiba was a secularist. He didn't like Sufis and shrines, and these slave shelters were often on the sites of shrines where runaway slaves had historically sought refuge (and brought with them *stambeli*, a music and dance known as *gnawa* in Morocco and *diwan* in Algeria performed on people believed to be possessed by *jinn* as a way of releasing them). Later it was popularised when white Tunisians would invite blacks to perform *stambeli* at their weddings because they believed they brought luck.

In 1964, a member of Bourguiba's party bought this shrine, knocked down its dome, reduced the size of the grave and ripped out the tiles. Around that time, the shelters that the *beys* established to reintegrate freed slaves into society were closing, including the one up the street in Hajj Ameen.

Ben Ali's wife, Leila Trabelsi, grew up in the Medina and her mother used to bring her here to read the *fatiha*. One night the saint appeared in her sleep, in the form of a black man with a sword, and introduced himself as Ali. After that, we'd be invited to the presidential palace to play Stambeli and our activities were supported. But now, because the building's inheritors want to sell it to build an apartment in its place, we've formed an NGO to try to stop it from happening, and are preparing a file to send to UNESCO so that Stambeli can be protected. But we live in a country whose state often doesn't know what Stembeli is let alone what an important part of Tunisian culture it is.

I distrust those who pray and praise God, and like those who drink and sing: they have compassion in their hearts. They ask me why I don't move to La Marsa or Carthage (chic suburbs to which much of the district's bourgeoisie departed). I reply to them that the only place I'm going to is the *jellaz* – directly from here.

Aboubaker Bouras, 34, an aeroplane engineer and amateur historian, descended from one of Montfleury's older Tunisian families

We're from Djerba. My grandfather was a clothes-merchant in the Medina. A Jewish *simsar* (real-estate agent) we knew got us a deal for the villa we

bought in Montfleury from the departing French in 1954, two years before Independence. In that era, many embassies had their ambassadorial residences in Montfleury, and we were neighboured by the Belgian ambassador. At the time, there were White Russians who had fled from the Bolsheviks living in Montfleury, and their presence is marked by street names such as Moscow and Kronstadt (currently Ali Riahi).

The big exodus from Montfleury happened at the end of the 1990s as there was a rise in criminality in the surrounding working-class suburbs, such as Mellaseén. The tendency was to go to La Marsa (a chic, seaside suburb) or emigrate, with Canada being particularly popular at the time. Usually, Montfleury's wealthy families would send their kids to study abroad, and they would stay behind, alone in these huge villas. Soon they'd either take an apartment somewhere else, or move abroad to join their children. There was a wave of selloffs, resulting in a general drop in the price of properties. Those who bought were considered *arrivistes* by the existing residents. The neighbourhood assumed a more defensive posture as some neighbours closed off their facades and fortified them to dissuade people from looking in, or sitting at their entrance drinking.

I'm not planning on staying in Tunis, let alone Montfleury. The only thing keeping me here is my father's love of history. But memory has become a luxury and I'm ready to forgo this luxury in order to emigrate to somewhere like Canada where I can finally have some anonymity.

I only see a further deterioration in the future of Montfleury and in the quality of municipal services offered. Even so, we feel a great nostalgia for what it has been, and wherever we meet, whether in the US or Switzerland, we pine for when we'll be able to go back, hang out on the *rondpoint*, smoking a cigarette and checking out the girls of Montfleury, whose beauty is renowned.

Mennoubi, 75, the keeper of the Torbet el-Bey Royal Mausoleum in Bab Jdid

I grew up in a working class neighbourhood called Ras el-Darb/Ma'aqel al-Za'im, a neighbourhood at the top of the hill close to Gorjani that was demolished in the 60s. Montfleury was for the *gauris* (foreigners) but we knew it as Nahj Essahel. As kids, we'd have fun by taking rides on three-wheeled carts down the hill. But then the mayor demolished our neighbourhood and moved the adjoining graveyard. Some who had joined Bourguiba's Dostur Party ended up with social housing in Bab Alioua but I moved in with my mother in Ben Arous (a suburb of Tunis).

Later I met my wife, whose grandmother had been a servant for the Hosseinid noble family and knew a lot about them by virtue of having lived among them. She was far-sighted and advised us to move and live here, as the place was likely to become a museum one day. The number of tourists has gone down since the Revolution. The mausoleum has been under restoration for the past few years and remains closed, but when people knock on my door I show them around.

I'm seventy-five years old now, and gave up smoking and drinking twenty years ago. People's mentality changed with the passing of time. We used to all live together, large families in one house with a courtyard, we'd stop in front of older men in the street, or run to help women if we saw them carrying heavy things. There were separate knockers on doors according to gender so that those inside the house knew who should open. My friends have got fewer and fewer, having left the neighbourhood and Tunis to return to their towns and villages, or died. I no longer have time or the appetite to go to the café, as life has got faster and faster in the effort to make money. Your only friend now is the cash you have in your pocket and your friends try to trick you out of it.

Latifa, the guardian of the shrine of Sidi Belhassan, one of the three guardian saints of Tunis. She lives alone on the shrine at the top of the jellaz

I'm from Gafsa, in the South, although my mother's from Aleppo and my father from Kerbala. I first came here nineteen years ago, after having already served Sidi Abdelqader for fourteen years in Libya and Algeria. I received my first (spiritual) key from Abdessalam al-Asmar in Zliten. My Syrian mother had taken the *tariqa* (path) and used to come to Tunis to visit Sidi Belhassan.

When Sidi Belhassan came to Tunis 650 years ago, he found forty thieves living in the *jellaz*. He tamed them, brought them into Islam, taught them, and together they built the mosque and *khalwa* that stand here until today. He's known as the Father of the Poor and the Learned because of his social services, and Seyyida Menoubiah, a female mystic whose shrine is on top of Montfleury, was among his students.

I spent fourteen years serving Sidi Belhassan in the cave a little further down from here, and moved up here five years ago. My relationship with the cave was spiritual, and I needed to have spiritual depth since during that time I was visited many times by *dajjal* and bad people.

Most of Sidi Belhassan's pilgrims are from Bab Jazira. Sidi Belhassan loved the area and dedicated himself to it, keeping a separate *khalwa* and home here, alongside the mosque. He used to gather the drunks and prostitutes, clean them up, and set them on the straight path. Even when some people threw stones at him, he had the spiritual depth to continue his work.

Bab Jdid is so full of the domes and graves of saints because of its proximity to the Zeituna Mosque and *madrassah*, the fourth most important in the world after Mecca, Medina and Jerusalem. And of course it's next to Bab Alioua (the high gate), a huge open-air market where farmers used to bring their produce and barter it. Many of the newcomers to the city would spend their first night in Tunis sleeping in the tombs and *zawaya* of saints, which were open to visitors. They would bring offerings to the saint, and some would get involved with the place and become a *maurid* (follower). It was a wild area with its own unspoken rules and laws and the saints were a part of this.

Today, the followers are the sons and grandsons of the people who moved to the area, and we have pilgrims coming from as far away as Sri Lanka, to which Sidi Belhassan travelled and established a *zawia*.

During the French occupation, this was a shelter which the authorities respected as a place of prayer and didn't enter, allowing it to be used to store weapons. Recently, I'm in constant struggle with the people around the *sheikh* who are involved in immoral transactions and dirty the place, physically and spiritually, to the point where I'm soon going to abandon it and leave.

Yassine Ben Cheikh is a psychiatrist who grew up in Montfleury

Two years after Independence, my grandfather came up from Mahdiya in 1958 to purchase a house in the capital. Because he wore traditional dress, the French owner, an engineer, didn't even let him in, let alone consider selling him the house.

Undeterred, my grandfather knocked on the neighbours' doors and asked them to take a look at the house from their balcony. Satisfied by what he saw, he returned to the house for sale – where they still refused to let him in – and signalled them through the railings that he was offering four million. That's how the deal went through.

The French were replaced by the Djerbians who moved into Montfleury in force. A new bourgeoisie developed, consisting of the remnants of the old beylical nobility, the high-ranking civil servants of the new state, a couple of Scandinavian ambassadors whose residences were here, and the professional classes. But as traffic increased, slums spread and students increasingly trespassed on properties, the residents began selling and moving out.

I lived in this ninety-year-old villa for a couple of years and then my father sent me to boarding school for seven years. I studied Medicine and then moved to France. I moved back thirty years ago and have been living here since then. My psychiatric practice is next to the Railway Station. Living here is ideal as you're high up with a privileged view of the city, but walking distance to everywhere. I only ever use my car to travel outside the city.

Because the house is large and heating it is expensive, we've stopped inhabiting the ground floor and moved upstairs to the first floor. Once you've got used to living in a house like this, high-ceilinged, with a beautiful garden, and an incredible view of the neighbourhood from atop the hill, it's hard to move anywhere else, much less into a modern home. At nights I pull up a seat on the roof and sit looking out at the view. I will only leave this house when I die.

Munira Fakheri, 75 is the daughter of an Italian who converted to Islam to marry her Tunisian husband. Munira lives in Bab Fella, site of an open-air market, where she runs a shop selling dates

I was born here in Bab Fella to an Italian mother at a time when there were Italians and even French living there and Montfleury, the area above us, was all French. There were only a few Arab houses. After the last foreigners left around 1970, the Arabs took over.

I bought my building from a coiffeur called Monsieur Seintre. My mother, Luisa, was Italian and Muslim, as her father had converted to Islam. She died recently, and we buried her in the Jellaz. I finished primary school, married and had five children, of which two died. I had my first daughter when I was fourteen. My husband and I worked as greengrocers. He died and now my eldest son runs this place and I've written everything to him in my will. Produce used to be delivered by horse-drawn carts, and there was a mortuary next to the mosque where bodies were washed and prayed over till the mid-80s.

My husband used to spoil me, buy me everything, cover me in gold. But I'd never wear lipstick and when I'd go out with my man somewhere, they'd think I was a German woman, because of my face and green eyes.

When Umm Kalthum came to Tunis, my husband's boss gave us tickets and told us to go attend. And in the *jardin* of Bab Fella, I remember Abdelhalim singing and people coming to watch dressed up. Warda came to Tunis, Oleya, Naama, Safiya (all singers of the 60s and 70s) all came to sing, and my husband would take me to attend the concerts. Then the *jardin* closed and now people sit around braziers getting drunk and smoking weed. It was another world, a splendid one. Now it's only strangers from the countryside, those who don't belong.

Relationships between people changed a lot. Now they're friends with you only for money or if they need you. They don't have a pure heart, they don't sit to share their bread. Real friends still come to kiss my hands and legs.

Times changed, presidents came and went, rulings were issued and changed. It's a different world now.

REVIEWS

DINNER AT POMPEII

Iftikhar H. Malik

Terracotta votive food: pomegranates (open and closed); grapes; figs; almonds; cheeses; focaccia; honeycomb; mould; long bread. 360 BC. Tomb 11, Contrada Vecchia, Agropoli, Parco Archeologico Di Paestum

On a fateful day in October 78 CE, Mount Vesuvius woke up from its 500-year long dormant sleep and began to spew thousands of tons of molten ash into the air above the Bay of Naples sealing down the fate of Pompeii, Herculaneum, Oplantis and villages around the Sarna River. The blast was so fierce that the ashes reached as high as 30,000 feet – the usual height of flying planes today – and the rocks and debris rained down as piercing rockets raising the temperature to 350 centigrade, engulfing habitation, valleys and even the Bay with ten to thirty metres of smouldering ash. Though there had been earthquakes and other signs preceding this dramatic eruption, the cataclysmic catastrophe caught everyone by surprise and in the process, humans, cattle, crops and vegetation all perished, mostly turning into sheer dark rubble. Trying to escape searing heat and suffocating ash and smoke, many desperate residents sought shelter within the inner chambers of their houses but to no avail as death suffused the city as a triumphant scourge.

Comparatively an affluent Roman region, Pompeii and its environ prided itself on prosperity, which often came through a rich and diverse cuisine with wine being a vital part. Largely a community of traders, wine growers, cattle breeders and soldiers, these residents had acculturated several Etruscan, Greek and Egyptian mores and religious practices. They mainly worshipped Bacchus, Venus and Hercules, to whom offerings were made through food and wine, and their human-like characteristics, as later discovered on murals and frescos, allowed a greater sense of conviviality. Bacchus, the god of wine, is shown in some of those excavated murals covered in grape bunches. Elaborate winemaking utensils, vases, pans, ladles, jugs and cups made of terracotta, bronze and silver once adorned shops and wineries all across the region. A mural shows people having a relaxed family meal when one of them starts to sing while being served wine and food by the slaves. Corn came in from Egypt, as did a few beliefs including the concept of life after death where the funerary customs and arrangements had to ensure enough provisions for the next phase. After cremation, ashes were buried in specially designed terracotta urns—not of minor sizes but more like raised tombs with the statue of the deceased anchored on the top. One mural shows a woman's journey in a covered kind of canopy in a standing posture—almost alive—led by priests and followed by maidens carrying food. Offering of food to Bacchus were a particular feature when warriors would return from battlefields.

Ashmolean Museum, Last Supper at Pompeii. 25 July 2019–12 January 2020. Oxford, UK
Paul Roberts, *Last Supper at Pompeii*, Ashmolean Museum Publications, Oxford, 2019

Wealthy inhabitants of Pompeii and the region, owned elaborately built houses with atriums boasting opulence as well as statues of the wine god. Inner gardens and fields all the way from the slopes of Mount Vesuvius to Sarno River provided an ample supply of staple food. The bay and the river were a reliable source of a variety of fish thus making Pompeii self-sufficient and even able to export surplus food items to other areas. Pompeii was located in a bountiful region in Italy, more like Tuscany— where diverse professions, multiple products and cross-cultural interactions underwrote leisure and pleasure with food and drinks heralding comparatively luxurious lifestyles, away from the drudgeries of a routine life further south. Commercially, an ideal location ensured a reasonable supply of wealth whereas cultural and ethnic linkages with the Mediterranean regions all the way from the Levant to France inducted an interesting blend of commodities and customs. Despite their propensity for more emancipatory habits, wealthy Pompeiians were not totally narcissist or hedonistic people, displaying a spiritual side, which manifested in their belief in deities. They made offerings of wine and food at temples and distributed food amongst less privileged residents. For instance, the bakery at the House of the Chaste Lovers reveals elaborate arrangements for raising flour, usage of efficient metallic utensils for baking bread and cakes besides extensive grain storage facilities making their set-up more than just a small outlet. Skeletons of donkeys and mules found in the bakery witness the significant volume of baking and trading activities at the premises.

The food and wine culture of Pompeii was well displaced at Oxford's Ashmolean Museum exhibition, The Last Supper in Pompaii. The exhibition benefited from the archaeological research carried out at Pompeii and Oplantis over the past many decades. The collection of statues, burial chambers, murals, frescos, utensils, tools, remains of the food particles and other historical evidence almost brought

Pompeii back to life. Collected from the sites, often scores of metres below the present surface, these artefacts successfully reconstructed the preparation and consumption of food in this part of Southern Italy where rich dwellers, often in reclining postures, would be served multi-course meals by their slaves. Interestingly, men and women appear together in murals, often in jovial moods. However, only men were allowed to recline while consuming food, although one cannot miss the amorous vibes among the couples. Archaeologists, following extensive excavations over the years, have numbered and named houses in Pompeii either in reference to the respective professions of the owner, or because of some unique artefact found in the debris. Chemical analysis of items found in shops has also helped scholars identify the nature of merchandise and the places of their origin.

While the communal meals were served in larger rooms overlooked by the statues and frescoes of gods and goddesses and neighboured by indoor gardens, the food itself was prepared inside the kitchens which, curiously, neighboured latrines. The residue of food found in some of the remaining pots, pans, dishes and the latrine pipes affirm a wide variety of items such as Indian black peppers, Egyptian barley and Tunisian grain. Bronze ladles, amphora and jugs, excavated from the sites and analysed in the laboratories, have revealed traces of olive, lime and special seasoning for fish called *garum*. Like recent natural disasters, including large-scale earthquakes, tsunamis, floods and enduring droughts, the destruction of Pompeii has refused to be a forgotten page of history, largely owing to archaeological research into its past and an undiminished interest in Roman history. Unlike Mount Etna and more like Krakatoa in Indonesia, Vesuvius caused total destruction, which, despite subsequent vandalism and human malfeasance, allowed Pompeii an enduring life that has been further reassured by a series of exhibitions in the last few decades. The very thick covering by the debris that was solidified over the subsequent era, ensured the preservation of some of these finds several metres deep down from the current surface. The vandals could not often reach those deeply buried chambers largely because of the thickness of the layers and also because the blocked gases would certainly hasten deaths for such diggers. Thus, more recent excavations have been undertaken in a more scientific way with greater care for safety and preservation.

The Romans, explains Paul Roberts, the curator of the exhibition and the editor of the excellent catalogue that accompanies the exhibition, were quite meticulous when it came to trade and feasting. In Pompeii alone there were 600 shops of all kinds including pub-like bars where food and wine were sold to patrons who, other than the locals, would include people from the other regions of the empire. Most shops and thirty-one bakeries were located on both sides of the main thoroughfare, Via delle Terme, with its surface deeply scarred with wheel ruts along with the featuring stepping-stones. The most frequently used word for 'shop', Roberts states in the catalogue, 'is *taberna* (plural *tabernae*), perhaps derived from the Latin word for timber (*trabs*) or board (counter?) (*tabula*), reflecting a shop's simple, wooden origins. The shop was also a home, however, in particular for the poor, and *tabernae* often had stairs leading to living quarters on the upper floor, sometimes with toilet facilities and/or cooking areas. In fact, *tabernae* may have accounted for around one-third of the housing stock in Pompeii.'

Frescoes retrieved and restored from the ruins reveal several religious and cultural practices of these early Italians who loved gardens, nurtured vineyards on the slopes under a temperate sun, sold all kinds of goods in their well-provided shops and then retired for expansive meals where offerings were made to Bacchus. While a human-size marble statue of Bacchus welcomed visitors to the exhibition, other murals displayed scenes such as a warrior returning from a battle followed by slaves, whose wife welcomes him by offering wine at the altar. In another mosaic, an apparently rich local is shown disbursing bread to several needy people whereas another mural depicts a couple that ran one of the several bakeries in the town. Like many other societies, Pompeiians ensured a good supply of food and fluids for a person's journey to the hereafter and thus burial chambers would include utensils, eggs and amphora containing olive and wine. In the same tradition, the exteriors of the graves were often sculpted with the deceased's figure—irrespective of gender—holding a wine goblet in his or her hand, almost mocking death itself.

While the exhibition displayed objects and artefacts from shops, temples, houses, orchards and surroundings, the catalogue attempts to reconstruct the life of this multi-layered society by focusing on family and communal life. The Pompiieans emerge as industrious, jovial but no less spiritual people, with their own sense of humour and self-importance. They did not leave much graffiti on their walls except for one on a bar where some patron claimed to have been able to bed the barmaid. The rich had elaborate dwellings where fountains, inner gardens, colonnades, bigger rooms with murals, expensive silver, art collections and elaborate furniture conveyed an impressive sense of prosperity and taste. 'The concept of dining—eating, drinking and everything that went with this—was central to Roman life and a common theme in the Roman art', notes Roberts, 'the banquet, as in so many areas of Roman society, was also about status and influence; the host had more than nutrition or hospitality in mind when he planned his dinner party. Dining brought the family and their guests together, affirming ties of kinship and dependence and the dominant role of the head of the household'. Farmers lived out on the farms with traders using space behind and above the shops as their residence while their shops would feature awnings to save the goods and the owners from the shimmering sun. Just near the mouth of River Sarno, archaeologists discovered the main seminary, which was partially reconstructed though even in Pompeii and Oplantis there are vast areas, which still remain covered by thick layers of soil since the eruption.

The archaeological search has been going on at Pompeii and other sites since 1748 despite the early thefts. Over the past few decades scientific tools have helped reconstruct life as it was before the decimation. Scholars of Roman history and arts find that Vesuviusian sites have preserved more frescoes than the rest of the Roman empire altogether. In the 1970s, archaeologists were able to dig deep inside the rubble to discover some remains of human skeletons, which were reconstructed by using plaster of Paris. One of the known residents is Lady Resin, whose human-size skeleton was on display at the exhibition, though as Roberts says, there was quite a bit of hesitation on including this human figure but eventually consensus was reached. Lady Resin was a younger woman from Villa B at Oplantis, who still had her ornaments on her fingers and arms while spread-eagled on her stomach on the floor with a jug in her hand. She lay in the same posture in one of the showcases at the exhibit while her jewellery was on display in separate boxes.

Guests at the banquets of the rich Pompeiians were attended by slaves who took their shoes, washed their feet, and served them wine distilled locally. Showing the mindfulness of such hosts for arts, a statue of Apollo was used as a tray bearer during the banquet at the house of Julius Polybius, whose palatial dwellings have yielded an impressive collection of Greek and Roman arts, some of which was on display at the exhibition. Other than silverware, glass vessels were also widely familiar in Pompeii on the eve of eruption though the latter had been invented by the

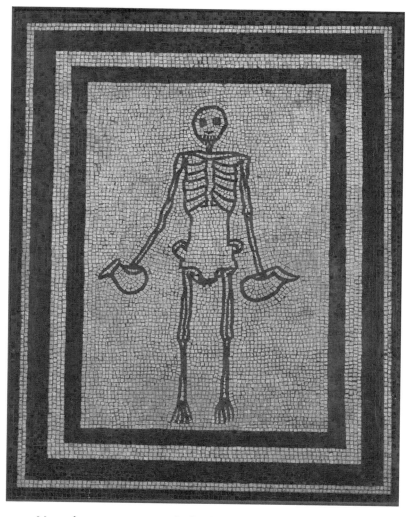

Monochrome mosaic panel of a skeleton holding two wine jugs
AD 1–50 Pompeii, House of the Vestals 91 x 70 cm
Museo Archeologico Nazionale di Napoli

Egyptians and not by the Italians. Possibly, the Roman term for kitchen was *culina,* mostly storing food and water besides a latrine, all operated by slaves. Cooks were often also slaves keeping a lower social status on the same level as the butchers and dancers. However, 'there was no concept in the Roman world of a bathroom with toilet and washing facilities combined. Instead, toilet facilities were often accommodated in the kitchen. Simple "squatter" toilets were built directly over a downpipe. Water for flushing, essential to keep the (relatively narrow) downpipes flowing freely, was kept in storage vessels', says Roberts. Following their conquest of Britain in 43 CE, Romans led the introduction of several new food ingredients, plants and crockery in the country. For the first time, cherries, cultivated apples, plums, olives and lemons were inducted into the British cuisine. Unlike Pompeii, they did not have any public places to eat and only the coastal Britons would consume fish: 'The Romanisation of the diet in rural areas of Britain occurred much more slowly than in the newly founded towns. Staple foods were little changed. Domestic fowl and oyster seem to have been some of the first new foods adopted in the countryside, but spices soon followed. The entire population of Roman Britain appears to have developed a taster for food flavoured with seeds of coriander, dill and celery', notes Roberts. An entire room at the exhibition was devoted to the British culinary traits and ingredients which revealed many permeating Italian influences including cuisine, arts, tomb stones and cutlery underpinning a whole plethora of cultural transfusions.

The people of Pompeii sought the gratification of drinking and dining right up the very last moment of their lives! The exhibition displayed an impressive mosaic: a skeleton representing Death, holding two *askoi* (wine jugs) in its hands. The underlying message is to highlight the pleasure of life before the finale. The accompanying text announces something like 'this is the moment', your last chance, make the best of it. Looking at the mosaic, I was reminded of a saying of my favourite Mughal writer-king, Babur: 'Oh Babur, enjoy this very moment as life is only too transitory!'

DESPERATE GAZA

Daniel Marwecki

On the day the US embassy opened in Jerusalem, in May 2019, 58 Gazan protestors died from Israeli fire. This, Donald Macintyre writes in a special dispatch for *The Independent*, was easily the bloodiest day since the Gaza war of 2014. The seasoned journalist describes both scenes, which also played out simultaneously on split-screen televisions around the world. On one hand you had the glitz and pomp of state power. On the other, Gaza's destitution after eleven years of smothering blockade. Stuck in a desolate status quo of unemployment, outside dependency, isolation and the threat of ever-recurring war, Gazans reminded the outside world of their existence, many protesting along the border fence with Israel, some trying to storm it.

Donald Macintyre, *Gaza-Preparing for Dawn*, Oneworld Publications, London, 2017

The controversial US embassy move, a strong sign of support for Israel's claim to an 'undivided' Jerusalem, was yet another reminder that despite rhetorical commitment to a negotiated two-state solution, Western policy towards Israel and Palestine is not primarily concerned with alleviating the problem of Palestinian statelessness, or with ensuring a modicum of human rights for Palestinians in the West Bank and especially Gaza. In the case of the embassy move, the Trump administration first of all catered to an important lobby and section of its voting base: the evangelical Christian movement.

The speakers opening and closing the embassy celebrations were Robert Jeffrees and John Hagee, both of them Texan megachurch pastors and Trump advisors. To them and their influential following, the State of Israel is the result of biblical prophecy and Jerusalem the site of Jesus' return. Upon this return, Christians will be 'saved' and adherents of other religions, including, of course, Judaism, won't. From this perspective of divine planning, 'Israel's occupation and oppression of Palestinians — including those who are Christian — is either ignored or perceived as required to achieve the end result.' The knowledge American evangelicals have of the Israel-Palestine conflict is not derived from much study of it. If your mind is bent on biblical apocalypse, your eyes remain closed to the apocalyptic imagery created a mere fifty miles away from the embassy opening in Jerusalem.

It is indeed one of the many striking things about the Israel-Palestine conflict that outside perceptions of it are so often based on factors that have little to do with the 'actual' history of the conflict. These factors can be antisemitism, anti-Muslim racism, orientalism or Christian Zionism, a mixture of all these and others. In short, there exists an array of lenses and projections that can be used to talk about the conflict, to frame it, to exert influence over its course. As for Gaza, however, it has, after now more than twelve years of blockade, been excluded not only from any 'peace negotiations', but also from any real political efforts on the part of Europe and the US. As Donald Macintyre remarks in a talk with Peter Beinart, it is only violence and war which catapults Gaza into the news cycle. The crippling everyday effects of the siege are not part of the Western debate. For the time being, Gaza is 'managed', kept on a lifeline, with no real discernible future.

In the conclusion to his new book, *Gaza – Preparing for Dawn*, Macintyre writes that Western powers treat the Gaza strip like a Mediterranean North Korea. A pariah state, ruled by an illegitimate regime, kept in isolation from the outside world, with only basic humanitarian aid coming through, which is strictly necessary for survival. In the 300 pages proceeding, this disturbingly illuminating comparison, Macintyre does what few European journalists before him have achieved: to provide a thorough, knowledgeable account of Gaza's recent political history which puts its people on the centre stage. He does this while lucidly describing those political and economic conditions which stifle, hurt or end their lives. Macintyre's careful yet authoritative account is a description of tragedy in the political sense of the word. Neither fate nor gods determine the course of Gaza, but political decision-makers and the combined destructive effects of their decisions.

In his column for the *Mail on Sunday*, conservative commentator Peter Hitchens, who doesn't share many political views with his colleague, called Macintyre's book 'rather noble'. The slightly quaint attribute is actually fitting, because the immense work Macintyre has put into his book, also after his years as Jerusalem correspondent for *The Independent*, may, sadly, not necessarily increase book sales. If anything, such nuanced and well-researched books about Israel and Palestine tend to sell less than the easily written commentaries seeking to validate this or that particular political stance, books which tell you what you think you already know anyway.

Macintyre's book is thorough, not tendentious and based on solidly researched facts and a myriad of personal stories from Gaza. In short, the author's motivation seems to derive from a maybe old-fashioned journalistic ethos and his genuine care, to put it too dramatically, for writing Gazans back into Western consciousness. He tells the stories which usually get buried under the loud sermons of messianic preacher men, solemnly reiterated commitments to a two-state solution, outcries over the BDS (Boycott, Divestment and Sanctions) movement and the like. Why, a critical reader may now ask, would Gazans need a European journalist to tell their stories? They don't, of course. But we, and here I mean a majority-society-European 'we', may do so. Macintyre's work helps bringing Gazans back into a discourse which is interested in them only when they build rockets or get killed in war.

The book describes in much detail the defining events of Gaza's recent past through the eyes of the journalist's interlocutors. The account ranges from Israeli disengagement in 2005, the Hamas election victory in 2006 and the strip's subsequent isolation, up until the wars of 2008, 2012 and 2014. Besides the 'general public' the book would also serve well to prepare journalists, UN-workers, tourists or diplomats going to visit and work in Israel and Palestine. Maybe somebody should send a copy to the new American embassy as well.

One effect of Macintyre's thoroughness is his fairness in apportioning blame for Gaza's condition. While he leaves us in no doubt that the blockade of goods and people is the main obstacle to development in Gaza, both economic and political, he doesn't cease to point out the contributions of Hamas, the Palestinian Authority in the West Bank, Arab and Western governments. Relatedly, another particular quality about the book is how well it interweaves all of the political levels which determine life in Gaza, from the local and family level to that of Palestinian politics up towards the high grounds of international relations. While Macintyre's prose is detached and observing, the subject of his book nevertheless makes for rather fast-paced reading. The quality of his writing and multi-level analysis come together especially well in his chapter about the kidnapping of BBC-journalist Alan Johnston by the hands of a rival Islamist-cum-criminal faction to Hamas. Making good use of Johnston's personal account, which manages to be equally ironic and harrowing, Macintyre integrates the story of Johnston's kidnapping into the broader dimensions of the intra-Palestinian war between Hamas and al-Fatah factions following the 2006 elections.

If true that tragedy and time are the key components of irony, Gazans should be able to tell good jokes. Macintyre relates his first ever visit to Gaza in 2003. He stands in front of the smouldering remains of an vehicle engine repair shop in Gaza city. The repair shop had been destroyed the previous night by an Israeli incursion into the strip, in response to Palestinian rocket fire during the Second Intifada. Mahmoud al-Bahtiti, the shop owner, grins sardonically: 'So Abu Ammar said Gaza was going to be the new Singapore.' Abu Ammar, *nom de guerre* of Yassir Arafat, had promised, nine years earlier as the Oslo-Process stirred hopes for a two-state solution, that Gaza would see an economic and political renaissance over the course of the peace process. Why has Gaza never turned into a second Singapore, but instead to a place which, according to the UN, will be 'unliveable' by next year?

A lot of space in Macintyre's book is devoted to stories of Gazans who are creative, inventive and willing to realize their ambitions, but are prevented from doing so. Presently, at least 70 per cent of Gaza's population depend on international aid, mostly foodstuffs, for their subsistence. With little production left, Gaza has one of the highest unemployment rates in the world. Throughout the book, Macintyre echoes what the American political economist and scholar Sara Roy has termed de-development: the creation of political conditions not only preventing but reversing economic development. Foremost of these conditions is the blockade, upheld by Israel and Egypt, supported by the US and the EU. There is little doubt that Macintyre would agree to Sara Roy's assertion that:

> Gazans are entrepreneurial and resourceful – and desperate to work and provide for their children once again. Instead they are forced into demeaning dependency on humanitarian aid, which is given by the very same countries that contribute to their incapacity. The policy is not only morally obscene: it is also outrageously stupid.

Why stupid? What Macintyre suggests is that easing the blockade and allowing for economic development and thus some form of normality would in turn improve chances for a political settlement. However, creating the conditions for economic development is a political decision. In short, key to Palestinian economic development would be an end to the blockade and the occupation. As may have been expected, the recent, grandiose economic plan for Palestinians developed under the aegis of Trump's son-in-law Jared Kushner, includes nothing of the sort. This is a plan according to which political impediments to Palestinian development do not exist. The document does not even mention the word occupation — when it does, it does so as in 'occupational training'. However, throwing money at a problem will not make it go away. The vocabulary of depoliticised neoliberal development, with which the plan is rife, doesn't even begin to explain, let alone remedy, the conditions of economic unfreedom under which Gaza subsists.

'It is too easy to blame Israel alone', writes Macintyre in his conclusion. 'If Gaza is an open prison, Israel is not the only gaoler.' He rightly lists Egypt and Jordan, with the first closing the Gaza border to its own territory and destroying its smuggling tunnels, the second imposing strict transit restrictions on Gazans. Furthermore, Gazans 'have also been betrayed by the chronic failure of Fatah and Hamas to resolve their differences, subordinating the interests of Gaza's public to their own in a conflict made especially disheartening because the power they are struggling for is so heavily circumscribed by Israel. And, perhaps least discussed of all, they have been abandoned by the international community and Western governments in particular.'

Why have Western government abandoned Gaza? Or rather, as Macintyre specifies the question, why have the US and EU countries not done more to exert pressure on Israel with view towards a two-state solution based on the 1967 borders? 'Here it is impossible', writes Macintyre, 'to escape the legacy of the Holocaust'. Israel is seen not simply as a powerful state occupying a weak Palestinian population, but through the historical lens of the Nazi genocide of Europe's Jews. Macintyre shares the view that Europe has an 'historic responsibility to understand Jewish fears of such a spectre ever being raised again' and that 'too few in the Arab world yet share that understanding.' He also thinks that there exists a causal chain of historical responsibility. Given that Israel's birth has been accelerated in the darkest possible way by the genocide in Europe and given that the creation of Israel also created the Palestinian refugee problem, it is in Europe's and especially of course Germany's responsibility to find a solution to this problem. Talking to a British and not German audience, Macintyre also draws attention to a specifically British post-imperial responsibility, as it was the Balfour Declaration which promised European Jews a state on a territory already inhabited by Palestinian Arabs. Here, of course, we enter the unstable and contested territory of political recommendations as derived from historical interpretation. For Macintyre, it is a cliché that the two parties, Israeli and Palestinian, have to come to an agreement of their own volition. He finds the opposite to be true, namely that an agreement would have to be enforced from the outside. Key to this would be a policy of separation between Israel in its 1948 territory and the territories it started to occupy after the Arab-Israeli War of 1967.

It seems that these are the two most widely established positions one can hear in European or broader Western political commentary at the moment: belated and enforced liberal compromise roughly along the 1967 border lines versus growing 'Iron Wall' Zionism of the Jabotinsky sort. On the one side, there are those who argue that a two-state solution based on the 1967 borders still constitutes the best possible option. On the other, there are those who maintain that the conflict of two nations struggling over the same territory will always be a zero-sum game, with any concession simply meaning lost territory.

The dominant political forces in Israel, as well as the rising 'far right' across the West, stick to the second position, if not always for the same reasons. This is a bizarre moment: While for Jews in the US, life has become more dangerous due to Trump's emboldening of white nationalism, as terribly evidenced by last year's massacre at the Pittsburgh Tree-of-Life synagogue, foreign policy ties with Israel have become tighter. The biromantic, cynical love affair between Netanyahu and Trump is quite contrary to the personal hostility that characterized the relationship under the Obama presidency. But the Christian Zionism of a Texan megachurch pastor is not based on an honest respect for Judaism and the Islamophobic glue which, for the moment, binds the Western far right to a right-wing Israel is not a stable basis for mutual relations.

In closing, the subtitle to Macintyre's book, *Preparing for Dawn*, should not be interpreted as an expression of hope against the odds, which at the moment point towards an impossible future for Gaza. What the title conveys is that Gazans are ready to build their lives — provided they are given half a chance to do so.

KILLING A MYTH

C Scott Jordan

A truly heart-breaking display of the tragedy of the commons plays out on the centralised table displays of your local book shops and across the entirety of airport bookstores. At first glance they seem a placing of the finger upon the pulse of 'what everyone else is reading.' Those a bit more savoy in the ways of bookselling know this is actually a combined effort of publishers telling you what you should read and the rubbish everyone buys, hidden beneath a cleaver cover. For those who frequent these fading vestiges of physical literary marketing, trends can be noted. The essential division is between your fiction books, a series of historical fiction pieces and the rubbish that has demented the meaning of 'popular' fiction, and nonfiction. Within the nonfiction, once brushed past the dietary and supposedly 'self-help' books, one actually gets a small pulse reading. That reading of the subject of the month that popular academic writers are latched onto at any given moment. The latest of this small sub-culture of popular fiction has deemed race the hot topic of our current epoch. Whether or not these books are worth reading, they give us a good idea of what the pseudo intellectuals will be squawking about between sips of champagne and can give us a dangerous forecast of the real tragedy of the commons. That tragedy being how ignorant the masses can truly be. And on the topic of race, a more nauseating example would be hard to come by.

Angela Saini, *Superior: The Return of Race Science*, Fourth Estate, London, 2019.
Jennifer Eberhardt, *Bias: The New Science of Race and Inequality*, William Heinemann, London, 2019.

It is hard to say whether it is more disheartening that a book can be so well written yet tell nothing new, or when such books are hailed as brilliant insights by the words printed on their covers. Both the dietary books and the self-help books that would be so familiar from walking by various windows use the excuse of genetics to explain everything from cosmetic imperfections to unhealthy behavioural tendencies. Every problem seemed to have a gene tied to it. It wasn't that alcoholism was anyone's fault, be that God or man, it was just genetic. The same went for other addictions, even to chocolate! What one could do in life from sports to having a great intellect all depended on what was passed from parent to child. Yet this was too simple and as exceptions piled up, popular science needed to make a quantum leap to catch up to the science that those in the field had known since the days of Darwin and before. Yes, what passed from parent to child via chromosomal multiplying, only provided an image of the potentials before an unborn child. Combinations of genes into complex phenotypic displays and the chance of random shifts and mutations provided for a much wider picture than the casual reader could have once imagined. Yet, even as popular science explored the much more complex world of genetics, a narrative survived that set out to explain why humans can be so different. It too was a discussion that dated back to Darwin, yet through a combined effort of certain scientist wishing not to be the bad guys of history and a greater, yet more private curiosity to many, asked why people from one part of the world look different from those of the other. Unadulterated genetics answered this question over a hundred years ago yet the concept of race remained an idea too great to simply dismiss or even scientifically disprove.

Angela Saini and Jennifer L. Eberhardt are two writers that rise to the top in bringing to light both the state of our ignorance and exposing the hopelessness that is faced by those hoping that the public sees the truth. Saini's *Superior: The Return of Race Science* betrays its subtitle in a cleaver twist as it is not so much the story of how Race Science returned into modern parlance, but rather how it has survived and thrived by hiding itself within both lies and the need to fill gaps left misunderstood by the uneducated. The proverbial fear of the unknown had its justification in the idea of race, a concept scientifically proven to be a false dichotomy. Sadly, the concept of race has permeated culture and language so deeply, that to dismiss it is nearly unthinkable. It fortifies and informs other major notions from identity to nationalism and social structures. Eberhardt's *Bias: The New Science of Race and Inequality* takes a less historical approach, building on her work with communities and turning the mirror on our own stereotypes and false assumptions as relate to race and society. Where Saini gives a more journalistic history of genetics which goes the way of a Shakespearian tragedy, Eberhardt's tale is a more personal account of her own fears of the world her son was growing up in, where even a black child in contemporary America grows up fearing the stereotypical caricature of other black people. She also shines light on the dark scientific history of race and especially notes how it has survived in American society. The authors are especially well read together in painting a picture of a deeply problematic social dimension of the Western collective conscious. A collective conscious that threatens to inoculate other non-Western desires to fuel hatred of the other. Hate is nothing new, but a true evil lies in the marriage of hate and scientific justification. One would think the lesson was learned after the horrors of World War II, yet since both sides were engaged in the dark art of race studies, its ruffling of feathers reverberates into the present world. It also helps that they come from opposing sides of the pond in the Western context, Saini being of the UK and Eberhardt of the US, both states facing a bit of an identity crisis as Far/Alt Right politicians garner more and more power fuelling the fascist and xenophobic tendencies of the powers who seek to win most in a world ran by such concepts as race.

The unique approach taken by each author provides a deeper insight to the larger problem. Saini begins by taking us on a tour of the British Museum. On her first trip she was drawn to the exhibits covering India, her ancestral homeland stating that everyone is drawn to discover where they came from. In her own quest she came to find the British Museum was a catalogue of civilisations vying to be the superior over the ones before it. The British Museum gives a wonderful narrative of how one civilisation conquered another to then show themselves the master race over the other. This would serve as the roots of modern eugenics, the science of discovering how to make humans of a more superior quality. When Hitler's regime and the Nazis showed a truly ugly outcome of the eugenics project, those who had dedicated their life to the science (especially in the victorious West) needed a way to survive and continue their vile world views on into the foreseeable future. Being a Heinz 57 mutt, a child of little discernible ethnic heritage (and not for lack of trying) and older beyond my schoolboy days, my first visit to the Museum had me exploring the African exhibit, the one geography that is most distant from any ethnicity my family tree has uncovered. This was largely out of convenience to avoid the crowds, yet since I lacked a heritage, it was nice to try on another. Yet, I am aware of the dangerous void and the ease for which something wicked can fill it in terms of identity. Saini's story illuminates this danger of idolising heritage as most of what we carry forward is what differentiates it, feeding the false narrative that one's heritage may be better than another's. These are not the ways we speak of such matters, but to look at it through this more macabre lens helps us to understand how terrible we humans have become in terms of xenophobia.

Bias begins with a much more poignant anecdote from Eberhardt. She tells of her speaking to groups of police officers about the stereotypes they hold dear to themselves and may carry into their working life. The most soul crushing encounter was not of a white cop discovering a deep seeded hatred for black neighbours, but rather, Eberhardt's own son, a black boy, fearing another black man, assuming him violent and a man dedicated to crime. Racism makes a horrid full circling when it comes around to justify hate for ourselves or what we may become. The self-becoming of the other can have disastrous fallout indeed. When stereotype is taken for granted, ugly narratives are allowed to fester. Eberhardt challenges all to check themselves in relation to this. Joking and linguistic norms often have some dark origins that need to be reflected on and actively pressured against.

Both authors go to great detail to expose an ugly truth and spare no energy in disproving lies and false beliefs linked to genetics and stereotypes. Sadly, both author's conclusions leave a bittersweet taste in the mouth. Overall, their message is one of hope, but it is such a faith-based hope that it wouldn't be hard for one to see the complete opposite of hope in the future before us. Dismay seems appropriate as both authors insist that their work is not ground breaking. No new wisdom can be taken from the pages of *Superior* or *Bias* but maybe this is the true spirit of 'popular' books, be they of science or any subject. For while hope can seem hard to find as the world seems only to fill headlines with horrible treatment between humans of different skin colours and civilisational histories, the fact is that these differences are, quite literally, only skin deep. The attempt to use science to justify and perpetuate lies is a great sin of another kind beyond what Human Rights groups know how to even advocate for. But the story doesn't end with these books. For those who peruse the central tables of bookshops and the occasional airport bookstore may see, more and more books on the myth of racism are being written. Perhaps page by page, bad myths can be killed or at least corrected. The public may one day, quite soon, change its mind on such notions, despite their grab on contemporary society. And maybe the commons need not be a tragedy.

ONLINE MUSLIMS

Josef Linnhoff

If God were to send a Prophet today, would he be active on social media? The question is not as glib as it sounds. Mobile technology has irreversibly changed how we experience the world. Facebook and Twitter dominate our lives to an extent that it is hard for many to live without them. In an age of hajj selfies and 'Sheikh Google', it is clear Muslims are no exception. The Qur'an notes that every prophet spoke the tongue of his people and its poetic beauty is seen as an appeal to its own seventh century, jahili Arab audience. Would revelation in the twenty-first century, then, be expressed through a modern medium like YouTube or Instagram?

I ask this after reading *Follow me Akhi*, the debut work of British Muslim journalist, Hussein Kesvani. The book examines how a new generation of British Muslims use the internet to explore and express their religious identity in new online spaces, far removed from traditional structures like the mosque. Kesvani's interest stems from what he felt were the out-dated ways that we try to find out 'what British Muslims think'. As a journalist, he recounts that this typically involved being sent on a day-return trip to Bradford or East London Mosque. The same applies to the wealth of academic and popular literature on the topic of Muslims in Britain. Referring to works by Sadek Hamid, James Ferguson, Sayeeda Warsi among others, he writes:

> The vast majority of these studies and volumes, while useful, have tended to focus on what 'British Muslim communities' are imagined to be in physical or geographical terms... the framework is constructed around physical Islamic spaces, meaning that mosques, imams and community centres have been the reference points for trying to understanding what a 'British Muslim' is.

Hussein Kesvani, *Follow Me, Akhi: the Online World of British Muslims*, Hurst, London, 2019

Against this, the book's core claim is that British Muslims increasingly live their faith online, that British Islam is defined less and less by mosques or self-styled 'community leaders', and more by memes, halal dating apps and popular YouTube preachers. The book uncovers a world where faith meets technology and where the internet has allowed a generation to contend with difficult and complex questions of religious identity in new ways. The argument is clear – to understand British Islam today, head first to Twitter, not Bradford. But in what ways has mobile technology impacted the lives of British Muslims, why have they embraced this so readily and is this a positive or a negative phenomenon? The book tries to get to the bottom of these questions. Chapters tackle diverse topics of religious authority, sexuality, extremism, Islamophobia, online gaming and Muslim minority communities. It cleverly interweaves these issues around a consistent theme that the internet is essential to understanding British Islam today. While echoing broader societal trends, the focus is clearly on the impact of new technologies in ways specific to British Muslims.

The book comes at an important moment in broader societal attitudes towards social media. Once seen as emancipatory and democratising forces, Facebook and Twitter are now increasingly linked to the problems of echo chambers, populist extremism and fake news. Yet the book neither champions nor condemns the impact of social media upon British Muslims and readers will find plenty of evidence for both sides. On the one hand, Kesvani provides a convincing account of the many ways in which technology allows faith to flourish. Away from the sterile and restrictive environment of the mosque, Muslims have turned to online platforms to further explore and deepen their understanding of the religion. Tied to this are the admirable, even inspiring, anecdotes littered across the book of young Muslims determined to make Islam a meaningful part of their lives. The book shows how online platforms can provide a vital sense of community and support to many, including women and minority communities (LGBTQI, Ahmadi's, Black Muslims), that have long felt ignored, marginalised or simply unwelcome in traditional settings. The discussion of online campaigns like #MosqueMeToo and 'Side Entrance' show the potential of the internet to tackle real injustices in the community. Throughout, Kesvani speaks not just in general terms but gives real case studies. We read of a Muslim women's Facebook support group rescuing one member from domestic abuse. Perhaps most moving and dramatic is the account of one young unmarried Muslim arranging for her secret abortion via friends on Tumblr. The theme of the internet as providing the only place for Muslims to discuss a range of taboo topics, for instance on sexual matters like masturbation and female orgasm, is also present. On the other hand, the book inevitably discusses the problem of online radicalisation of Muslims. Kesvani skilfully illustrates a tension wherein we do not know if the internet is the cause of violent extremism, or simply exacerbates it. Readers get a vivid account of the reality of Islamophobic abuse encountered by many Muslims online, leading some to quit social media altogether. Yet the book also discusses how British Muslims don't just receive online abuse, they also provide it. We find many accounts of the sexism, sectarianism, homophobia and racism easily found on Muslim online spaces. The sections on Muslim minorities captures this perfectly. LGBT, Ahmadi, Black Muslims and even Muslim women create online spaces as a refuge from both the Islamophobia outside the Muslim community and the discrimination they often encounter within it.

If for no other reason, the book deserves to be read for its account of the true diversity of British Muslims, creedal, racial, sexual and political. Social media is often accused of peddling a false vision of life that bears little relation to reality. We don't give a true account of ourselves online, critics claim, only the idealised image that we want others to see. But the book makes a convincing case that the opposite might apply for British Muslims. That is, the online world of British Islam is a far more accurate and candid reflection of the community than one visible at the mosque. Consider Kesvani's treatment of the political diversity of Muslims. The book interviews members of a WhatsApp group of women, mainly mothers, who support the UK government strategy Prevent. As the book notes, this goes against the common narrative. Yet Kesvani quotes one Muslim mother as claiming:

> I do think that Prevent probably has more support from Muslims – especially Muslim women – than you would expect…At the end of the day, I am a mother and a parent, and I want what is best for our children. And for me, the biggest danger isn't about my daughter not being able to practise her religion…My fear is that she might get influenced by some bloke who tells her she

isn't a proper Muslim unless she goes to Syria and gets married. That sounds crazy, until you remember that it actually happened just a couple of years ago.

Or, consider the section on 'Alt-Right Muslims'. Kesvani points to a small but growing number of young Muslims gravitating towards the more extreme fringes of the right-wing internet. It is the strict social conservatism endorsed by figures like Jordan Peterson and the alt-right MiloYiannopoulos, their rejection of feminism and transgender issues, that appeals. The blatant Islamophobia often found on alt-right channels does not dissuade. As one 'Alt-Right' Muslim, Abu Muawiyah, puts it;

> Even though they are not Muslim – and, inshallah, one day they will be – the values they are advocating and supporting are not that different from those that most Muslims should be supporting. They believe marriage is between a man and a woman; they believe that men and women have different roles… These are all things that Islam already teaches.

It is true that the extreme right does endorse values shared widely among Muslims: a defence of family, faith and traditional social values. So one wonders: if only the far right toned down its anti-Islam rhetoric, how many more Muslims would join? These are but two of the many ways in which the book points to a complex and even surprising reality of British Islam. So it seems that it is not social media that gives a fake image, it is the mosques, community centres and even a media discourse that gives a false sense of unanimity to British Muslims.

The section entitled 'Preachers and Mosques' tackles the question of religious authority in a digital age. This seems to be the heart of the book. It raises issues and themes that run throughout. Kesvani discusses in detail how previous generations' attachment to local mosque and imam is being supplanted by a new breed of online religious authorities, typically YouTube preachers and tech-savvy scholars, who are able to reach a far larger global audience online. The book notes that religion-related content is the second largest category uploaded ontoYouTube, after music. Within that, the majority of the content relates to Islam. Islam-themed apps and podcasts, fatwa live stream sessions and online lectures also abound. The potential benefit of this is clear. It is hardly a surprise that the book is littered with stories of Muslims whom turn online to further explore and understand their faith. Yet the sense remains that all that glitters is not gold. Faced with endless choice and mass information, for example, how is a young generation of British Muslims, largely un-rooted in the Islamic intellectual tradition, meant to navigate this digital terrain? The book discusses how the internet has made it easier to claim religious expertise and develop an online brand and following, with most Muslims lacking the requisite tools to discern true from false scholarship. The book also considers the most extreme shift from traditional, pre-digital methods of learning about Islam, the phenomena of Sheikh Google. It is indeed staggering just how common this process has become. For many Muslims the will of God is sought at the click of a button. No effort, struggle or patience required. This says much for how the internet has fragmented the nature of religious authority in modern Islam. It may also be an apt metaphor for our transactional, consumerist age. Again, Kesvani is well aware of the pitfalls of this approach and cites the dystopian warning of British Muslim scholar, Yahya Birt:

> Sheikh Google will lead the unified madhhab of the virtual umma in which a billion-plus, atomized Muslims project their subjective musings… into the ether in a dialogue of the deaf. Sheikh Google's *umma* would be protean, individualised, samizdat, postmodern, unregulated and without any agreed standards in interpretive technique.

Kesvani thus neatly captures a tension wherein the digital world is both a friend and foe for Muslims. It can be used to deepen knowledge and strengthen faith. It can also cause no end of further chaos and confusion. But it should perhaps be underlined that this is the new reality. The genie is out of the bottle. The digital world cannot be tamed or regulated.

It is worth noting that almost all the online preachers and scholars that the book discusses follow the Salafi school. This is perhaps no coincidence. A platform like Twitter or Instagram is hardly conducive to explore the nuances of fiqh, the subtleties of classical kalam. Nor, from reading the book, is this what British Muslims seek when they go online. They want clarity, not complexity. Conviction, not confusion. The self-styled strictness and simplicity of the Salafi method, its claim to draw largely from the scriptural sources, neatly fits a social-media world of short, flashy answers and limited attention spans. Try explaining ibn Rushd's *Bidayat al-Mujtahid* ('The Distinguished Jurist's Primer') in 280 characters. Or the intricacies of al-Ghazali's *Alchemy of Happiness* in a Facebook post. Kesvani never makes the point, but there is perhaps enough in his book to suggest that, revenue streams aside, a one-dimensional stupefying Salafi Islam will continue to dominate the British Muslim scene that increasingly takes place online.

The question of Salafi Islam is tied to broader debates over the place of Muslims in wider British society; and, on this point, *Follow Me, Akhi* makes a valuable contribution. For a segment of Britain, Muslims are the worrying 'fifth' pillar of society, in need of 'integrating' into 'British values' (problems of definition aside). For others, the very suggestion that Muslims are not 'just as British as everyone else' is met with outrage. In between these poles, the book points to a more complex and layered reality: one of British Muslims occupying a liminal space, both indelibly British and yet clearly distinct from wider society in important ways. Like everyone else, Muslims have hardly been hesitant to embrace new technology. But if British Muslims use dating apps, these apps are called Minder and Muzmatch, not Tinder or Bumble. If Muslim youth also flock to new YouTube 'influencers' and Instagram icons, these figures give hijab tutorials or have names like Ali Dawah. It is also clear from the book that some of the most prominent Salafi-style figures that have emerged online are indebted to inner-city gang culture and the UK grime scene. Consider the description of Imran Ibn Mansur, also known as Dawah Man, a huge if controversial Muslim online presence and one of the first to use YouTube to upload videos of his proclaiming 'dawah'

> Ibn Mansur's aesthetic is a blend of traditional Islamic clothing and contemporary streetwear, popular among young people living in London. In most of his videos, he wears a black skullcap and designer sports jackets, under which he wears traditional *thawb*… [He also] sprinkles his speech with Arabic words and citations from the Qur'an and hadith, with the tonal inflections of South London 'road' talk more commonly associated with grime musicians.

Those familiar with Dawah Man would agree. It's a kind of fusion of Salaf and Stormzy. Kesvani hints time and again at an indication of what 'British Islam' really looks like, particularly among the young. This is far more than what is to be found in a think-tank paper or government report. In this way the book also defies simplistic attempts to posit either the radical sameness or difference of British Muslims vis-à-vis the wider populace. If our lives are increasingly tied to our online presence, UK Muslims appear both similar and distinct. The second half is no less important than the first.

Much of what Kesvani does is explore these problems and possibilities of social media. What he doesn't do is position himself on these difficult issues. Beyond the claim that the internet has become essential to understanding British Muslim identity, we never get Kesvani's own take. Kesvani speaks not with his own voice but hides behind the voice of others. In addition, the sense remains that even his account of the problems associated with social media is too reductive, too focused on questions of utility. Online platforms can promote extremism, Islamophobia, sectarianism. But I suspect that many readers know this and there are surely some deeper ethical questions that arise from the mass embrace of new technology. On these, the book is silent. Fears over big data, mass surveillance and invasion of privacy, for example, are never raised. The growing body of evidence linking social media use to anxiety, self-harm and depression, particularly among younger users, is nowhere discussed. Little is made of the deep sense of narcissism, voyeurism and inanity that seems to dominate so much social media discourse. It is also worth questioning at what point the evident Muslim taste for social media becomes an unhealthy, dopamine-fuelled addiction. It seems no exaggeration that some would easier fast from food and drink in Ramadan, than Twitter. The point is that if social media is part of the new reality of British Islam, as the book makes clear, these questions must surely be raised. A cynic could claim that the book gives an insight into British Muslims as the keenest consumers of new technology, while among the least alive to some of its deeper, moral quandaries.

Nevertheless, *Follow Me, Akhi* is a timely reflection on some of the concrete ways that new technology has effected real change in the Muslim community. One need only look around: Qur'an and Islamic-themed apps are an everyday fixture. Muslim podcasts abound. Masjid Ramadan in Dalston, East London, now accepts donations in Bitcoin. Kesvani notes that a Danish virtual reality company even offers VR Karbala, producing simulations that will allow users to 'travel back in time and experience the tragedy of Karbala'. This is the new Muslim reality. No one can predict where this will lead. But it is clear that these rapid and unprecedented changes and the response of traditional structures will define the future of the British Muslim experience. For this reason alone, as a valuable snapshot into the present reality and a hint into the future of British Islam, this book is required reading. Those from an older Muslim generation, however, should perhaps be forewarned. They may be shocked at much of what they read.

ET CETERA

ON RELICS OF MODERNITY

Liam Mayo

What sphinx of cement and aluminium bashed open their skulls and ate up
their brains and imagination?

Moloch! Solitude! Filth! Ugliness! Ashcans and unobtainable dollars! Children
screaming under the stairways! Boys sobbing in armies! Old men weeping in
the parks!

Moloch! Moloch! Nightmare of Moloch! Moloch the loveless! Mental Moloch!
Moloch the heavy judger of men

Allen Ginsberg, *Howl*. 1956

Allen Ginsberg's *Howl* underscored the disenfranchisement of a group of
avant-garde white urban Americans of late 1940's post war United States,
a group that became known as the Beat Generation. The poem, both
lauded and reviled, captured the dichotomy of life during the Cold War.
Behind the pleasant exterior of idealised domesticity, suburban wealth
ascent and nuclear families, an anxiety, paranoia and restlessness plagued
the collective psyche of the West. *Howl* begins with an enumeration of
various embodiments of middle American dissent—addiction,
homosexuality, political radicalism — frequently invoking the social
margins, deliriously unconcerned with sexual differentiation – the poem
quickly shifts in tone in section two where Ginsberg evokes the Caananite
god Moloch, the god who demanded child sacrifice.

For Ginsberg, Moloch is the industrialised metropolis; 'whose mind is pure machinery', 'whose blood is running money!', 'whose fingers are ten armies!', and 'whose eyes are a thousand blind windows!'. Moloch is capitalism; 'whose love is endless oil and stone!', 'whose soul is electricity and banks!', and 'whose poverty is the spectre of genius!' Moloch is rationalism and order, with its 'robot apartments! invisible suburbs! skeleton treasuries! blind capitals! demonic industries! spectral nations! invincible madhouses! granite cocks! monstrous bombs!' Moloch is the grand narratives of modernity, faith in inevitable social, scientific and technological progress, rationalisation and secularisation, the development of the nation-state, representative democracy. 'They broke their backs lifting Moloch to heaven! Pavements, trees, radios, tons! Lifting the city to Heaven which exists and is everywhere about us!' The myth of Moloch, indeed the myth of the modernity project, is that human sacrifice will take us to Heaven.

Howl narrates the modern experience as, philosopher and Marxist humanist, Marshall Berman, points out, not a hollow wasteland, but as an epic and tragic battle of giants. This battle, we may now understand, is the battle between the past and the future; between the nostalgia of the thought past and ignorance of the unthought future. The battle between nostalgia of the imagined past and ignorance of the unimagined future. A battle for our very essence. Moloch is Ginsberg's modernity and its will for relentless progress and the impacts, both physical and metaphysical, cultural and spiritual, this has on identities, individual and collective.

In the wash up of the Enlightenment we found ourselves alone, without a creator or fear of condemnation, steadfast in our determination toward self-improvement, and equipped with seemingly infinite resources (and resourcefulness), our modernisation quickly gained force and momentum. Modernity that followed, set a framework that exposed the fragility of things and then set about to reforming them. This reform involved the rejection of traditional ways of life, the prioritisation of individualism, freedom and formal equality, achieved through the advancement of industrialisation, secularisation, representative democracy and the proliferation of market economy. Life, in modern times, was no longer seen as a given owed to divinity and fate, rather a vocation for us all to face up to. As the sociologist Zygmunt Bauman put it, one's identity exists only as an unfulfilled project.

This ideation for reform placed humans, specifically white men of the West, as the apex of wisdom and central to advancement. Principles where developed and disseminated to assure advancement and the maintenance of established power dynamics. Exploration, discovery, export and trade, and more recently, human rights, education and development, motivated colonialisation. Rationalism, order and normative societal structure articulated purpose for patriarchy. In modern times linear time is necessity, the importance of the self-development celebrated, and values are disposable if they impede the advancement of self-interests. To borrow a phrase from the futurist and neo-humanist Sohail Inayatullah: the modern world is not god-centred or nature-centred or myth centred; rather it was man-centred. For Friedrich Nietzsche, modern society had found itself in possession of a remarkable abundance of possibilities, yet a distinct lack of morals and values. His response, the now infamous; 'death of God' and the advent of nihilism.

More than this though, in many ways 'Moloch' is the answer to the question Ginsberg poses in the opening section of *Howl* – what is it that caused the madness he saw engulf his friends and family – that engulfs him?

I saw the best minds of my generation destroyed by madness, starving hysteri-cal naked, dragging themselves through the negro streets at dawn looking for an angry fix, angelheaded hipsters burning for the ancient heavenly connection to the starry dynamo in the machinery of night.

The dialectic between modernity and it influence on the way we perceive ourselves – our universe and our existence – has been a source of enquiry and inspiration for centuries. In *Julie*, Jean-Jacques Rousseau's protagonist Saint-Preux moves from the country to the city and is rapidly overcome by the experiences of metropolitan life. He writes to his love: 'with such a multitude of objects passing before my eyes, I'm getting dizzy. Of all the things that strike me, there is none that holds my heart, yet all of them together disturb my feelings, so that I forget what I am and who I belong to'. For Rousseau, who is widely considered to have used the word *modernise* in the way we now use it, life in the city – with its rational moral principles – was a heady and intoxicating turbulence that engulfed and overwhelmed his sensibilities. Indeed, as we learn in *Julie*, even as Saint-Preux reaffirms his love for Julie, he fears that, in this new world, he does not know who (or what) is he going to love from one day to the next.

The sociologist and philosopher Max Weber argued the inextricable order of society – with its economies and bureaucracies – meant that, not only is society an 'iron cage' but all the people in it are shaped by its bars. For Weber, owed to modernity, we are beings without spirit. The social theorist and historian of ideas, Michel Foucault, argued there is no emancipation from societal institutions that shape us. These institutions are forces of power, they are all around us and they are within us. For Foucault, this profound enslavement is enacted through forms, which he calls 'normalising power', where-by societal ideologies not only inspire people to believe that the decisions that they make are their own, but convince them that they indeed possess a free will and that they are discharging this freedom with the manner in which they live their lives. Ginsberg, again in *Howl*, decries: 'Moloch who entered my soul early! Moloch in whom I am a consciousness without a body! Moloch who frightened me out of my natural ecstasy! Moloch whom I abandon!'

However, he cannot abandon Moloch. The madness is already within him. The cunning of modernity is its ability to adapt and colonise for survival. In a world devoid of divinity, the past becomes sacred; to be worshiped, revered and adored. In modernity, the past provides us certainty through uncertainty. It assures us that our experiences are shared, not just across our lifetime, but by those who have lived before, all be it from a different temporal perspective. It also provides us a sense of responsibility, to continue to strive forth as our ancestors did. For their sake, as much as ours. Of course, the past can be controlled, framed and shaped. It can be put into a museum, a text book, cordoned off and protected by government policy. A monument can be built in honour of it, a public holiday announced, and gift cards printed. The past is taught as a subject called 'history', written into curriculums, disseminated through schools and student progress is measured through a series of indicators that quantify their level of knowledge. The past is easily accessible, it sits in wait to reflect back to us the things we already know. The past is a relic we visit, not only to pay homage, but to fulfil cultural practise. In this way, we see, the past influences our images of the universe and our places in it.

Becoming humanity, thus, has been a project built in past worlds from the plane of the present day. For if our very meaning for existence is defined in a realm that we can never have the ability to shape or control, the will to modernise is with us from birth. Modernity becomes our fate.

Significantly, the success of the modernity project (and its propensity for progress) has been built on the foundations of man-made lineal time. So, if humanity constructs time, man can control time, and if man can control time, he has a tool for overcoming the all too restrictive entity of space. And if man can control time and space, then man is all powerful. Entire systems have been set-up on these very foundations: world markets, governance, communications, education – all complex systems thatched against the premise of the past, present and future as fixed entities on a lineal spectrum characterised by their certainty and reliability. Yet, the very notion of humanity, as we understand it, has only existed epistemologically for a few hundred years – knowledge was ordered differently in feudal and religious eras. As Inayatullah points out, macro historians – those who study social systems, along separate trajectories, through space, time, and episteme, in search of soft laws of social change – understand that all things rise, and all things fall. The Muslim macro historian Ibn Khaldun proposed a cycle of degeneration, whereby the ideology that enabled conquest becomes progressively less relevant as the conquerors settle down. What follows is disunity in the systems of powers – revolutions take place, new rules rise up, power is centralised once again – and a new myth for a new world takes its place. We see this degeneration, I argue, all around us right now. The perversity of the global economic system, the widespread disillusionment with the democratic process, ongoing civil unrest regarding inaction over climate change and the absolute proliferation (and normalisation) of cyber surveillance by corporations all indicate that transformation is afoot.

The social, political and economic progress that is celebrated by neoliberalism suddenly has caveats that precludes portions of the population. Decidedly undemocratic decisions are made in the name of democracy and populist ideals are projected, reiterated and churned through the perpetual media feed. Of course, this is counter to our conventional understanding of the projected future for humanity. The myth of early modernity has all but lost its appeal; the forces of Western civilisation – democracy, human rights and capitalism – were supposed to have saved the planet by now. However, what we are experiencing is the converse – a rise in totalitarianism, an escalation in the systemic dehumanisation of marginalised people and the significant disparity in the distribution of global wealth.

We have reached a fulcrum point in the modernisation agenda. Across disciplines, the contemporary epoch has gathered a variety of pseudonyms: liquid modernity, post-industrial, post progress, post truth, global weirding, 'the age of surveillance', 'the sixth mass extinction', 'the new dark age' – to name a few. Different names, yet the commonality they all share is that modernity has led us to a point of no return. The normal by which we have lived our lives is no longer feasible. A transition to a new normal is not only imminent, but vital for our very survival. The hyper-interconnectedness of a globalised world means that the slightest incidence in any geographical corner of the globe has the possibility of triggering a tectonic social, political, economic and environmental shift in any number of other places, if not universally. Chaos ensues, as we scramble anxiously to understand the experience and adjust to a new norm. This is compounded, as one incidence precedes another, then another; each intersecting with one another, each incrementally affecting the other. And as communities seek to adjust and settle into the new normalcy, they cling on to the little they have that provides them certainty: nostalgia for the glorious past, naked nationalism and protectionism. Indeed, contradictions prevails.

In modern times – normal times – we understood our place. The past was a place to find meaning through homage and reflection. We were to strive for self-improvement; develop ourselves personally, professionally, sexually and spiritually, whilst grappling with the anxieties and tropes of inadequacy amongst peers, for the betterment of ourselves and ultimately humankind. With this certainty, we built images of the futures that nourished us and gave us something to believe in. Today the past is no longer a fixed point in the rear-view mirror of our life. The past is now a space where a diversity of voices and agendas converge and grapple for legitimacy. The past is not a monolith, rather the past are spaces for plurality. The linearity of time now runs at breakneck speed as we attempt to occupy the multiplicity of spaces contemporary life insists that we preside over. We are attempting to build and sustain our identities under duress; we are transitioning to a new normal and this will involve a new way of constructing our identities and how we are influenced by our pasts.

In these times of change, the past has also become a space for those that modernity kept outside history, and therefore without a future and without agency. Those people, who have for centuries, been maligned, subordinated and ostracised, may find opportunity through the turbulence of change and step off the straight line of modern time, reclaim their pasts and rewrite their histories. Indeed, we already see real social innovations, community cooperatives, peer to peer economies, First Nations movements and climate defenders enacting anticipatory action through this change. The chaos of degeneration becomes a tool for these agents of change. These may very well be the madness of Ginsberg but they are also our own angel-headed hipsters.

Berman's contention is that *Howl* dares us to take on modern giants. Ginsberg's mission is to inspire our imagination and creativity. In *Footnote to Howl*, the final section of his opus, Ginsberg attempts to find divinity: 'Everything is holy! everybody's holy! everywhere is holy! every day is in eternity! Everyman's an angel! The bum's as holy as the seraphim! the madman is holy as you my soul are holy!' And then, after his long and emphatic condemnation of Moloch, Ginsberg doubles-back seemingly to retract his earlier sentiments: 'Holy the solitudes of skyscrapers and pavements! Holy the cafeterias filled with the millions! Holy the mysterious rivers of tears under the streets! Holy the lone juggernaut! Holy the vast lamb of the middle class! Holy the crazy shepherds of rebellion! Who digs Los Angeles IS Los Angeles! Holy New York Holy San Francisco Holy Peoria & Seattle Holy Paris Holy Tangiers Holy Moscow Holy Istanbul!' And it is here that Ginsberg's decisive message is revealed to us: whilst Moloch is the destroyer, the cause of our madness, our fate, these forces are indeed holy. It is these forces that expose the true nature of the world to those of us who live with madness. This madness, no longer tragic, is a joyous illumination. Only in madness can we truly appreciate the divinity of life.

But how do we break the shackles of modernity and spread the joy of madness around? Change is an inevitability; Khaldun's degeneration is upon us. Where we go from here is entirely dependent on the actions we take today. Inspiration for change can only be found from within the institution. Modernity is both the oppressor and the inspirer. Surely it is Ginsberg's madness that we need now more than ever? As the philosopher and historian of science Jerry Ravetz, states 'people must believe in something that makes their sacrifices worthwhile, something that makes their meritorious acts become real 'sacrifices' or holy deeds. This belief need not be an explicit religious doctrine; experience shows that the religious seem just as vulnerable to corruption as the irreligious. But it must exist'. In light of this, rather than perpetuating the modernist bent for finding meaning in the past, historian Eelco Runia advocates the concept of 'presence' in our approach to exploring the past: that is to say 'being in touch' – either literally or figuratively – with people, things, events, and feelings that made us who we are. Presence 'is having a whisper of life breathed into what has become routine and clichéd – it is fully realising things instead of just taking them for granted'. So, Ginsberg engages Moloch, just as I engage Ginsberg, because the past is a form of presence that lives among the chaos of the everyday. We cannot control chaos, rather, we can call on our creativity and imagination to navigate it.

But modernity is a wily character. Its ambition is to commandeer Khaldun's cycles of degeneration to usurp the abdication of power. And with technology modernity may now have the tools to achieve this. Indeed, with theses faculties we may attain the power of gods. But to what end? And at the sacrifice of who? And what? But if we are to become gods, we must act with divinity; learn that there is holiness all around. This requires a level of morality that modernity is simply bereft off. Ours is a time where we cannot return to any past we have known and with no confidence in any path to a desired, attainable or sustainable future. Ignorance and uncertainty infect our very core. The futurist and cultural theorist Ziauddin Sardar tells us that to transition to the new normal we should look to the age-old virtues of humility, modesty and accountability to begin a coherent debate about the future we wish to have for ourselves. This is by no means a nostalgic rouse, designed to insight a return to religious doctrine. Rather, as Sardar elucidates, 'modernisation, progress, bureaucracy, science and all the disciplines of modern knowledge emerged complete with a rich sustaining mythology whose most basic tenet was the delusional notion that they were value neutral, universal and inherently good.' In these ignorant and uncertain times, it is the chaos, complexity and contradiction where we must focus our attention. From here we must negotiate, with the diversity of voices, and their plurality of opinions, all invited, and all heard, toward an ethical response for our transitional dilemma. This requires leadership.

As we transition to a new normal, we must excavate the relics of modernity and find within them holiness; something for people to believe. While postmodernists may have believed to have announced the end of modernity, this thesis has now proven to be misguided. The grand narratives, characteristics, vices and virtues of modernity remain, albeit ratcheted up to absurdity. The industrialised metropolis is now becoming the mega-city, as cities around the world are projected to hold two thirds of the global population by 2050. Built by the virtue of capitalism, global tech giants now hold greater power than any nation state. Rationalism and order are now contained in our personalised intuitive technologies, with all their algorithms and anticipatory functions at our very command. And of course, in our time, it is within digital culture that our identities are formed and performed.

To be modern, Berman argued, is to experience personal and social life as a maelstrom – to be modernist is to make oneself somehow at home in the maelstrom, 'to make its rhythms one's own, to move with its currents in search of the forms of reality, of beauty, of freedom, of justice, that its fervid and perilous flow allows.' This is good instruction – and provides us a head-start in thinking about how we should approach our transitional age. However, the maelstrom of the contemporary experience goes well beyond what Berman was speaking to. Much of that which we have considered to be normal has reached it limits. The Newtonian absolute chronological time, for example, is inadequate in a hyperconnected world of rapidly accelerating temporalities. Not to mention the impacts of climate crisis.

In his book *21 Lessons for the 21st Century*, the historian Yuval Noah Harari outlines his position that the next decades may be characterised by intense soul-searching and the formulation of a new social and political model. I agree with him. I have excavated the relic of Ginsberg's *Howl* to enact the sense of presence Runia confers. Many years ago, Ginsberg travelled across time and space, across generations and geography, to find me as a teenager to inspire me through uncertainty. Again, in a time of uncertainty, I seek out Ginsberg, and *Howl,* for inspiration. For they are not fixed points on a lineal time scale for to us to reflect on in search of meaning but exist with us here today – amongst the chaos, complexity and contradictions. In doing so, we may find something new to believe in; something that was always there, but something that we are yet to fully realise.

There is one final point, for me, that Ginsberg inspires us to do with *Howl,* namely, while we are looking around us, in search of holiness, it is within us that the search should begin. For surely all the divinity and morality already exists within. After all, as Harari says, it is our 'soul' we must be searching for. If modernity has become the way with which we view ourselves, then modernity has not just colonised our lives, its colonised our very souls. However, for Ginsberg, our souls exist outside of modernity, we just need to revive them. So perhaps the last word here should go to Ginsberg, with the final line of *Howl,* with his reminder that: 'Holy the supernatural extra brilliant intelligent kindness of the soul!'

TEN SURPRISING RELICS

Go anywhere in the Muslim world and you will bump into a shrine, tombs, sacred relic, or footprints of the Prophets. No doubt you have witnessed the footprint of Prophet Muhammad at the Eyüp Sultan Mosque in Istanbul, and climbed the Adam's Peak in Sri Lanka to see the footprint of Adam. But there are even more marvellous vestiges out there from blessed tortoises to sacred crocodiles, moving walls and revered trees, and even a celebrated shrine on the sex mountain! They all come neatly, not to say sacredly, wrapped in mythology, legends, traditions and what have you. So here is our list of some noteworthy relics for you to seek out.

1. Footprints Everywhere

Sacred footprints are ubiquitous all over the Islamic World. Widely discussed in scholarly circles has been a pair of carved footprints at the Rozabal shrine in Srinagar, Kashmir, which is sometimes ascribed to Jesus, but more often to a local Sufi saint who may very well just be an Islamised version of the Buddha. An object of fervent devotion up until today is the Qadam Sharif, the footprint of Prophet Muhammad in Paharganj, Delhi. A complex of dargah, mosque and madrassa was built around this footprint in medieval times and an 'urs' festival is held in its honour once a year. Other holy traces can be found across the Muslim World as well: An imprint of the hand of Imam Ali is revered on Maula Ali Hill in Indian Hyderabad. A royal eunuch (*khwajasara*) of the Nizam once discovered this imprint after being guided to it by a dream vision of the Imam himself. Another imprint of the hand of Ali can be found on the Khyber Pass, in local Pashtun legend often identified with the Arab city of Khaybar.

Hoofprints of the horse of Imam Ali's son Hazrat Abbas can be seen at the Murad-Khani shrine in Kabul.

2. The Tomb of Seth, Son of Adam, in Ayodhya

Islamic mythology relates that Adam touched down on Earth in Sri Lanka, so it's not too surprising that according to some traditions his son Seth spent his life in India and is buried there. A tomb of Seth can be found in Ayodhya, of all places. Its existence once helped eighteenth century scholar Azad Bilgrami make his point about South Asia being the original Holy Land of Islam. The tomb's dimensions are unusual: Seth's grave is nine metres long, supporting pious traditions, which claim that human beings in the age before the Great Deluge were much taller than humans today. South Asia is not the only region on earth that claims special proximity to the Garden of Eden, however. Similar claims have often also been made about Mesopotamia, and so it does not come as a surprise that another tomb of Seth, with equally surprising proportions, can also be found in Mosul, Iraq. Tragically, the tomb in Mosul was destroyed by ISIS in 2014. Given Ayodhya's troubled recent history of religious extremism, we are lucky that the Indian tomb still remains largely unharmed today.

3. Narrow Passages

At several shrines devotees try to pass through narrow passages of different kinds to gain the blessings of particular Muslim saints. At the shrine of Bahauddin Naqshband in Bukhara, visitors are shown the fallen trunk of a mulberry tree that once grew out of the staff of the saint. It is said that whoever is able to crawl under that trunk will have a prayer answered. Near Hacibektas in Turkey, on the other hand, visitors able to pass through a hole in a particular rock at the retreat cell of the saint are promised all their sins will be forgiven. Success in passing under such tree trunks or through tight holes may be attributed to the powers of fate and divine intervention. Nevertheless it is probably not a bad idea to go through a careful and honest assessment of one's physical proportions before attempting such ventures.

4. Walls That Moved

A legend appearing in several parts of the Muslim World tells us about a saint riding on a wall, defeating another saint riding on a lion in a battle of supernatural feats. The Dutch anthropologist Martin van Bruinessen once traced several variants of this legend from South and Central Asia to Kurdistan and Anatolia. The identity of the two battling saints shifts according to local context. But the detail of the victorious saint making a lifeless wall move as his mount is always the same. The wall in question can still be visited at several locations. Most notably in Turkey in Hacibektas, where Hajji Bektash himself once rode it, and in India at the shrine of Shah Mina Sahib in Lucknow. There apparently also exists a shrine erected on the spot where the Punjabi Sufi Bu Ali Qalandar rode a wall in an occult battle with the Sindhi saint Lal Shahbaz Qalandar.

5. The House of Khadijah

Many relics from the early Islamic period have been destroyed by the zeal of both: Wahhabisation and modernisation of the two holy cities, Makkah and Madinah. Yet, believers of a more traditional persuasion still try to find remains of these blessed sights during Hajj or Umrah. This has turned into a painful experience for those pious visitors who have tried to discover the remains of the house of Prophet Muhammad's first wife Khadijah, the very house that was the centre of the early years of the Prophet's mission. The original site is now partly covered by a block of public toilets. A very visible sign of the divide that separates modern Islam from the Islamic past.

6. Bayazid Bistami's Turtles

It is unexpected enough that ninth century Persian Sufi saint Beyazid Bistami has a tomb in Bangladesh's Chittagong (besides having one in Iran and another one in Afghanistan). Even more unexpected are the sacred turtles that live in the pond belonging to the shrine. According to local legend, the turtles were once evil djinn who incurred the wrath of the saint and were transformed by him. The species inhabiting the pond is rare and endangered. Scientifically the species is known as the 'black softshell turtle' but the locals call them 'Bostami turtle'. Believers feed them out of reverence for the saint.

7. The Crocodiles of Manghopir

Pir Mangho was a descendant of the Prophet Muhammad and Imam Ali, as well as a Sufi who settled in the area of modern Karachi. He became the patron saint of the Indo-African Sheedi community in particular. Hundreds of crocodiles live in a lake by the shrine and devotees regard these large reptiles as manifestations of the sacred presence of the Pir, revere them and feed them. The late German scholar of Islamic spirituality and mysticism, Annemarie Schimmel, made it a point to mention in one of her books that she found the turtle shrine in Chittagong far more horrifying than the crocodile shrine of Manghopir. We wonder what was her problem with cute little turtles?

8. Musa the Burqa-wearer

The Iranian city of Qom, which is the centre of Shi'a Muslim learning, sports numerous remarkable shrines. Most well-known are of Fatima Masumah, the sister of Imam Reza, and the tomb of Ayatollah Khomeini. A little more obscure is the shrine of Musa Mubarqa (or, in Iranian Persian pronunciation, Musa Mobarregheh), Musa the Burqa Wearer. This son of Imam Taqi, the ninth of the twelve Imams of the Shi'a, was so beautiful that during his life-time he had to wear a burqa in public to not distract the businessmen in the bazaars of Qom. If Musa Mubarqa were alive in our day and age, he would find travelling through several European countries more challenging than walking through the bazaars of Qom. Or do modern burqa bans in Europe also apply to young men?

9. The Shrine on Sex Mountain

Legend has it that in medieval Java, prince Pangeran Samodro fell in love with his stepmother Nyai Ontrowulan; and fled to Kemukus Mountain with her, where the two were eventually killed by the king's soldiers. A shrine developed around their graves. And since at least the nineteenth century, devotees have been visiting the shrine, engaging in eyebrow-raising rituals that involve having mandatory sex with someone who is not one's legal spouse. Pilgrimage to (and illicit sexual activity on) Kemukus Mountain is supposed to ensure material success and wellbeing. The ritual may have its roots in pre-Islamic Tantric ideas, but most of the Indonesian pilgrims nowadays see themselves as devout Muslims. Not surprisingly, the shrine and its rituals have drawn the anger of other Muslims and several times in recent years authorities have attempted to ban religious and sexual activities on Mount Kemungus, colloquially often referred to as the Sex Mountain.

10. Sacred Relics at the Topkapi Museum, Istanbul

Another footprint of the Prophet can be found in the Topkapi Museum in Istanbul. Together with other relics: The pot of Abraham, the turban of Joseph, the staff of Moses, the sword of David, the sword of Ali, the mantle of the Prophet, a hair from the beard of the Prophet, and others. Most of these relics came into Ottoman possession from their Abbasid predecessors as Caliphs of the Sunni world. During Ottoman times, these *kutsal emanetler* (sacred relics) were exhibited to the public during special occasions. Believers longed to offer reverence to them and gain blessings from the prophets as a result. With the advent of the Turkish Republic, these objects were displayed in the museum. A Qur'an recitation plays all day in the chambers of the *kutsal emanetler*. Is this out of respect for the relics, or staged drama for tourists? Your guess is as good as ours!

CITATIONS

Introduction: Things to Remember by Samia Rahman

Atiye (The Gift), directed by Ozan Açıktan, written by Jason George, Nuran Evren Şit, and Fatih Ünal, Netflix Studios, 2019. *CM 28: Narratives*, (Hurst, London, 2018).

The Lost Mosaic by Boyd Tonkin

The two volumes of John Julius Norwich's history of *The Normans in Sicily*, *The Normans in the South 1016-1130* and *The Kingdom in the Sun 1130-1194* (Faber & Faber) remain unmatched as a portrait of the period and its culture. Alex Metcalfe's *Muslims and Christians in Norman Sicily* (Routledge) offers more recent research in a more specialised study. Ibn Jubayr's travel journals are generously extracted in Horatio Clare's *Sicily Through Writers' Eyes* (Eland). Barry Unsworth's novel of Arab-Norman Sicily, *The Ruby in Her Navel*, is published in by Penguin, and Tariq Ali's *A Sultan in Palermo* by Verso. Justin Marozzi's *Islamic Empires: Fifteen Cities that Define a Civilization* (Allen Lane) vividly evokes almost every other centre of Mediterranean Islamic culture – but not Palermo. Dirk Booms and Peter Higgs edited the invaluable catalogue-book that accompanied the 2016 exhibition *Sicily: Culture and Conquest* (British Museum Press). The island's UNESCO-registered monuments are described and illustrated in Maria Antonietta Spadaro and Sergio Troisi's bilingual guide *The Arab-Norman Itinerary* (Edizioni Kalós, Palermo). Leoluca Orlando's manifesto can be found (9 November 2018) at climate2020.org.uk. 'Palermo is again a migrant city' by Jason Horowitz appeared in the *New York Times*, 22 May 2019. 'Palermo to Europe: Leoluca Orlando's Political Vision' by Harold Bauder (14 May 2019) is at citiesofmigration.ca. For a colourful, erudite and gripping journey through Sicilian history and culture, see Peter Robb, *Midnight in Sicily* (Vintage Classics).

Ignorant Antiquities by Aaron Tugendhaft

This is an expanded version of Aaron Tugendhaft's article 'Archaeology and Jihad' that appeared in *Cabinet Magazine* in October 2019. For further reading see Al-Tabari. *The History of al-Tabari.* Volume 2: *Prophets and Patriarchs.* Translated by William M. Brinner. Albany: State University of New York Press, 1987. Vincent Blanchard, ed. *Royaumes oubliés. De l'empire hittite aux Araméens.* Paris: Musée du Louvre, 2019. Nadja Cholidis, and Martin Lutz, eds. *Tell Halaf. Im Krieg zerstörte Denkmäler und ihre Restaurierung.* Berlin: De Gruyter, 2010. Lionel Gossman, *The Passion of Max von Oppenheim: Archaeology and Intrigue in the Middle East from Wilhelm II to Hitler.* Cambridge, UK: Open Book Publishers, 2014. Sean McMeekin, *The Berlin-Baghdad Express: The Ottoman Empire and Germany's Bid for World Power.* Cambridge, Mass.: Belknap Press, 2010. *The Qur'an.* Translated by M. A. S. Abdel Haleem. Oxford: Oxford University Press, 2004. Sayyid Qutb. *Milestones.* Karachi: International Islamic Publishers, 1981. Sayyid Qutb. *In the Shade of the Qur'an.* Volume 4. Translated by Adil Salahi and Ashur Shamis. Leicester: The Islamic Foundation, 2001. Rayyane Tabet. *Fragments.* Beirut: Kaph Books, 2019.

Lingering Scents of Hyderabad by Rita Sonal Panjatan

On the history of the city, see Eric Beverley, *Hyderabad, British India, and the World: Muslim Networks and Minor Sovereignty, c.1850–1950*, Cambridge University Press, 2018; on its heritage, see Madhu Vottery, *A Guide to the Heritage of Hyderabad: The Natural and the Built*, Rupa, New Delhi, 2010; and on their demise, A G Noorani, *Destruction of Hyderabad*, Hurst, 2014. Geeta Devi's *The Jewels Of Nizam: Recipes from the Khansamas of Hyderabad*, Rupa, New Delhi, 2013, provides a flavour of Hyderabad's famous cuisine.

Death and Burial by Andrew Petersen

For further reading see James Boone and Garnett P. McMillan, 'Population History and the Islamization of the Iberian Peninsula: Skeletal Evidence from the Lower Alentejo of Portugal' in *Current Anthropology* Vol. 40 No. 5 December 1999; A R Gatrad, 'Muslim Customs surrounding Death,

Bereavement, Postmortem Examinations and Organ Transplants' *British Medical Journal* 309: 521–3 1994; Y Gleize, F Medisco, M-H Pemonge, C. Hubert, A.Groppi, B. Houix, M-F Deguilloux, J-Y, Breuil. 'Early Medieval Muslim Graves in France: First Archaeological, Anthropological and Palaeogenomic Evidence' *PLoS ONE* 11(2), February 2016; and A Petersen, 'Death and Burial in the Islamic World' in L Nilsson Stutz, and S Tarlow, editors, Oxford *Handbook of the Archaeology of Death and Burial*, Oxford, 2013, pp241-258.

From Minaret to Minaret by Leyla Jagiella

The Dżemila Smajkiewicz-Murman quote is from Harry Norris, *Islam in the Baltic* (I B Tauris, London, 2009). On Polish Tartars, see Barbara Pawlic-Miskiewicz, *Performance of Identity of Polish Tatars: From Religious Holidays to Everyday Rituals* (Peter Long, New York, 2018). See also, 'Polish Muslims: An Unexpected Meeting', a documentary directed by William Barylo and produced by the Cordoba Foundation, 2013. Olga Tokarczuk's *Flights* is published by Random House, New York, 2019; and *The Books of Jacob* is available in German edition and will be published in English in 2021.

Three Faiths City by Hafeez Burhan Khan

On the history of the holy city, see Simon Sebag Montefiore, *Jerusalem: The Biography*, Phoenix, London, 2012; and https://www.history.com/topics/ancient-middle-east/history-of-jerusalem and https://www.bbc.co.uk/news/world-middle-east-26934435. To discover the importance of Jerusalem to the Abrahamic faiths see https://www.theguardian.com/commentisfree/2015/may/20/why-jerusalem-important-google-autocomplete. Also watch the Al Jazeera documentary on the first Crusades: https://www.aljazeera.com/programmes/the-crusades-an-arab-perspective/2016/12/shock-crusade-conquest-jerusalem-161205081421743.html.

Reclaiming Manuscripts by Nur Sobers-Khan

The works cited in the essay are: Michael Taussig, *What Colour is the Sacred* (Chicago, University of Chicago Press, 2009), p. 196; Liana Saif, 'What is Islamic Esotericism,' in a special edition of *Correspondences* 7, no. 1 (2019), pp. 1–59, p. 2; From MacDonald, D.B. and Gardet, L., 'al-Ghayb', in: *Encyclopaedia of Islam, Second Edition*, Edited by P. Bearman, Th. Bianquis, C.E. Bosworth, E. van Donzel, W.P. Heinrichs, Brill, 1954-2005; Toufic Fahd, *La Divination Arabe* (Leiden: Brill, 1966); Matt Melvin-Koushki, 'Persianate Geomancy from Ṭūsī to the Millennium A Preliminary Survey,' Nader El-Bizri and Eva Orthmann, eds., *Occult Sciences in Premodern Islamic Culture*, Beirut: Orient-Institut Beirut, 2018, p. 184; Stefano Carboni, *Following the Stars: Images of the Zodiac in Islamic Art* (New York: Metropolitan Museum of Art, 1997), p. 4; Liana Saif, *The Arabic Influences on Early Modern Occult Philosophy* (Houndmills, Basingstoke: Palgrave Macmillan, 2015), and the review of this work by Matt Melvin-Koushki, '(De)colonizing Early Modern Occult Philosophy' in *Magic, Ritual, and Witchcraft* Spring 2017, pp. 98-112, p. 100; Matt Melvin-Koushki, 'Introduction: De-orienting the Study of Islamicate Occultism,' in his special edition of the journal *Arabica*: 64 (2017), ed Matt Melvin-Koushki and Noah Gardiner, pp. 287-295, p. 288; Ayesha Chaudhry 'Islamic Legal Studies: A Critical Historiography' in the *The Oxford Handbook of Islamic Law*, ed. Anver M. Emon and Rumee Ahmed (Oxford, 2017), p. 5; Ibid, p. 5.

Other works referenced: Meredith-Owens' *Handlist of Persian Manuscripts in the British Museum 1895-1966* (British Library, London, 1968); Shahab Ahmed's *What Is Islam?* (Princeton Univeristy Press, 2017); and Nur Sobers-Khan, 'Dreaming' *Critical Muslim 28: Narratives* (Hurst, London, 2018).

Touba by Yovanka Paquete Perdigao

For further reading on Cheikh Ahmadou Bamba and Touba see semanticscholar.org. See also: Michelle R Kimball, *Shaykh Ahmadou Bamba: A Peacemaker for Our Time*, The Other Press, Kuala Lumpur, 2018. For the annual trek to Touba, see: http://news.bbc.co.uk/2/hi/africa/1330324. stm. Read *Time* magazine's piece on the Museum of Black Civilisations in

Dakar at: https://time.com/collection/worlds-greatest-places-2019/5654118/museum-of-black-civilizations-dakar-senegal/ and for more on the report commissioned by President Macron calling for looted African artefacts to be returned see: https://www.theguardian.com/world/2018/nov/21/france-urged-to-return-looted-african-art-treasures-macron.

Desperate Gaza by Daniel Marwecki

Donald Macintyre report on the May 2019 deaths in Gaza can be read at: https://www.independent.co.uk/news/world/middle-east/gaza-protests-latest-palestinians-killed-border-embassy-jerusalem-trump-a8351761.html. Jared Kushner's plan for Palestine can be seen at: https://www.dw.com/en/jared-kushners-plan-for-palestinians-whats-not-in-it/a-49350560.

Donald Macintyre and Peter Beinart conversation is available at: https://fmep.org/resource/occupied-thoughts-gaza-w-peter-beinart-donald-mcintyre/.

Sara Roy quote is from her article 'If Israel were Smart' in *London Review of Books*, 39-12, 15 June 2017. See also: Mimi Kirk, 'Countering Christian Zionism in the Age of Trump', *Middle East Report Online*, August 08, 2019.

On Relics of Modernity by Liam Mayo

All quotes attributed to Allen Ginsberg are from *Howl and Other Poems*, City Lights Books, San Francisco (1956). The citations mentioned in the text in order of appearance, are from: Berman, M, *All That is Solid Melts into the Air: The Experience of Modernity,* Penguin Books, New York (1988); Bauman, Z. 'Identity in the Globalizing World', *Social Anthropology,* 9(2), 121-129 (2001). doi:10.1111/j.1469-8676.2001.tb00141.x; Inayatullah, S., 'Cycles of Power', *Edges* (1990); Burnham D. and Jesinghausen, M., *Nietzsche's Thus Spoke Zarathustra*, Edinburgh University Press, Edinburgh (2010); Rousseau, J.-J., Stewart, P., & Vache, J., *Julie, or The New Heloise: Letters of Two Lovers Who Live in a Small Town at the Foot of the Alps* (Vol. 6), UPNE (2010); Weber, M., *The Protestant Ethic and the Spirit of Capitalism,*

Routledge, Abingdon (2013); Foucault, M. *Discipline and Punish: The Birth of the Prison,* Vintage Books, New York (1995); Foucault, M., *The Order of Things*, Routledge, Abingdon (2005); Inayatullah, S., 'Cycles of Power', *Edges* (1990); Ravetz, J. , 'Ibn Khaldun and the Arab Spring', *Critical Muslim 1: The Arabs Are Alive,* Hurst, London (2012); Runia, E. 'Presence', *History and Theory,* 45(1), 1-29 (2006); Sardar, Z. 'Welcome to Postnormal Times, *Futures,* 42(5), 435-444, (2010); Harari, Y. N., *21 Lessons for the 21st Century,* Random House, London (2018).

CONTRIBUTORS

Alev Adil, writer and academic, combines poetry, anthropology and art practice to explore the borders between memory and identity ● **Shahbano Alvi** is a Karachi-based writer ● **Iason Athanasiadis** is a multimedia journalist dedicated to Mediterranean issues ● **Dalia De Gondi** is a Tunis-based architect focused on heritage preservation ● **Aaftaab Haider** hopes to continue to live and work in Europe, and as soon as he has a proper residence status and proper papers he wants to travel back to Punjab, play with his children and cry at the grave of his mother ● **Aamer Hussein** is a well-known short story writer ● **Tam Hussein** is an award-winning journalist and writer ● **Leyla Jagiella** is a cultural anthropologist exploring orthodoxy and heterodoxy in South Asian Islam ● **C Scott Jordan** is Executive Assistant Director of Centre for Postnormal Policy and Futures Studies ● **Hafeez Burhan Khan** was an archaeologist before becoming a teacher ● **Josef Linnhoff**, a Middle East researcher for BBC Monitoring, has just completed his doctorate on the meaning of *shirk* in classical and modern Islamic thought ● **Iftikhar H Malik** is Professor of History at Bath Spa University, and MCR, Wolfson College, Oxford ●**Daniel Marwecki** is converting his PhD thesis on West Germany's Israel and Palestine policy in a book to be published by Hurst in 2020 ● **Liam Mayo**, a Fellow of the Centre for Postnormal Policy and Futures Studies, works in and with communities to bring marginalised voices into the mainstream ● **Rita Sonal Panjatan** is Berlin-based Research Fellow at Zohre Esmaili Foundation ● **Yovanka Paquete Perdigao** is a Bissau-Guinean writer working to champion Lusophone African stories ● **Andrew Petersen** is Director of Research in Islamic Archaeology at University of Wales Trinity Saint David ● **Samia Rahman** is Director of the Muslim Institute ● **David Shariatmadari** is a *Guardian* editor and writer ● **Nur Sobers-Khan** is Associate Professor of Islamic Studies at Habib University, Karachi, Pakistan ● **Boyd Tonkin**, journalist and critic, was literary editor of *The Independent* newspaper from 1996 to 2013, and is the author of *The 100 Best Novels in Translation* ● **Aaron Tugendhaft** teaches humanities at Bard College Berlin; his book *The Idols of ISIS: From Assyria to the Internet* will be published by University of Chicago Press ● **Sahil Warsi** is an American anthropologist residing in the UK.